# The Art of the
# American Film

Poet, teacher, critic, **Charles Higham** brings an especially sensitive eye to bear on the American film. For this major study, he worked closely with archives on both coasts, including the Library of Congress and George Eastman House. He is the author of *Hollywood in the Forties, Hollywood Cameraman, The Films of Orson Welles,* and *DeMille* and has been Regents Professor, teaching poetry and film, at the University of California, Santa Cruz.

# The Art of the American Film

## CHARLES HIGHAM

**ANCHOR BOOKS**

Anchor Press / Doubleday,  Garden City, New York

*The Art of the American Film* was originally published in a hardcover
edition in 1973 by Anchor Press/Doubleday.

Anchor Books edition: 1974


ISBN: 0-385-06971-5

# Acknowledgments

I am deeply grateful to James Card and George Pratt of George Eastman House, Rochester, New York, for their open-hearted generosity in showing me the magnificent collection of films in their establishment. My debt to them can never be repaid. I also thank David Bradley, who was kindness itself, Tom Luddy of the Pacific Film Archive at Berkeley, Anthony Slide, and the staffs of the Academy of Motion Picture Arts and Sciences and the Library of Congress, for much valuable assistance. Some passages in the book appeared in a slightly different form in articles in *Sight and Sound, Film Quarterly, Film Heritage* and *The London Magazine.*

# Contents

PART THREE: The Forties and After

PART FOUR: Toward the Contemporary Film

■ ■ ■ ■ ■ ■ ■ ■ ■ ■ ■ ■ ■ ■ ■ ■ ■ ■ ■ ■ ■ ■ ■ ■ ■ ■ ■ ■

# Preface

■ ■ ■ ■ ■ ■ ■ ■ ■ ■ ■ ■ ■ ■ ■ ■ ■ ■ ■ ■ ■ ■ ■ ■ ■ ■ ■

The film in America is a collaborative professional activity, a business first and an art second. An American film is not, like a painting, a poem, a novel, or a composition in music, the work of an individual talent imposing its will upon a medium and a public. It is a combined artifact in which the writer and the director, the cameraman and the editor, the designer and the costumier, and—in sound films—the composer of the score are all of major importance. A good film emerges from the successful collaboration of these main figures and of the cast, welded together by the force of a good director. It may well be argued that casting and a first-rate script are the most important single ingredients of all, since in this highly commercial medium it is the story and the players that have to command the public's interest before anything else. Without characters and actors with whom the public can identify and a story which involves its deepest immediate concerns, a film cannot succeed. No film maker in America can afford to ignore public taste. If he does, he is certain to be destroyed.

If the story is interesting and the stars are acceptable reflections of the masses—or, in times past, idealizations of the masses—then more than half the battle is won. These statements were as true of *Birth of a Nation* and *Gone With the Wind* as they were of *Airport* or *Love Story*. The job of seizing and holding the audience's attention is the director's. But even this is not his job alone. Most directors know nothing about lighting, so it is necessary for a lighting cameraman to make certain that the film is continually and vividly exciting to the eye. It is up to the lighting expert to keep the eye busy, and to select telling details. The composer holds the ear, underlining scenes with subtle dramatic strokes, while the editor makes the film move fluently, so that the audience is never bored by the pace.

An exhaustive history of every aspect of the American motion picture would fill as many volumes as the Encyclopaedia Britannica, and, in view of the disappearance of innumerable important films, cannot now be written. Of necessity, any historian tackling the subject must condense the material, omit many figures, and at times seem arbitrary in selection and judgment. I do not plead innocent to the charge of being prejudiced in many areas. No *critical* historian—that is to say, a chronicler of responses to a vast variety of films made over a period of almost sixty years—can within any degree of honesty sustain an impersonal tone. If I have seemed to be unfair to favorite figures, that is because, after a most careful reviewing of their films, I have found that even in the light of the conventions of their own period, they have seemed to be overrated. I have seen and reseen each of the films discussed in this book, where possible on 35 mm.

I have omitted sustained discussions of certain overwhelming "camp" favorites such as Mae West and Fields, because an immense literature already exists on them and it seemed unlikely that anything more could usefully be said. In one matter I am unregenerate. I prefer talking pictures to silent films. It seems to me that the invasion of Broadway dramatists at the dawn of sound gave the American cinema its adulthood. It provided it, more or less consistently until the fifties, with a tough, insolent mind of its own. And new directors from Broadway gave a new depth to acting undreamed of except in the performances of great Broadway figures like Pauline Frederick and Laurette Taylor and the very rare silent star like Lillian Gish in silents.

Some words on the structure of the book are necessary. With the exception of those major directors who bridged the gulf between silents and sound I have preferred to deal with creative figures in single sustained sections, beginning with the decade in which their careers began. Inevitably, this has caused some compression in dealing with films outside of their first decade, but this seemed more satisfactory than dividing their careers into sections separated by scores of pages. Each part of the book is introduced by a special prefatory section giving the over-all background of a particular period in broad general terms. The director has been followed as the main creative force in the American film. Actually, the writer and the cinematographer have been equally influential, but it has proved impossible to show a sustained line of thinking in the works of writers (with rare exceptions like Ben Hecht, Jules Furthman, and the writer-director Joseph L. Mankiewicz and a book following *cinematographic* personal expression should be an entirely separate volume. I have discussed the collaborative nature of the art form in the first chapter.

Since this book is concerned with the art of the American film, an art which has survived the businessmen who run it, I have omitted any consideration of the history of that business. Conservative and rearguard in their thinking, impatient of artists, and disastrously shortsighted, the people who have operated Hollywood deserve a book to themselves. I have been chiefly concerned with their enemies, the men who have fought them to achieve a measure of personal expression.

I have followed a number of main traditions in the writing of the book. The first tradition sprang from Griffith, a rural romanticist whose roots go back to the literature and drama of the nineteenth century. It was a tradition purified by directors of the caliber of King Vidor and Henry King, who retained the rural values but simplified the excessive writing and acting techniques. Against this line of thinking came the Belasco-like tradition of De Mille and Ince (also stemming from epic painters like Alma-Tadema and from novelists like General Lew Wallace) and the Viennese-Berliner traditions of sophisticated boudoir comedy introduced in the work of Lubitsch. The second half of the book deals with the emergence of entirely new traditions. The book has been organized so that all of the successive and complementary modes are clarified.

I have deliberately condensed the final section, on the contemporary film. Most of the directors mentioned there are at the outset of their careers and it is far too early to give them the kind of sustained critical discussion one would accord a Wyler, a Milestone, or a Cukor. I have simply tried to express some of the themes that have centrally concerned them for a mixture of commercial artistic motives—most notably, the theme of the young rebel—and the way in which they have reflected contemporary taste, that fundamental necessity of the crowd-influenced film-maker. At the conclusion I have endeavored to point to possible developments in the future. An account of animated films and documentary (including Flaherty) has been omitted from this survey.

Numerous minor figures have been left out since I have found it more valuable to discuss the major directors in great detail than to make lists of the films of those less important. I have also omitted a discussion of those whose films (e.g., William De Mille's and Mal St. Clair's) have largely disappeared, those whose most important work has been made outside of America (e.g., Fred Zinnemann and Stanley Kubrick), and some figures whose *oeuvre* discloses no perceptible sustained visual style (Allan Dwan, Sidney Lumet, Robert Rossen).

# PART ONE
# The Silent Era

■ ■ ■ ■ ■ ■ ■ ■ ■ ■ ■ ■ ■ ■ ■ ■ ■ ■ ■ ■ ■ ■ ■ ■ ■ ■

# 1. Principles and Beginnings

■ ■ ■ ■ ■ ■ ■ ■ ■ ■ ■ ■ ■ ■ ■ ■ ■ ■ ■ ■ ■ ■ ■ ■ ■

Even in the earliest days of film, collaboration instead of individual
artistic creation was the rule. Griffith has generally been credited exclusively with the excellence of his best films, but he owed a great deal
to his cameraman Billy Bitzer and to assistant writers, few of them
acknowledged. The great silent comedians have tended to claim extravagant things for themselves, including absolute command of every
detail of their films. Actually, such writers as Tim Whelan, Sam
Taylor, and Clyde Bruckman had a great deal to do with the success
of the work of Lloyd, Keaton, and Langdon. Chaplin, despite certain
claims to the contrary, owed much of the refined look of his films to
that neglected cameraman Rollie Totheroh. Erich von Stroheim and
Josef von Sternberg owed a great deal to their cinematographers and
writers, though they were scarcely prepared to admit as much. Cameramen in their films often had a major creative influence, an important
fact which to the dissatisfaction of the cameramen has gone unmen-
tioned in most film histories.

The American cinema, aggressively commercial, artistic often by
accident, grew up during the presidencies of Theodore Roosevelt and
Woodrow Wilson. Their energetic reforms—powerful thrusts against
monopolies early in their careers, Roosevelt's conservation schemes,
and so on—were earnestly supported by many of the new film-makers
in California, but little of their zeal found its way into pictures. The
reasons were twofold: film-makers were working for business people and

banks, and they had to bear in mind that the public was not as progressivist as some politicians in Washington like to suppose. Film was an escapist form, made in an escapist community. After the general removal of the film industry from New York in the teens of the century to southern California, it became the factory and the focus of the world's dreams. It also provided a convenient escape route from process servers to the Mexican border, a not inconsiderable fact at a time when crooked interests were deeply involved in the new industry.

It is unfortunate that the majority of American films did not continue to be made in New York in the late teens of the century when the great emergence of sophistication and urbanization in the mass of Americans took place. Holloywood was, as late as 1919, a largely rural community, and film-makers sometimes even rode to work on horseback. This rural character, reflecting a feeling of agrarian realism and lyricism, continued to flourish until the advent of Lubitsch, though there were brilliant exceptions, including Frank Lloyd's *Madame X* (1920) and Clarence Brown's and Maurice Tourneur's *Foolish Matrons* (1921). While the telephone system, the wireless, electric light, and new improvements in transportation bound America into a largely urban community, and the entry into World War I brought it closer to the rest of the world, the cinema sustained the attitudes of nineteenth-century comedy, melodrama, and rural romance. Seeing many films made between 1918 and 1921 almost convinces one that America was peopled by pretty girls out of a late-nineteenth-century Valentine with large luminous eyes and flowing curls, broad-chested stalwart men in riding boots, and barefoot boys with Tom Sawyer hats who defeated the villain at the wooden garden gate. Even the comedies of Mack Sennett, Hal Roach, and Al Christie kept looking backward to nineteenth-century traditions of knockabout. It was not until 1923–24 that the cinema really began to catch up with Americans. Suddenly, the dimpled darling was partly replaced by the eager flapper. The stalwart hero was replaced by the smooth lounge lizard and the attitudes to sex became somewhat more sophisticated.

Perhaps because of their innocence—or assumed innocence—and their largely rural moral character, early silent films have the charm of primitive paintings. Their visuals often seem modeled on period drawings: They have a silvery quality or a diffused calendar art charm which was expressed in the use of orthochromatic film, in general use until 1924. Because glass stages and ranches were used for film-making, natural light, carefully diffused, gave many silent films a beautiful clarity. The rapid cutting and unpretentious playing again gave a reflection of the energetic life of a booming and still young country. Despite the conservative sentiment I have referred to, the actual appearance and execution of silent films were wonderfully in step with a dynamic people. The great directors, chief among them Griffith and Ince, were robust executors of the basic principles. These principles—aesthetics would be too pretentious a word—were centered on a need to tell a story as economically as possible by means of cutting. Since it was not usual to move the tripod camera (although Griffith did so from time to time) the film must progress by the rapid juxtaposition of fixed images and by as much movement as possible within the frame. A galloping horse, a train chugging along a railroad, a vehicle crammed with police in full cry after a fugitive provided the vivid thrusting movement that the camera did not.

Acting must be constantly animated, every movement larger than life, in order to engage the eye. Silent screen acting by such figures as Valentino, Nazimova, Novarro, Garbo, Mary Pickford, or Douglas Fairbanks always had to be enormously explicit and fluent to prevent a look of static tableaux. Beyond that, realism was the norm. Light sources —the sunlight from a window or the gleam of an electric light bulb, candlelight seeping under a door or shining on a face on a pillow— must be accurately simulated, and the American landscape of fir forest and lake, mountain and river, must be shown with a luminous accuracy that caught its effulgent beauty.

Until the advent of Lubitsch, the silent film script—almost uniformly inferior to the other elements in a work—tended to be based on a number of predications. It was aimed at a public which industry leaders thought to be of the mental age of twelve. Characters had to be drawn in blacks and whites; heroes were staunch and villains beetle-browed; heroines were wiltingly innocent and vamps theatrically menacing.

The "authorship" of silent films was divided between the scenarist and the title writer. Title writers like George Marion, Ralph Spence, the prolific Julian Johnson, formerly of *Photoplay*, and John Colton were responsible for the poor quality of most silent title writing, with its calendar sentiments, the panels wreathed in flowers. Griffith can be charged with having set the tone of these: he wrote his own titles, many of which were lamentable in their humorless sententiousness. Often, titlers would "improve" scripts after the film was completed, adding panels, under the director's supervision, if the screenplay was thought to be lagging. Sometimes the titles interrupted the flow of a performance. At the end of the silent film period, when the silent picture form reached its brief apogee, American directors—taught by such German directors as Murnau and Dupont—began to cut written material to the absolute minimum. The writing was as much a handicap to the expressiveness of the medium as the camerawork was its finest glory.

The best features of silent films were their universality and their sense of spaciousness and freedom: the best comedies, Westerns, and epics had an exhilarating sweep and dash, reflecting the youth and energy of the people who made them. When the Europeans arrived to give a new sophistication to the American film, men like Lubitsch, Leni, and Sjöström were able to use the superb technical resources of the American movie to express their vision in fluid visual terms. Before the studios became consolidated and operated by banks or combines, film-making was fun, a vigorous activity like group sport.

The best silent films still have the power to captivate, in spite of the nineteenth-century dramatic values, stemming from Augustin Daly and Ellen Price Wood, among others. Today, with the increased pace of living, we are conscious of the lethargic pace, the plethora of lengthen titles which make many films of the time look like illustrated books, and the laborious introductions of the players in cameo. We are also aware of the extremely stagy interiors with the camera permanently at medium distance, and the endless dialogueless versions of Broadway successes. Yet the silent era still fascinates and excites. The first thirty years of American cinema may not properly reflect American truths, but rather the charm, the energy, and the fantasies of the American people. The spirit of the period, energetic, forceful, and inventive, as well as Philistine, aggressive, and crass, comes through vividly in this massive volume of work.

# 2. The Advent of D. W. Griffith

Before the advent of the first artist of the American cinema, the field had already been extraordinarily rich in material. The first American film director of consequence was Edwin S. Porter, who followed an early career of manufacturing cameras by joining Thomas Alva Edison's primitive studios in 1900 at the age of thirty. Porter's *The Life of an American Fireman* consisted of 425 feet of excitement showing the rescue of a woman and her child from a burning building. Porter introduced the technique of cross-cutting, showing how to awaken audience interest by building suspense through carefully isolated happenings. Because of the camera's selectivity, it proved more gripping to see such a rescue on the screen than it would in real life. It would not be possible for any single individual to see every particular of the rescue from every point of view. Not even a news report by the most diligent reporter interviewing everybody concerned and braving the fire himself could equal the startling impact of focusing on the details in a compact movie narrative. It became evident at once that film was superior to journalism in isolating the reality of day-to-day experience. It also had the effect of making events more easily absorbable; the movement of images was more exciting than the movement of prose. In 1903 Porter made *The Great Train Robbery,* which again singled out particulars of a gripping incident, and in 1907 *Rescued from an Eagle's Nest,* in which D. W. Griffith appeared.

These primitive films made clear that the motion picture was not a novel in pictures brought to life nor was it photographed theater. It was, in fact, a carefully telescoped, somewhat distorted but brilliantly concentrated visual abstraction of the flow of life itself. The cutting together of images—each one of which presented a highlight of human experience—was designed to provide a more lucid and moving way of telling a story than the narrative line of prose fiction. It became obvious from the outset that movies did not merely reach the vast masses who did not read, but could provide those who did with a more immediate experience. Yet the shortcomings of the medium became apparent from the beginning. A novelist could explore feelings that could not be seen. A brilliant verbal image could cast resonances, making the reader use his imagination, while by its very nature film was literal, spelling out what a writer might imply. The fascination of movies was entirely different from the fascination of reading. There may be some basis for believing that film reduced the intensity of the human imagination in the twentieth century by filling out realistically what might be imagined in reading. The stars, of course, were developments of the heroes and heroines of the popular literature and theater. It was comforting to know that they came from the ranks of the masses, that they were frequently shopgirls or soda fountain boys raised to the pinnacle of fame.

Another pleasure in films was in seeing, probably for the first time if you lived in Omaha, the great stars of the Broadway stage. It was magnificent to see the great Laurette Taylor or Pauline Frederick on the screen when a trip to New York plus the price of a theater ticket might be well beyond the pocketbook. Chiefly, though, a film star meant someone created by the movies. For instance, two of the earliest dominant companies, Vitagraph and Biograph, developed newcomers and effectively launched them on the public consciousness. Vitagraph offered Florence Turner, a charming and talented girl who played Topsy in the first screen version of *Uncle Tom's Cabin.* Vitagraph also developed John Bunny. This fat comedian became the prototype of the burlesque screen clown and his quarrels with his screen wife Flora Finch became prototypes of husband and wife comedy almost up to the present. Florence Turner was the original innocent heroine, spirited and resourceful but still pure and virginal, who, stemming as she did from the girl-woman ideals of a Gene Stratton or Eleanor Porter, set the style for Mary Pickford, Blanche Sweet, and scores of others later on.

Other companies included Essanay, Kalem, and Keystone, home of the pie-wielding Keystone Cops, but the only studio that seriously

approached film as an art form was Biograph. It was Biograph that used
literary classics widely as its sources of inspiration (not always acknowledged). It was at this primitive and stimulating New York studio
that the young D. W. Griffith's genius flourished and grew, that this
extraordinary man fitted together the forms of film into a medium of
artistic expression. Griffith was first and foremost a nineteenth-century
man, working precisely within the established traditions of film already available by 1915. His many short films at Biograph established
his approach to individual shots: exteriors glowing with a silvery light,
interiors soft with fire or candle, heroines' faces large and carefully
backlit, a style as fixed as that of Sickert. Lake and forest, living room
and bedroom had an accuracy so authentic we seemed to be living
among the characters. Yet their miming was often painfully overemphatic; it took a Chaplin to understand the subtle possibilities—
learned from the English music hall—of screen mime. We recognize
Griffith's created milieu, but we cannot, except when they are played
by Lillian Gish or Mae Marsh, feel for its inhabitants. When a poor
actor—a Robert Harron, a Carol Dempster, or a Henry B. Walthall—
takes the stage, the results are markedly inferior.

Griffith began as Lawrence Griffith, a stage name he preferred to his
own, acting in traveling companies, writing plays and poems on the
side. He first met the Reverend Thomas Dixon, author of the inflammatory *The Clansman,* while appearing as leading man in Dixon's
play *The One Woman* in New York in 1906. Shortly thereafter, he
wrote a panoramic spectacle called *War,* based on the events of 1776
and later incorporated in his film *America.* Finally, he secured a job at
the American Mutoscope and Biograph Company as an actor. He wrote
a number of screen plays (at $15 each), eventually obtaining the oppor-
tunity to direct *The Adventures of Dollie,* the story of a girl stolen by
gypsies. Griffith directed from a kitchen chair, using few or no sets, and
instead the fields and forests of America. Florence Lawrence, a former
child actress called Baby Flo, became his first star, and among his actresses was Jeanie Macpherson, who later became Cecil B. De Mille's
chief scenarist. Mack Sennett was an extra for Griffith. Formerly a
boxing trainer and member of a musical comedy chorus, he specialized in
portraying comic policemen who later became the bases for the characters of the Keystone Cops.

Griffith made many of the early pictures at Cuddebackville, near
New York, moving to California for a time in 1912. A young film-maker

named Thomas Ince went out at the same time, taking over the 101 Ranch near the ocean at Santa Monica. Among those who left on the same historical train journey were Mary Pickford, Mack Sennett, Billy Bitzer, and Robert Harron. Griffith set up a small studio at Grand Avenue and Washington Street downtown with a stage for interior shots. A loft on Spring Street and Second was rented for processing. A two-reel version of *Enoch Arden* was his most ambitious production, shot in Santa Monica. And Griffith made primitive Westerns, beautiful in their simplicity and feeling for the wild.

Griffith's first feature was the four-reel *Judith of Bethulia* (1913), a slight and halting account of the Apocryphal heroine who decapitated Holofernes. Although the film is the work of a very young man, with little or no psychological cogency, it has a strong period feeling, summoning up an era with effortless skill. The peaceful life of the simple people is effectively placed in contrast with the barbarous maraudings of Holofernes' army, galloping through clouds of dust to attack a walled city. Alas, for all his command of spectacle, Griffith had not yet learned the ability to affect an audience emotionally: the all-important scene, when Judith, driven by an irresistible attraction for her victim, kisses him and then raises the knife above his sleeping form, goes for little, in part due to Blanche Sweet's inexpressive playing. In this sequence, Griffith does succeed in making an important advance in dramatic technique: as she pauses before the death blow, Judith looks out toward the right of frame, when the dead and dying compatriots with whom she grew up appear to haunt her. She turns back, resolved to strike the fatal blow.

Griffith's next films, *Home Sweet Home* (1914) and *The Avenging Conscience* (1914) among them, did little to advance his career, indicating instead his shortcomings at the time: an inability to cast satisfactorily and a tendency to present elaborate, pretentious, and pseudo-literary plots. *The Avenging Conscience* was a pastiche of Poesque elements, badly played by Henry B. Walthall as the murderer of an ancient relative whose spirit returns to haunt him. *The Tell-Tale Heart* was the chief inspiration, but *The Black Cat* also cast its influence. The subject, despite Griffith's fondness for Poe, was quite unsuitable for him, his nostalgic expansive Protestant character the precise opposite of Poe's inverted pagan psyche.

It was *The Birth of a Nation* (1915) which firmly established Griffith's reputation, making him an international celebrity and giving the new medium itself a degree of respectability. It was the first motion picture to open in the Broadway area of New York. The Reverend Thomas Dixon's *The Clansman,* on which the film in part is based, was the work of an unreconstructed Southerner, and its bias against black people was notoriously severe. At the first night in New York, Dixon appeared and told the audience that he would not have dreamed of letting anyone but the son of a Confederate soldier make the picture. Griffith's portrayal of blacks in the production stemmed from a deeply rooted southern sensibility: he had all the passionate naïveté which can so often bring about unintentionally evil results. By glorifying the Ku Klux Klan, which, a title informs us, was "the organization that saved the South from the anarchy of black rule," and by showing Federal and Confederate rallying together after reconstruction in a "Holy War to protect their Aryan birthrights," Griffith presents us with a naked and dangerous racism. At the end of the original version of the picture, Abraham Lincoln actually advocated the shipping of the black population to Africa. Griffith's opening title is: "If in this work we have conveyed to the mind the ravages of war to the end that war may be an abhorrence these efforts will not have been in vain." Yet a moment later he offers us the words: "The bringing of the African to America sowed the first seeds of dissension."

At one stroke, Griffith had established the intolerance and conservatism that marked much of the silent screen. The founding father of Hollywood, he imparted to it a provincialism, a bourgeois Philistinism from which it has never quite escaped. As is well known, the film used with unprecedented skill all of the many techniques previously developed: the iris and the wipe, the fade and the dissolve, the use of rapid cutting to provide an exciting picture rhythm and momentum. Yet it also helped to improve the fortunes of the Ku Klux Klan at a time when that infamous organization was suffering from widespread criticism; gave President Wilson, who admired the film as "history written with lightning," a grossly distorted view of the southern states of the nation of which he was President; and caused an increase in racial dissension which continued for more than a year.

Griffith with his ironclad naïveté was astonished when delegations of liberal-minded citizens called on local police chiefs and demanded that the film be removed from theaters. Mayor Thompson banned all showings in Chicago. Ohio, too, prevented showings for a period. In the northern states the reaction was unequivocal: the New York *Evening*

*Post* reported that "[Audiences] clapped when the masked riders took vengeance on Negroes, and they clapped when the hero refused to shake the hand of a mulatto who had risen by political intrigue to become Lieutenant-Governor."

The whole purpose of the film is to attack northern liberalism as personified by the well-meaning politician Austin Stoneman, and to suggest subjugation, mass export, or extermination as the only solution to the black problem. The message is delivered with all the fervor and dazzling technique for which Griffith had already been noted. For all Griffith's rudimentary portrayal of character—white and black—from the Stoneman family with its irritating frisky children down to the humblest mulatto servant, and his inability to provide a satisfactory history of the Civil War, all of his work here is in the highest degree physically impressive. Between dull passages of exposition weighed down by Griffith's vainglorious titles boasting of every historical reconstruction before we see it, there are fine stretches of screen narrative: the first call for volunteers; the celebration of the victory at Bull Run; the raid on Piedmont, its succession of shootings, rape, and pillage conveyed with all the immediacy of Brady photographs; and above all the siege of Atlanta, a magnificence of cathartic imagery.

Shocked by his critics, Griffith in the same year poured his earnings into an even more extravagant spectacle which attacked, of all things, *Intolerance* (1916). He returned from the inflammatory to the sentimental mode, viewing not just one period of history but four, in the grossest and most naïve terms. By doing so, he succeeded in turning the greatest intellects against the cinema for some fifteen years. Magnificent in execution, foolish in content, *Intolerance* convinced many that the American cinema was a strictly commercial medium, that for film-making of high and austere dedication, the critic must look to Europe. It was thought that, divorced by a 3,000-mile land mass from New York, the Hollywood film under its leaders would never be anything but a side show or circus for the enjoyment of the masses. For all that it advanced the technique of film, *Intolerance* damaged Hollywood's prestige even more seriously than its epic predecessor.

It is unnecessary to dwell again on the film's inspired use of parallel narrative in telling four stories: of Babylon, of Christ, of the Huguenot revolt, and of the threat of capital punishment in more modern times, all accompanied by a recurring image of Lillian Gish endlessly rocking a cradle to the printed words of Whitman's poem. And it is needless to

Scene from INTOLERANCE

Scene from INTOLERANCE

comment on the masterful handling of details of siege, murder, cruci-fixion, and trial. The film's primitive grandeur is real, but it is a false portrayal of history, reflecting the director's ignorance of actual events. As an example, the entire siege of Babylon is fictitious, since that city in fact fell to the invader without a struggle at the time.

Griffith next turned to a semi-documentary war story, *Hearts of the World* (1916), made at the behest of the British Government. Despite its many effective shots of the trenches, the film was marred by Griffith's inadequate portrayal of the lives of British soldiers, and its official back-ing ensured that the picture of the generals was excessively flattering. A series of unremarkable features followed, including *True Heart Susie* (1919); but *Broken Blossoms* (1919) was impressive—a poetic, per-sonal work, and a great advance for Griffith.

Based on Thomas Burke's Limehouse story *The Yellow Man and the Girl, Broken Blossoms* even survives its dated opening title: "It is a tale of temple bells, sounding at sunset before the image of Buddha; it is a tale of love and lovers; it is a tale of tears." The three central figures are symbols: Battling Burrows (Donald Crisp) is a boxing champion, who symbolizes the cruelty of life; Lucy, his daughter (Lillian Gish), is feminine weakness personified; the Yellow Man (Richard Barthelmess) is a representative of the downtrodden, shrink-ing upon contact with violence. Griffith moves in this film from senti-mental romance and the epic documentary to the lyric form. Extraor-dinarily concentrated, *Broken Blossoms* is at its best deeply moving: the sequence in which her father drags Lucy from her hiding place and she pleads for mercy before he strikes her down is, due to the dynamic editing and Miss Gish's playing, made a piercingly lifelike visual experience. The last sequence shows Griffith's new mastery of sus-pense—the Yellow Man picking up a knife to stab himself to death following his murder of Lucy's father; the police breaking in; then a shot of a man striking a gong, and ships sailing out toward the Thames basin. A short textbook of editing in itself, it is a sequence that rewards many reviewings. Photographed under the supervision of Hendrik Sartov by Billy Bitzer, the film offers consistently rewarding images, its evocation of misty streets, piers gleaming, the tracery of rigging on a skyline, cramped lodginghouse rooms foreshadowing and superior to von Sternberg's *The Docks of New York*.

After minor works, Griffith returned to popularity with *Way Down East* (1920), adapted by Anthony Paul Kelly from the novel by William

Scene from **BROKEN BLOSSOMS**

A. Brady and the long-running Broadway play by Lottie Blair Parker (1898). The first two thirds of the film are indifferently directed: a humble servant (Lillian Gish) arriving at a rich New England house, betrayed by a lecher, left to raise her baby out of wedlock, forced to baptize it herself, and fleeing to a windswept town. Not even Gish's sensitive playing can save this narrative, based on the traditions of nineteenth-century moral melodrama. The film gains momentum with the exploration of the sewing circle in the small town, the gossip Maria Poole bustling along a snowy road to inform her friends of the unwed mother's behavior, and Gish's flight into a blizzard, all brilliantly shot by Bitzer. It is impossible not to be excited by sequences like the search for the lost girl by her friend (Richard Barthelmess) at night by lantern and her journey by ice floe. Once again, Griffith's greatest strength is his ability to involve the audience in the lives of the characters, his Dickensian sense of realism and evocation of a lived-in place. The New England environment, with its wooden houses and fences, its carriages and silent muffled figures moving against snow, is very fully achieved.

Unfortunately, Griffith seldom reached that level again. His *Dream Street* (1922) (played at the first screenings with sound accompaniment) was a failure; and *Orphans of the Storm* (1922), adapted from the novel *Two Orphans* by A. D'Ennery, a major disappointment. The latter begins with a typically specious title: "The lesson—the French Revolution rightly overthrew a BAD government . . . But we in America should be careful lest we with a GOOD government mistake fanatics for leaders and exchange our decent law and order for Anarchy and Bolshevism." The plot is a rigmarole: the De Voudrays, outraged at the marriage of their daughter with a foreigner, snatch the baby away, kill the husband, and finally leave the child as a foundling on the steps of Notre Dame, where she is discovered and raised with another foundling. The two girls—played by the Gish sisters—grow up during the Revolution, a simplified portrait of which is given by the film (Danton is described in one title as "the Abraham Lincoln of France"!) Both luxury and poverty are vulgarly realized, the Rescued by Rover climax in which one of the girls is snatched from the jaws of Madame Guillotine does not wear well, and the film's one redeeming feature—apart from some well-staged crowd scenes and Lillian Gish's warmly felt performance—is the playing of Joseph Schildkraut as the feline Chevalier de Voudray, a role he repeated in the thirties in his portrait of Philippe Egalité in Van Dyke's *Marie Antoinette*.

In 1924 Griffith attempted a new major work, an epic in which he essayed a portrait of the events of 1776: *America,* based on a story by Robert W. Chambers. Characteristically, he attempted nothing less than a physical re-creation of a whole era. In historical-documentary terms, *America* is almost as remarkable as *The Birth of a Nation*. Such scenes as the opening in Lexington, Massachusetts, a glimpse of George III in the House of Lords (a ceilinged set seen only for a moment), the carousing of the renegade Walter Butler surrounded by his doxies, Paul

Revere's ride—we might be actually present at the events, the roles not so much acted as lived. In many ways, the portrait of historical figures was superior to anything Griffith had attempted before, and his account of Walter Butler's career was entirely convincing. The sequence of Valley Forge, in particular, pleased many an educated child.

With *Isn't Life Wonderful?* (1924) Griffith moved back to the mood of *Hearts of the World,* evoking the lives of Germans in the period after the First World War. Interesting for its use of locations, the film suffers from a meandering narrative; the central love story is particularly repetitive and vexing, and Carol Dempster, Griffith's new star, was a decided liability.

Griffith's later career was depressing. Outclassed by the sophisticates of the Twenties generation, he was already an anachronism by 1928. He seemed an old-fashioned figure with his great nineteenth-century hawk face, and his attempts to keep up to date were pitiful. He was reduced to making films like *Drums of Love* and *Lady of the Pavements*, a travesty of Diderot's *Jacques le Fataliste*, which was later made by Bresson as *Les Dames du Bois de Boulogne.* The advent of the sound film destroyed him completely. *Abraham Lincoln* (1930) a series of tableaux, was a faint echo of *The Birth of a Nation. The Struggle* (1931), though a worthy attempt to show accurately the lives of the poor, and though less sentimentalized in this area than any other Griffith film, was somewhat dry and sterile in execution. Griffith's last years are sad to recall: appearing on radio in Los Angeles to discuss his former successes, living in the sterile ambience of the Hotel Knickerbocker, wandering down Hollywood Boulevard like some dress extra, "supervising" a British remake of *Broken Blossoms,* or faced with the final humiliation of acting as a special adviser on the looks of primitive women in *One Million B.C.*

■ ■ ■ ■ ■ ■ ■ ■ ■ ■ ■ ■ ■ ■ ■ ■ ■ ■ ■ ■ ■ ■ ■ ■ ■ ■ ■ ■

# 3. Followers of Griffith

■ ■ ■ ■ ■ ■ ■ ■ ■ ■ ■ ■ ■ ■ ■ ■ ■ ■ ■ ■ ■ ■ ■ ■ ■ ■ ■

Of Griffith's imitators, the most distinguished was Henry King, who
had worked as an actor for Thomas Ince. King was not, strictly speaking, an artist. He had no strong ideas of his own, he had a somewhat
stolid style. He drew his films from proven successes of fiction—all the
way from Hergesheimer's minor classic *Tol'able David,* down to Olive
Higgins Prouty's *Stella Dallas,* and worse. Yet though he lacked Griffith's
sense of rhythm and epic sweep, he improved on him in one important
respect: he had the ability to penetrate character, to make his performers—especially his actresses—show not simply one aspect of human being (envy, meanness, weakness of spirit, heroism, ecstatic adora-
tion) but also ring a whole series of changes, creating mirrors for the
unpredictability of life.

*Tol'able David* (1921) was drawn from a screenplay by Edmund
Goulding and King himself based on Joseph Hergesheimer's short story
about a West Virginia mountain boy ruled by a stern code of honor.
David comes to manhood when confronted with the pitiless realities
presented by the marauding Hatburn family. Innocence has been stripped
of its illusions, the outside world has broken up the sleepy enclave of
the village, and Tol'able David is ready to face life. The production was
fluently and excitingly put together, a fine model of the action film.

*Stella Dallas* (1925) was an improvement on anything King had done
hitherto. For example, there is a sequence, shot with exquisite tact,
when mother and daughter, abandoned by their friends, sit down to a

lonely birthday dinner together, bound by a common sadness. King sur-
mounts even the major hurdle of the titles ("Springtime and her twin
sister—romance"). Olive Higgins Prouty's famous soap opera, adapted
by Frances Marion, traces the misadventures of Stella (played with
consummate skill by Belle Bennett) in a small town. She sets her cap
for a newcomer, Dallas; he marries her out of boredom. Their daughter,
Helen (Lois Moran) grows up scarcely knowing her father; Stella becomes more and more fluffy and profligate; finally turned into a drunken
tramp, rejected by her lover, she presses herself against a symbolic iron
railing to see her daughter's marriage in the rain.

King managed the film with remarkable flair, a constantly expressive
camera style, and a strong grasp of narrative, convincing us that we are
seeing a portrait of the truth. The small factory town where Dallas
works and marries is starkly evoked, and all the other backgrounds,
aided by some marvelously accurate sets, are fascinating to watch. Best
of all is the episode in the resort where Helen Dallas meets her future
husband: the mother rejecting Ouspensky's *Tertium Organum* ("sounds
like stomach trouble") for the latest Elinor Glyn novel, couples leaving
for summery boat rides or tennis games, all capped by one superlative
moment: the daughter looks up as someone says, "There's that awful
woman!" and we see Stella Dallas far off in the trees; slowly her image
dissolves over the first into a larger one, marching relentlessly forward
in vulgar frock and flourishing a parasol; we are at once made aware
of the embarrassment of the vision. Frequently, King uses visuals in
this manner to underline the sharp pain of an emotion, making the
film, for all its novelettish elements, a moving achievement.

Following *Stella Dallas,* King's most important silent picture was
*The Winning of Barbara Worth* (1926). Harold Bell Wright's famous
novel of pioneer life was perfectly rendered by King, whose unit worked
in harrowing conditions in the Nevada desert; the screenplay by Frances.
Marion was a model of construction. During a brief prologue, Jefferson
Worth (Charles Lane), a banker, hears of the plans to build a railroad
across the desert; in a sandstorm which almost kills him, he learns the
value of taming the wilderness. His adopted daughter—her parents are
killed in the storm—inherits her father's dreams, and after she grows to
adulthood she falls in love with a pioneer engineer. Despite the limitations of Ronald Colman and Vilma Banky in the leading roles, King's
direction was full of vigor and imagination: the sandstorm, the arrival
of the settlers, the magnificently staged river flood, above all the evoca-

tion of the lives of courageous pioneers—Harold Bell Wright's somewhat banal pages were greatly improved in this adaptation.

Another director influenced by Griffith, using simple, realistic settings for often romantic and sentimental subjects, but improving on him in his plain, untheatrical, and unforced direction of the players, King Vidor did not make his best films until the sound period. His fondness for medium shots and his rather pedestrian editing gave most of his silent works a rather stodgy flavor; the personality behind the silents has a mild, detached geniality and coolness in contrast with the intensity, the passion of his great work in talkies. Vidor's first films, which do not appear to have survived, were made in his birthplace of Houston, Texas; he made an example of Christian Science propaganda, *The Turn of the Road*; finally the directors of First National gave him a serious opportunity to make a drama, *The Jack-Knife Man* (1919), which established his rather dry and distant style, his interest in the lives of the common people, and his concern with shooting films in pastoral surroundings.

*The Jack-Knife Man* is the story of an old-timer, Peter Lane, a Mississippi shanty boat owner with a gift for whittling toys. In Potter's Cove, a sleepy settlement at a river bend, he conducts an uneasy flirtation with a widow who finally marries him, after complications ensuing from his harboring of two fugitives from a storm—an exhausted woman and her baby. It is in every respect a Griffithian subject, both in its sentimentality and in its technical execution, decorated by lighting effects ingenious for the period (at one point, the entire screen is dark save for the light of a single match flame) and enhanced by authentically grubby lived-in sets of the shanty boat interior. The titles are in the tradition of the period ("The only home he had ever known is sacrificed for a little one's need"; "At bedtime the childish heart is too young to understand and is vaguely troubled"). The playing, though naturalistic enough, is scarcely above the average.

The film's degree of surface realism earned Vidor a reputation sufficient to make such films as *Three Wise Fools* (1923) and *Peg o' My Heart* (1923), in which the great Laurette Taylor repeated her famous stage success. Another Laurette Taylor vehicle, *Happiness* (1923), was typical of Vidor's work in the period. Modeled on Mary Pickford, Miss Taylor was in her forties made to seem (almost) a girl of seventeen or eighteen, a dress shop messenger who gets into a series of scrapes, winning the affection of a rich woman (Hedda Hopper) despite her disgraceful table manners. The film has a neo-Victorian charm. In the opening scene Laurette Taylor removes a mask during a children's party, to disclose an identical mask of makeup which hides Miss Taylor's middle-aged countenance. There is also an amusing dinner party sequence, in which Miss Taylor misbehaves delightfully at the expense of her hostess, Miss Hopper. Both screenplay and titles assume a condescending attitude to the poor and at the same time perpetuate the then common film myth that the rich are uniformly cruel and the poor uniformly kind.

For most of the Twenties, Vidor was handicapped by vehicles of this kind, exploitation pieces like *The Wine of Youth, His Hour* with Elinor Glyn, or that well-made version of Hergesheimer, *Wild Oranges*. His most famous films of the period remain *The Big Parade* (1925), *La Bohème* (1925), *Show People* (1928), and *The Crowd* (1928).

Of these, the first two are the least satisfactory. *The Big Parade* does not wear well: the portrait of World War I is softened and senti-mentalized out of existence, soldiers portrayed as innocents thrust into the maw of battle, the cannons wreathed—to paraphrase the contempo-rary critic Iris Barry—in scriptwriter's roses. Laurence Stallings' false and attitudinizing screenplay in fact represents the worst of silent film "thinking"; even the most grievous talkie writer never matched these pretty printed lies. The scenes on the Western Front look trivial along-side contemporary photographs: the lice, rats, and roaches, the urine and blood, the disease, fear, and horror of the true events are altogether lost in this version.

*La Bohème* is as false about life in Paris as Mürger's novel and Puccini's opera; directed with cold detachment, it is redeemed only by Lillian Gish's accomplished playing as Mimi. *Show People* is a sport among Vidor's films, a satire of Hollywood which contrives to give the public the illusion it is seeing the real place. Marion Davies (an obvious but witty comedienne) arrives in Hollywood dressed up as a southern belle, simpering like Mae Murray; hired at the Mack Sennett studios, she is showered by a soda siphon, deals out custard pies, and is chased by the Keystone Cops. Achieving stardom and bad manners, she sees herself in a tennis outfit ("Marion Davies? Who's *she*?"), unwittingly rejects Charlie Chaplin's request for an autograph, and reaches the apogee of her career: being directed by King Vidor. There were skilled impersonations by Miss Davies of Gloria Swanson and Joan Crawford, "fun" appearances by John Gilbert and other stars. The movie is an escapist farce rendered in cheerfully artificial terms.

In the same year as this amusing but trivial contrivance, King Vidor's career received a fillip: for the first time since *The Jack-Knife Man* he made a really personal work, *The Crowd,* a film made at the very end of the silent period which sparked off an extremely interesting talkie career. Admittedly the central couple played by James Murray and Eleanor Boardman are prettified versions of real people, devoid of tension, cruelty, and unpredictability. Yet this story of two young people coming to the Big City is executed with such skill that its sentimentality can easily be overlooked. It is a superb piece of craftsmanship.

The film is full of good sequences: the hero's first discovery of New York from the Hudson ferry; his honeymoon train journey to Niagara Falls, flexing his muscles and brushing his teeth before going to bed with his wife; the introduction to the gigantic city office, with rows of desks and white-collar workers; the death of the couple's child; the final moment when the hero is swallowed up in the masses, another anonymous face among millions of New Yorkers.

Rowland V. Lee, who had worked as an actor and a director for Ince, and deeply admired his editing skills, made a number of accomplished films in the silent period marked by a lyrical realism. They included *The Secret Hour* (1928), the first of several versions of Sidney Howard's *They Knew What They Wanted,* with Pola Negri in a very skillful performance (Pauline Lord had played the role on the New York stage) as a city girl married to a rancher (Jean Hersholt). Lee shot the film in the San Fernando Valley's Italian vineyard district, in a romantic style that conveyed the environment's natural beauty.

Lee's *Doomsday* (1925) is in every way a remarkable film, alive with intelligence, movingly and beautifully made. The subject matter—a novel by Warwick Deeping adapted by Donald W. Lee—was not particularly interesting: a young woman (Florence Vidor) is torn between the love of a simple young man of the woods (Gary Cooper) and an older and richer but impotent husband. It is as though D. H. Lawrence's *Lady Chatterley's Lover* had been rewritten by Ethel M. Dell. Nevertheless—and despite the handicap of Florence Vidor's expressionlessly stolid heroine—Lee's direction is in every way extraordinary. The English setting—a village and the forests and fields that surround it—is flawlessly realized. The feeling for the open air, the freshness of the scenes in the sun and rain of high summer, the devices whereby we see the heroine's agony of decision—a room transferred as she imagines the problems of cleaning it, her tension conveyed by the

*Gary Cooper, Florence Vidor,* DOOMSDAY

moving minute hand on a clock—indicate a directorial talent of a high order. Henry Gerrard's camerawork is quite beyond praise, capturing the softly lit interiors, the sweep of meadow and hill with equal felicity. Like King and Vidor, Lee was a director who learned his Griffith lessons of realism well, but whose cool intelligence prevented any Griffithian sentimental excesses.

Another important film, composed as Paramount's "answer" to Metro-Goldwyn-Mayer's *The Big Parade,* Lee's *Barbed Wire* (1926) offered Pola Negri as a Renée Adorée-like peasant, not quite to the manner born. The John Gilbert role was filled by Clive Brook, equally miscast

*Claude Gillingwater, Pola Negri,* BARBED WIRE

as a German soldier imprisoned in Negri's native village. Hall Caine's novel, and the script by Jules Furthman, attempt a pacifist argument, bringing the proceedings to an unsatisfactory close as Negri's blinded brother returns from the war to forgive her passion for the Hun in a sequence inspired by a dream of Lee's, the dead come marching out of the sky to approve his "liberal" decision. Yet Lee manages to salvage much from this confection: the creation of the village life in the opening scenes; the evocation of the grain harvesting; the ringing of the Angelus to summon young men to war; the tracking shots along barbed wire already entangling the countryside—with the aid of the great camera-man Bert Glennon Lee evoked a mythical, archetypal France as convincing as the Lawrentian England of *Doomsday*.

Perhaps the most underrated of Griffith's followers was Monta Bell, another former actor who had worked with Chaplin as an assistant on *A Woman of Paris*. All of his films had imaginative touches: in the opening sequence of *Lady of the Night* (1924), Norma Shearer, *sans* makeup, leaves jail after a long incarceration, stopping for a moment to paint her lips, using as a mirror the window of a hearse. It is for *Man, Woman and Sin* (1927), written by Alice Duer Miller, that Bell most deserves to be remembered: from beginning to end, this is a very well directed film. The opening shot indicates Bell's mastery, as in a composition (by Percy Hilburn) worthy of Mathew Brady at his greatest, we see a small boy picking up bottles along a railroad track observed by a rich brat and his mother on a train ("Don't point, dear!"). In the slums of Washington, D.C., a complete portrait of a life of poverty is created, in images that succeed each other with assurance and the silvery delicacy of period daguerreotypes. Al Whitcomb, the Tom Sawyerish boy hero, experiences rejection from a fashionable child's birthday party, sells a few articles of clothing, and finds consolation in a haunted house where the cobwebs and flickering penny candles create an enchanted world. After these early scenes, which capture with economy the heightened intensity of childhood feelings, we move to Al Whitcomb's adulthood (he is now played by John Gilbert). Here again Bell does not falter. Whitcomb obtains a job on a newspaper, and the physical grubbiness of the life of the printshop, the spiritual grubbiness of muckraking newsmen are conveyed with great force (Bell was a newspaperman in his youth). The second half of the film is dominated by the performance of Jeanne Eagels as the society editor who has been given her job because she is the mistress of the proprietor. Willful,

*John Gilbert, Jeanne Eagels,* MAN, WOMAN AND SIN

callous, a platinum blonde chain-smoking with a Scott Fitzgerald air, she seems to sum up all the brittle doomed women of the late Twenties (herself included: two years after the film she was dead).

Another Griffithian of great talent was William Wellman, whose *Beggars of Life* (1927) had much of the pastoral lyricism that distinguished Rowland V. Lee's best work, without the handicap of the conventional writing. Drawn from an autobiographical work of the tramp Jim Tully, *Beggars of Life* is in its way a masterpiece, among the most excellent of all the films influenced by Griffith's talent. At the opening, Wellman builds the audience's concern for its central characters with sure strokes: a drifter (beautifully played by Richard Arlen) wakes by a railroad, peers through a nearby window, and salivates at the sight of bacon and eggs on a table. Seeing a man apparently asleep at the table, he finds him dead and the murderess, a pretty, orphaned girl (Louise Brooks), cowering on the upstairs landing. Tramp and girl hop a freight train, journey across Minnesota, and dream of escape to Canada. Outsiders intervening in this fugitive romance are shown to

*Wallace Beery, Louise Brooks,* BEGGARS OF LIFE

be mindlessly cruel, because, as Arlen remarks, everyone is unhappy, all of us are "beggars of life." When the runaways meet a group of itinerants, the tramp's offer of help inevitably points to a mass rape of the girl and the boy's murder. Shot in cool grays by the great Henry Gerrard, the picture evokes with striking freshness the America of the open road, railroad tracks stretching across wheat fields, the relief that comes from finding a place to rest, the uncrushable optimism of the fugitive. Fourteen years later the film was echoed in Preston Sturges' *Sullivan's Travels* (1941).

Far less talented than Henry King, King Vidor, Monta Bell, and William Wellman, two sentimental Griffithian directors have mysteriously achieved a reputation: Frank Borzage and Marshall Neilan. *Humoresque* (1920) was probably the most skillful of Borzage's silent films, though Fannie Hurst's story of the love affair of a violinist and a rich woman demanded the soundtrack and the unbridled enthusiasm Jean Negulesco brought to the Forties remake in order to make tolerable its essential absurdity. *Lazybones* (1925) and *Seventh Heaven* (1927) were lavish exercises in romanticism, embarrassingly dated today. Borzage persisted in making old fashioned sentimental films in the talkie period,

*Joan Crawford, John Garfield,* HUMORESQUE

including *Little Man, What Now?* (1934), a travesty of Hans Fallada's book. He did achieve some distinction with *No Greater Glory* (1934), his version of Molnár's 1907 play *The Boys of Paul Street,* in which children act out the events of a war in a European street. And his *A Farewell to Arms* (1932) and *History Is Made at Night* (1937), the latter of which offered a well-shot shipwreck sequence suggested by the *Titanic* disaster, were superior examples of Hollywood craftsmanship.

Neilan had none of Borzage's polish and all of his sentimentality; his series of Mary Pickford vehicles were particularly tiresome, encouraging her worst mannerisms as an actress. His career fizzled out in talkies; he re-emerged finally as an actor in Elia Kazan's *A Face in the Crowd* (1957).

■ ■ ■ ■ ■ ■ ■ ■ ■ ■ ■ ■ ■ ■ ■ ■ ■ ■ ■ ■ ■ ■ ■ ■ ■ ■

# 4. Originators of Screen Comedy

■ ■ ■ ■ ■ ■ ■ ■ ■ ■ ■ ■ ■ ■ ■ ■ ■ ■ ■ ■ ■ ■ ■ ■ ■

The chief progenitors of American silent comedy, Mack Sennett and Hal Roach, both owed their plain and direct style and insistence on fluid cutting to Griffith. Like him, they combined interior settings and natural landscapes, blending actual daylight and night-for-night shooting with stylized and unrealistic plots and situations. Sennett began as a vaudeville entertainer, and introduced vaudeville traditions of knockabout farce into his films. He learned from Griffith while working for him at Biograph; in fact, he appeared in a Griffith slapstick film, *The Curtain Pole,* in 1909. In 1911 he made his first comedy, *The Diving Girl,* starring Mabel Normand. His settings were natural and charmingly recognizable: a beach, a pier, a woodland, and the seemingly endless streets of Los Angeles flanked with telephone poles and leading into humpbacked hills like giant sand dunes. In 1916 *Mickey* appeared, with Miss Normand as its star. Versatile, possessed of a flawless sense of timing, Mabel Normand was a forerunner of Carole Lombard in the 1930s. Sennett also developed the ill-fated Fatty Arbuckle, Chester Conklin, Charlie Chase, Raymond Hitchcock, and of course Chaplin, whose best-known Sennett feature was *Tillie's Punctured Romance* (1914), which featured a chase by the Keystone Cops and was the blueprint for screwball comedy later on.

Artless by today's standards, Sennett's films had a signal virtue: they used landscape and recognizable people for an extension of vaudeville techniques, and they showed how expert cutting could drive home the

point of a visual joke. His chase scenes were dreamlike and hallucinatory, releasing farce from the theatrical proscenium. Hal Roach
also did much to develop the medium. He began the exploitation of
Harold Lloyd and, later, the delicious absurdities of Laurel and Hardy,
Lloyd's *Bumping into Broadway* (1919) established a mode with its
brash naïveté and sophomoric humor. By the mid-1920s American
silent comedy with all of its boisterous energy and pace had become established as a new art form, and in the hands of the very great figures
it outgrew the awkward growing pains of the Sennett school.

The major silent comedies of Lloyd, Keaton, Langdon, and Chaplin
followed Sennett's lead in being devoid of *photographic* invention. The
inventiveness lay in the handling of the actors, and in a large amount
of photographic improvisation on the set. However, Chaplin's films,
especially *The Gold Rush,* were beautifully lit. The *situations* were inventive due to the expert collaboration of the actors with their gag
writers, Chaplin alone creating his scripts virtually in their entirety.
The plots were of classic uniformity: an underprivileged young man,
not rich as a rule and certainly far from handsome, is generally regarded as something of a misfit until circumstances drive him to perform acts of bravery and he invariably wins the hand of a girl. It was
a shrewd reworking in popular terms of the plays of old in which the
clown becomes the knight in shining armor and wins the fair lady. The
shrewd formula worked, since most American males at that time had
not acquired the sexual confidence and financial affluence of today, and
saw themselves if they lived in big cities as social pygmies in whom
virile, powerful men were struggling to be let out. The end of each
film perpetuated the pleasant legend that with sufficient effort, any
young man, no matter how poor or physically weak, could capture the
young lady of his choice if he merely set his mind to it. No doubt, in
its way, the celluloid dream combined with Griffithian fantasies in fos-
tering the romantic illusions of two generations.

As in the other films of the period, the camera remained largely
stationary in the silent comedies, in some ways an advantage because in
this fashion the talents of the entertainers could be studied without
fragmentation. Keaton's films offered the most fluid editing style of
the comedians' films—and his films therefore gave an illusion of camera
mobility. Lloyd had the surest command of the *energy* of the medium
and his films have a vitality not found to the same extent in his peers'
work. It is a vitality not of camera movement or of editing, but of move-

ment within the frame. The influence of silent comedy did not extend satisfactorily into the sophisticated world of sound, since talkie writers and directors worked with the comedians to produce anti-heroic and anti-romantic images of man. Only Frank Capra managed to pursue in films like *Mr. Smith Goes to Washington* and *Mr. Deeds Goes to Town* the theme expressed in his Langdon comedies: the shrimp defeats the bigwigs to everyone's surprise.

In his early *A Sailor-Made Man* (1921), Harold Lloyd established his famous prototype of the scholarly, bespectacled mother's boy who by means of an extreme and unexpected resourcefulness succeeds over considerable odds. In this film, he played a spoiled scion of a wealthy family who was told by his girl friend's father that he must prove himself to be a man before he could marry her. He therefore becomes a sailor in the Merchant Marine and coincidentally meets her in a tropical backwater where she is made a prisoner of a native tribe. With hilarious improbability, he rescues her and wins her hand.

It was a pattern, an approach which was to prevail in most of Lloyd's films. Sam Taylor, whose career was later damaged when he worked on the Pickford-Fairbanks *Taming of the Shrew*, wrote the scripts with a constant inventiveness aided by Lloyd's own ideas. In *Grandma's Boy* (1922), Lloyd as a meek young man is given magical powers by the presence of an umbrella from his grandmother. The handle is enchanted and enables him to conquer the villain in a manner familiar to the reader of fairy stories. This brilliant film achieved something rare in American comedy: the release of the audience into a fantastic instead of a worldly daydream. By 1923 Lloyd was established firmly as a popular figure, and in *Safety Last* (1923) he and Sam Taylor devised a wholly inspired work. Lloyd played a counter clerk in a big Los Angeles department store, extremely nervous and in the opening scenes trapped in a series of awkward situations. In one episode, he is swamped by predatory women swooping into his department to grab up everything in sight in a holiday bargain sale. Emerging battered but victorious he nevertheless loses his job and tries desperately to find a way to justify himself to his out-of-town girl friend. He attempts to win $500 in answer to a challenge for a human fly to crawl up a downtown building without the aid of pulleys or platforms. Although suffering from fear of heights, he manages to succeed, and Lloyd's direction is dazzling in its confidence as we see the perilous ascent. *The Freshman* (1925) saw Lloyd challenging the very best on the football field. In *Welcome Danger* (1937), directed by Clyde Bruckman, an extremely gifted craftsman whose name has been somewhat overlooked, he was a humble, shy botanist who foils a gang. Lloyd's chases, often featuring streetcars in downtown Los Angeles settings, were more expert than those of anyone else in his time. He also had a more likable masculine vigor than the other, rather more passive clowns.

Buster Keaton, who also worked with Bruckman, was an effective equal of Lloyd in terms of comedic skill, using very similar plots. Keaton was a sad-faced revised version of the legendary Divine Fool. In *Our Hospitality* (1923) he was involved in a fued of rival hillbilly clans, proving himself a man by bravely rescuing his drowning girl from a falls. *Three Ages* (1923) was more ambitious. Here Keaton portrayed the underdog defeating the overdog in three ages of man, the Stone Age, the Roman period, and modern times. In *The Navigator* (1924), co-directed by Donald Crisp, he sets sail for Australia after being jilted by his girl. Through a series of circumstances he finds himself on a gigantic liner and makes himself into the captain and crew. This was an effective wish-fulfillment fantasy for suburban males. In *Sherlock Jr.* (1924) he is the projectionist and janitor of a small movie theater who foils the villain. At one stage he enters the screen—where he lives out his fantasies—to do so. Not only was this a comedy unleashing male dreams, it was by implication a comment on the exploitation of those dreams by the cinema. In *The General* (1927), made by Keaton and Bruckman working together and in this case sharing the job of direction, Keaton is in Georgia during the Civil War, a young railroad engineer who has been turned down by the Confederate Army because his job is too valuable to permit him to serve. Abashed by this, he emerges a hero anyway when he rescues a train which has been stolen by Union troops after giving chase in a dazzlingly shot locomotive sequence. *The Cameraman* (1928), co-directed by Edward Sedgwick, shows Keaton as a struggling photographer trying to achieve his ambition of becoming a Hearst newsreel man. After a series of mishaps, including leaving the film out of the camera during a shooting of a tong battle in the Chinese district, he wins the job and the girl.

Harry Langdon is an altogether odder figure of the comedy screen. Isolated and fragile, as bewildered as a recent arrival from Mars, he was exquisitely expressionless, every movement as disciplined as that of a kabuki clown. Langdon was the passive sufferer to whom everything happened, but as controlled as a ballet dancer. His life on screen was a pattern of misfortune: it was typical that, upon going to extraordinary lengths to rescue a worthless girl from a box where she has been trapped in *Long Pants*, he should at last pry it open only to find a crocodile snapping at him and the girl run away. Unlike the other comedians aforementioned (except Chaplin) he came almost too close to the realities of the underprivileged for comfort. With his moon-face, shoe-button eyes, and huge out-pointing flat-footed shoes, Langdon was almost too real to be funny at all. While Keaton and Lloyd were extroverts, Langdon and Chaplin were introverts. But Langdon was more extreme in his introspection, his loneliness, than any other comedian in screen history.

Langdon began to appear as a star later than the other great figures. He had the advantage of a tough and resilient talent in the director's chair: Frank Capra, who later emerged as a major figure. *The Strong Man* (1926) was more sophisticated and complex than the works of Lloyd and Keaton. Langdon did not even play an American, thus removing himself from the mass identification enjoyed by his peers. He played a Belgian soldier who receives letters from a pretty pen pal in America. After the war the soldier comes to America with the strong man Zandow the Great, a version of the Great Sandow whose exploitation had launched the vivid career of Florenz Ziegfeld. From this point on, the comedy plot is predictable: when the girl's father objects to the Belgian, he proves himself worthy of her by tossing a bootlegging gang out of her small town. This film was most ably directed by Capra.

*Tramp, Tramp, Tramp* (1926) was very well-written by Capra and directed by Harry Edwards. This time, Langdon has to win a walking contest organized by his sweetheart's father if he wishes to marry her. There is a slight twist in which after being jilted by the object of his affections he meets and marries another, but generally speaking the approach is the same. *Long Pants* (1927) again shows Capra's accomplished skill. The opening scenes in which Langdon struggles to graduate to long pants are echoed in the introduction to Welles' *The Magnificent Ambersons*. Langdon cycles with infinite grace to show off his splendor to the local folk, falls in with a bad-lot girl, and finally discovers true love. The typical plot, though, is simply a disguise: Langdon and Capra disclose the reality of life for the poor—drab, depressing, devoid of charm, the antithesis of most flattering silent film concepts.

The greatest of the silent comedians, Charlie Chaplin was a major creative artist both as director and player, despite his flaws, which included a degree of theatrical self-consciousness, a tendency to preach and an inability to escape traditions of the late-nineteenth-century vaudeville stage. He was handicapped also by a certain romantic softness, a slow pace well behind that of Keaton or Lloyd and an occasional monotony of approach, so that not only the clown's uniform but the clown's gestures were repeated in a narrow range. The public, of course, preferred the range to be narrow: they liked to see again and again the pathetic black derby, the size 13 flat-soled shoes, the nervous, half-bold tweaking of the villain's nose, or the casual twirl of the cane at the moment of triumph. To have extended his range might have cost Chaplin some of his popularity, but to see his films as a group today is to be aware of their self-consciousness, of their cool calculation, and of their mathematical working out of detail. Chaplin's feeling for the underprivileged was authentic, based on his own Vic-

*Joan Crawford, Harry Langdon,* TRAMP, TRAMP, TRAMP

torian childhood and the grind of music hall life; he was, through his over-whelming popularity, able to work out his ideas and feelings untrammeled by the system.

In *Shoulder Arms* (1918) Chaplin's condemnation of trench warfare was bitterly on target, far superior to Vidor's and Laurence Stallings' *The Big Parade*. *The Kid* (1920), an enormous success in its day, was the story of a tramp who adopts the infant Jackie Coogan, and saves him from an orphanage, but loses his custody, a harrowing and rather obvious assault on the audience's tear ducts. *The Pilgrim* (1922) was more interesting, about an escaped convict who poses as a preacher, pantomiming the sermons; Chaplin here attempted to expose the foolishness of religious orthodoxy. In *The Gold Rush* (1925) he established a genuine visual style. The snowy wastes of the Klondike, the silent muffled figures in the streets are effortlessly realistic. The superb comedy routines do not suffer from reviewings: the tramp eating his boots as though they were the finest steak, unraveling the laces like spaghetti; the exquisite ballet of the rolls, albeit copied from Fatty Arbuckle; the scene as the cabin teeters on the edge of a precipice: all this is inspired, reminding us that in *A Woman of Paris*, made two years earlier but not starring Chaplin, his comedy direction had been extremely polished, deeply influencing Lubitsch.

*The Circus* (1928) is a delicious work. Here the figure in the bowler hat and enormous out-pointing shoes is once again starving, encountering a circus owner and the owner's daughter, a bareback rider who secures a job for him after he has been reduced to snatching the food from a baby's mouth or posing as an automaton. Thenceforth he becomes an "act," hilariously compelled to perform in the lion's cage.

The opening is beautiful: a star glitters on a circus hoop, and a girl bareback rider pierces it at a sudden gallop. Now the scene is framed in the hoop ring as though in an iris: the crowd waiting, the tight little circular ring of figures, the circus manager with his top hat. At the end of the film, Chaplin brings the dramatic wheel full circle: he holds a star in his hand, and the paper from a hoop; he crumples them and throws them away; that part of life is over. Whether facing a lion or walking a tightrope when the funambulist is unavailable, Chaplin is superb; and the atmosphere of the circus, its sad glitter, its pathetic small rivalries, has seldom been better seen. In the sound period Chaplin went on to make such excellent films as *City Lights* (1931), *Modern Times* (1936), and *Monsieur Verdoux* (1947).

# 5. Rivals of Griffith

Thomas Ince was Griffith's greatest rival in the field of the historical film. Working first at his great ranch at Inceville, later at his studio at Culver City, Ince was not so much a creative director as the first producer, a precursor of men like Darryl F. Zanuck in the 1930s, with over two hundred people in his stock company. He controlled creative people with a kindly despotism, and spent long hours in his Benedict Canyon mansion late at night, cutting their work into what he regarded as an "Ince picture." He was long known as the best editor in Hollywood. Unlike the more poetic and leisurely Griffith, he liked a hard edge, a raw toughness in his films, particularly in the harsh truth of William S. Hart Westerns. His finest achievement, *Civilization* (1915), too often written off as a cold and undistinguished work, showed an impressive grasp of screen construction, a sense of realism superior to Griffith's since it was not undermined by sentimentality.

Like Griffith and De Mille, Ince in *Civilization* was preaching a simple Christian message. He introduced the film with the following: "Not until Hatred, Greed, Envy is plucked from the heart of man can we hope for Eternal Peace . . . Love Thy Neighbor as Thyself . . . If only those who profess to follow Him would practice what they preach, we would at last see the rising Dawn of Civilization."

With this onslaught on hypocrisy in religious bodies, also the target of De Mille, the work begins. We are plunged into a mythical state, based on Germany, but totally "created" down to the uniforms and the horses' accouterments. The reconstruction of a European township is flawless, the cobbler with his horseshoes, a girl wandering through trees, a suggestion of sunlight, flowers, and peace. A struggle among soldiers in the streets during a royal procession has the look of a period newsreel, as freezing in its accuracy as the news shots of Princip's assassination of Franz Ferdinand. We are aware, in scenes of soldiers riding down citizens, of a state committed to barbarism, and a single figure, Count Ferdinand, who has invented a war submarine, is used as the King's instrument of war.

Without preamble we see the results of his workmanship, the U-boat sinking of the S. S. *Propatria*. Supervised by Irvin Willat, it is a magnificently staged sequence, possibly the most authentic scene of a ship's demolition in the history of the screen: Ince cuts with overpowering effect from slanting deck to struggling mass of people, from engine room to couples trapped in cabins. He shows in a crescendo of action the scenes below decks, with unerringly placed close-ups of men slipping down companionways, hands clinging to black pipes, figures writhing in an inferno in a brilliantly effective masking device, as two thirds of the screen is blacked out; the intense coal blacks and blazing whites of the images, the oil-smudged faces and gleaming torsos—these shots are worthy of a Pudovkin, and probably influenced him. Nothing else in the film comes near this sequence, but other episodes are extraordinary: the tension of the Count's crisis of conscience—humanism vs. duty—conveyed by means of expressive cutting and close-up, the scene in the nunnery symbolizing the remoteness of Christianity from real life: compositions slashed by sunbeams, figures of nursing sisters grouped like the occupants of Vermeers. Tragically, Ince never equaled this great work again.

Other specialists in the spectacle film who worked more or less in the Ince tradition were legion. Among them may be enumerated Fred Niblo, whose vigorous epic *Ben Hur* (1926) had a mindless appeal for the public, glorifying warrior and peace lover alike. Also in this tradition was Clarence Brown, creator of the lavishly mounted Garbo-Gilbert vehicle *Flesh and the Devil* (1927); that well-made Valentino movie *The Eagle* (1925); and *The Goose Woman* (1925) and *Smouldering Fires* (1924), both portraits of women in their decline.

*Smouldering Fires* (1924) is a hypnotically fascinating demonstration of Clarence Brown's professional skill. The story is only average— an aging woman (Pauline Frederick) flings herself at a much younger

man only to lose him to her younger sister. But the writers have worked
out some interesting new variations: Jane Vale is not only past her youth,
she is still a virgin, working out her frustrations through the pitiless cruelty she hands out to her employees in a garment factory. Mannish, neck-
tied, Germanic, her face a mask, she issues dismissals without feeling,
stopping only at the task of removing an ambitious young man (Mal-
colm MacGregor) who attracts her. Miss Frederick plays with piercing
intuition the role of the termagant turned soft and self-pampered woman
of the world: Brown introduces her with Lubitschian details—a shoe
tapping irritably on the floor, hands nervously playing a tattoo on a
board meeting table, the eyes full of hatred for a world that has rejected her. Later, as she watches a younger couple, her finger is stabbed
by a rose thorn; as she preens herself at a mirror, her husband reaches
out in a dream for her rival. Again and again Brown makes crushingly
accurate observations on the "generation gap." His camera isolates
brilliant images of frustration: an aging face emerging from a Turkish
bath contorted with pain, the reflection in a window that tells Jane
Vale that her marriage is doomed. The film is a companion piece to
Lubitsch's *Three Women*, with the same female star and a very similar
story.

*The Goose Woman* opens with a static but fairly impressive scene
in which Louise Dresser, as the former opera star Marie de Nardi
(who lost her voice in 1901 when her son was born), is sitting in a
dilapidated cabin, accompanied by flocks of geese, and listening to her
one aural memento, a cylinder recording of one of her most famous
performances. She accuses her son in a hilarious title, "You changed
me from a nightingale to a frog!" referring to the professional disaster
of her pregnancy. Rex Beach's story, adapted by Melville Brown, is
dime fiction, and Clarence Brown is unable to raise it above the average,
although the scene in which the Goose Woman recounts her observations of a murder is dramatically lit by Milton Moore. There are some
sly touches of humor worth noting, in particular Marie de Nardi's humiliation of a newspaperman who has insulted her.

One figure who specialized in the big film had a major talent: Rex
Ingram. More a painter than a movie director, with little sense of pace
and rhythm, he had at best a superb pictorial flair. His finest work
was *Mare Nostrum* (1926).

Drawn by Willis Goldbeck from the novel by Vicente Blasco-Ibañez,
*Mare Nostrum* is an allegory of man's enchantment by woman and the

*Antonio Moreno, Alice Terry,* MARE NOSTRUM

sea, a deeply romantic, impassioned work. The opening shots are lovely, as John F. Seitz' photography evokes an underwater world, and we see fish picking their way through boxes of treasure, the spines of a sunken ship. We are aware that the naval officer Ulysses Ferragut (Antonio Moreno) is, like his namesake, captivated by the image of Amphitrite which occupies all his dreams, and dreamlike shots evoke his visions of the sea goddess riding in her coach across the waves.

In Italy, among the ruins of Pompeii, Ulysses meets an earthly temptress, Freya Talberg (Alice Terry), who is traveling in the company of a gross lesbian archaeologist. At Paestum, Ulysses tries to attract Freya, at first without success. She reveals herself by degrees as an Austrian spy working for the Kaiser, toasting Admiral von Tirpitz with champagne.

When Ulysses' son dies in a shipwreck, Ulysses blames Freya for betraying the ship's whereabouts, but amid the fish of the Naples Aquarium—an exquisite sequence echoed in Wells' *Lady from Shanghai*—he is finally lured to his doom. The rest of the story concerns Freya's and Ulysses' choices: between lover and country, sex and the course of duty.

Many sequences are admirably realized, but none as admirably as the account of Freya's downfall and ruin. Caught up with by her own side, she is imprisoned and shot: Amphitrite is mortal after all. No one who saw it could forget the execution at Vincennes, her arrival by limousine, dressed in fashionable clothes ("I shall die in my uniform"), her lofty bravery quenched by an actual sight of the rifles, her single horrifying glimpse of a coffin waiting to carry her away.

Ingram never again equaled this sequence. Too often his static arti-

*Vicente Blasco-Ibañez* visits *Alice Terry* on set of MARE NOSTRUM

Montage prepared by *Rex Ingram* for MARE NOSTRUM

ficial approach resulted in films that looked like animated paintings. His *Four Horsemen of the Apocalypse* (1921), though superlatively shot by Seitz, was an emptily elaborate version of another Blasco-Ibañez novel, with Valentino seen in an amateurish display of theatrical mannerisms, at ease only in the classic tango sequence. *The Prisoner of Zenda* (1922), like John Cromwell's version of Anthony Hope's

Ruritanian romance some fourteen years later, was stately, aristocratic in tone, accomplished, but a trifle dull. Romantic imagery, pellucid and deeply appealing, illuminated Ingram's version of John Russell's South Seas tales, *Where the Pavement Ends* (1923), a film which influenced the images of W. S. Van Dyke's poetic *White Shadows of the South Seas* and *The Pagan*. Unfortunately, *The Magician* (1926), though clearly influencing the art direction of Whale's *Frankenstein* and that film's final torchlit onslaught on the mill, is a labored, artificial work, except for the opening in a Paris studio, a grotesque statue looming over the slight figure of its creator.

Ingram did succeed in making a very interesting film of Rafael Sabatini's *Scaramouche* (1923), not quite as beautifully stylized as George Sidney's version some thirty years later but still displaying a talent to be reckoned with. Written by Willis Goldbeck, photographed by Seitz, it was characteristic of Ingram's spectacle films in that it was more sophisticated and less sentimental than Griffith's, while lacking his dynamic force. We are not swept along as we should be by the events. Sabatini's novel is given some additional pressure by Ingram's

*Lewis Stone, Ramon Novarro,* SCARAMOUCHE

emphasis in the early stages on the casually ruthless dispatch of a young divinity student by a Marquis (admirably played by Lewis Stone), an event which becomes a symbol for the rebellious hero André Louis de Moreau (Ramon Novarro) of the evils of the aristocracy of Louis XVI. The incidentals are sketched in with all of Ingram's pictorial mastery: the close-ups of the face of the king's justice, a bloated caricature worthy of Daumier; the lascivious greeting of the traveling

Scene from BAROUD

show's proprietor when Moreau enlists, kissing his new acquisition full
on the lips; the particulars of the Blue Boar Inn; Danton's pock-marked
face; the convention of the deputies; the feverish faces of the mob as
it storms the Tuileries. Alas, though, much of this cultivated and careful film fails to hold together: the escape of the Marquis from an en-
raged crowd at a theater is improbable, the back street duel in which
he confronts Moreau is quite thrown away, and the climax—in which
he is shown to be Moreau's father—is foolish. Ingram's later career
included a misguided version of Robert Hichens' *The Garden of Allah*
(1927) and another love affair with North Africa, *Baroud* (1932), in
which Ingram himself appeared, and which Alice Terry skillfully co-
directed.

Among those many directors who at once rivaled Griffith and emu-
lated aspects of his style were Herbert Brenon and James Cruze. Quintessential journeymen of the Twenties, neither brilliant nor mediocre, these
were reliable professional craftsmen whose later counterparts in the sound
period were men of the caliber of Sam Wood, Victor Fleming, or
John Cromwell. Highly paid and highly regarded, they neither added to
nor took away from the art of film. Brenon had by a small margin the
more critically successful record: his versions of J. M. Barrie's *Peter
Pan* (1925) and *A Kiss for Cinderella* (1926), both of which all too

*Mary Brian, Betty Bronson,* PETER PAN

faithfully rendered the writer's romantic lies about life, were skillfully made, beautifully lit by James Wong Howe and J. Roy Hunt respectively, but essentially theatrical and uninventive. *Peter Pan*'s encouragement of kidnapping, vengeance, and murder deserves a whole psychological study in itself, and Brenon's direction brings out its viciousness in the scenes when the children slowly prod a pirate to death at sword's point, force Captain Hook to walk a plank, or giggle at his doom in the maw of a crocodile. *A Kiss for Cinderella* celebrated materialistic acquisition with equal repulsiveness, and Brenon adds many vulgar touches to Barrie's scenes when the little London skivvy dreams of a socially successful marriage to Prince Charming, the epitome of bourgeois money-grubbing fantasy. The best sequence in this work is the opening, a wonderfully staged Zeppelin raid on London with England past (a carriage) and present (a new automobile) meeting in mid-street and a bobby emerging seemingly from beneath the camera to warn the occupants of their mutual danger from the terrible engines of the future.

Brenon's best-made film was *Beau Geste* (1926), a production into which Paramount put much effort, sending the entire unit and cast into the Mojave Desert for weeks to ensure realistic results. The P. C. Wren story about courage, brotherly love, and self-sacrifice and the supposed theft of the priceless Blue Water sapphire from Lady Brandon is a constant annoyance, but Brenon's handling, replete with all the sadistic relish of *Peter Pan,* is more cinematically interesting than usual. The scenes at Fort Zinderneuf, last outpost of the Foreign Legion in the Sahara, have a harsh authenticity, conveying the pain of constant sunlight, the rough humors and tensions of the Legionnaires, the sun-black figures riding down burning dunes, the maraudings of the Touaregs, seen lined up in battle formation against the sky. The most impressive sequence in the picture occurs in the fort's dormitory, when William Powell—sharply portraying a greasy liar and thief—is crucified on a table, knives thrust through the palms of his hands.

James Cruze was one of the leading box office figures of his day, but, like Ingram, he was a director with little sense of movie rhythm. *Hollywood* (1922), a mild-mannered account of life in the film settlement, has apparently been lost. His *Beggar on Horseback* (1925), despite an inspired performance by Edward Everett Horton as the clerk haunted by surrealist dreams, failed, to judge by extant footage, to escape the expressionist theatricality of the stage production. The film substitutes some very laborious titles for the verbal wit of the play. Even

*Ralph Forbes, Ronald Colman, Neil Hamilton,* BEAU GESTE

Cruze's famous box office success *The Covered Wagon* (1923) moved very slowly. Its account of the pioneers trekking across the American wilderness was so stately and carefully composed that today it seems empty of all energy and effect. Cruze's best film is *Old Ironsides* (1927), disliked by many industry figures at the time and not a great success at the box office.

Made with the cooperation of the Navy Department (the Secretary of the Navy, Curtis D. Wilbur, cheered the film on its opening night in New York), shot off Catalina, and using a full-scale re-creation of Old Ironsides herself, the USS *Constitution,* the film was based on contemporary records by the writer of the original story Laurence Stallings, covering the essential points in the *Constitution*'s battle against the corsairs of Tripoli. Cruze's direction is spacious and energetic, opening with a vivid sequence during the Fifth Congress at Philadelphia, followed by the singing of "Hail, Columbia," and gradually narrowing down to the romantic adventure of a young salt (Charles Farrell) shanghaied onto the bark *Esther*. In the original version Al Gilks' cool gray photography opened up into wide screen when the beautiful frigate *Constitution* first set sail, and during the attack on Tripoli, rousingly staged in the Lloyd or Curtiz manner. Masts crash on sailors, cannons rake decks, rigging frames the dead and dying in a series of expertly managed compositions, and there is one ravishing shot of a group of sailors in the crow's-nest, perched also on the mizzen to the left of frame, as the pirate ship sails across to windward and the sea sparkles in the sun. Stallings creates witty and shrewdly drawn characters, including two veteran sea dogs, played with inspired crustiness by George Bancroft and Wallace Beery.

A director superior to both Brenon and Cruze in his polished craftsmanship and advanced control of the language of physical gesture, Frank Lloyd was to go on to a very distinguished career in talkies. His best silent film, the exemplar of his fastidiously careful, measured style, was *Madame X* (1920), the second of five versions of Bisson's famous 1908 tearjerker. The melodramatic story concerns a woman who abandons her position as the wife of a legal official, sinks to prostitution in Buenos Aires, murders her lover and is defended at the subsequent trial by her son, who does not suspect her identity. In other hands it could have been mawkish, and it became so in later remakes. But Frank Lloyd's direction turned it into a masterpiece of commercial cinema. In the first place, he ensures that every minute detail of French life, the diplomat's mansion, the shoddy apartment where Madame X hides, the Hall of Justice at the end, is perfection itself. And then there is the matchless command of film pacing, the brilliant use of the iris, the unerring cutting, the pitiless precision of observation. Instead of being a novelette, the film is the equivalent of a Zola novel. We enter a completely realized world, charged with meaning to the last bottle and flowerpot. In the silent period, only *Greed* surpassed the physical detail of this creation. And Pauline Frederick confirms her reputation as one of the handful of great silent stars. Her entrance is magnificently timed. Dressed in deep mourning, her head swathed in a heavy veil, she pauses at the foot of a flight of ornate marble steps, gazing longingly at the tall chateau windows that half hide from view the life she has just left. Later, she is equally striking: in the Buenos Aires cafe, disconsolately awaiting a new conquest; and above all in the trial and its aftermath when, hunched over with grief, she takes her own life. It is one of the triumphant performances of the screen.

■ ■ ■ ■ ■ ■ ■ ■ ■ ■ ■ ■ ■ ■ ■ ■ ■ ■ ■ ■ ■ ■ ■ ■ ■ ■ ■ ■

# 6. De Mille: Commercial Giant

■ ■ ■ ■ ■ ■ ■ ■ ■ ■ ■ ■ ■ ■ ■ ■ ■ ■ ■ ■ ■ ■ ■ ■ ■ ■

Griffith's greatest rival was Cecil B. De Mille. While Griffith, as we have seen, worked in a primitive vein, with heroes and heroines from a Victorian fiction, De Mille was a great showman, his characters drawn with a knowing sophistication, his scenes larger than life. At his best, he was a director of spectacular talent, who because of his great commercial success has never had his critical due. Even at the end of his career in the 1950s, he never lost his flair for spectacle.

Following the shock of the public reaction to *Birth of a Nation*, De Mille developed a moral argument pressing for peace, understanding, and kindness for the poor and underprivileged. Like Griffith's, his was a simple Christianity. He seized on a variety of subjects ranging all the way from women's lib to Jesus Christ, not even quailing at the prospect of showing the devil in goatish garb tempting Christ on a mountain in *King of Kings*. We are fortunate that the big De Mille silent films have survived, that he ensured their preservation together with all of his scripts, bound in leather, lining the walls of his study at De Mille Drive in Hollywood, which has been kept exactly as he left it the day he died. Even his first film, *The Squaw Man* (1913), has been retained, as vigorous and clean-cut as the day it was made. De Mille's first important film (with Fannie Ward), *The Cheat* (1915), is chiefly of interest for the fact that Bette Davis, playing in *Mr. Skeffington* some thirty years later, imitated the mannerisms of Miss Ward (Davis' costumer, Orry-Kelly, was instructed to copy the earlier star's clothes and headdress). Edith Hardy, wife of a prominent New York stockbroker, becomes entangled with an unscrupulous Burmese ivory king, Hara Arakau (cleverly played by Sessue Hayakawa), who attempts to buy her with a loan to cover a debt; when she fails to give herself to him, he brands her. Despite the fundamental triviality of the affair De Mille's command of the material is undeniably showmanlike, proving him to be the Belasco of the screen. Fannie Ward had a legendary beauty still worth seeing, and Hayakawa's branding of her is affecting. There are some vivid uses of shadow play, rare in the early stage-bound American cinema. One recalls particularly the cameraman Alvin Wyckoff's shot of Sessue Hayakawa injured in silhouette, his blood gradually staining a paper screen.

*Joan the Woman* (1916) is the most impressive De Mille silent spectacle film, more modest in scale than *The Ten Commandments* (1923) and *King of Kings* (1927) but superior to both. Sensibly, De Mille and his writer Jeanie Macpherson settled on a portrait of Joan as visionary —she is haunted by images of death, most poignantly a black horseman who accompanies her on her ride across France, and by images of fire, which her precognitive powers tell her will be the means of her destruction. This sense of a short-lived career, of a limited future, gives the character its impetus and the film its strong sense of the workings of fate. Joan rejects without hesitation the British soldier who loves her, shrinks in horror from the Bishop of Cauchon's ring when she senses that the hand she is about to kiss has placed poison in the royal cup, stares horrified at a candle flame which presages her death. The film is full of portents and the last scene is staged with a skill even Belasco might have envied: the cool gray dawn and the carter arriving in the empty square bringing the sticks for the stake, the citizens gathering as though for a festival, the final unsparing account of the burning itself. Geraldine Farrar—broad-shouldered, raven-haired, a general to her fingertips—makes a thoroughly convincing Joan.

With the possible exception of *The Ten Commandments, King of Kings* (1927) was De Mille's most celebrated silent spectacle, displaying his talent at full stretch. The opening scenes were shot in Technicolor: a portrait of the corruption of the Roman province of Israel, women dancing ecstatically, flowers strewn, zebras pulling a chariot through a banqueting hall. Unerringly, with superb shrewdness, De Mille builds the suspense that will make the audience long for the arrival of Jesus. De Mille's introduction of Christ is an inspiration, a Belasco-like master

*Geraldine Farrar,* JOAN, THE WOMAN

stroke. The focus narrows to a single blind girl, stretching out her arms
to the Divinity: the camera takes her eyes, and lights begin to shimmer
in an otherwise black screen. More light appears, pulsing across the
darkness. Then suddenly, a curtain is torn open, and she sees the Savior.
Vulgar as the film undeniably is, as an example of mass entertainment
it works with frequent brilliance, slow expository passages alternating
with wonderfully staged set pieces: the sequence on the Mount of Olives,
the storm that accompanies the Crucifixion, the magnificent Resurrec-
tion scene, with the stone rolled back, the intense blackness, and the
figure emerging in the funerary robe like a grub emerging from a
chrysalis into the eager corrupt world.

In terms of influence, De Mille's most important silent films were
not his spectacles but his comedies, beginning with *Old Wives for New*
and *Why Change Your Wife?* (1919–20). In a deliberate break with
the Griffith tradition, he paved the way for a new style in American
film-making, sharp, sophisticated, and alert. In particular, *Why Change
Your Wife?* was an extraordinary film for its period, entirely disrupting

the Hollywood conventions in its portrait of human relationships. As De Mille and his writer, Jeanie Macpherson, saw it, women were not melting, fragile, and vulnerable creatures as Griffith portrayed them, but tough, aggressive, and unscrupulous in their pursuit of men. Immensely long and wordy titles exhorted the audience to face problems in marriage: women were to remain seductive or their husbands would look elsewhere; other women were always waiting, grimly competitive, to pounce on their prey. De Mille provided a mode that was to engage the American cinema for almost forty years and was to influence Chaplin (*A Woman of Paris*) and, through him, Lubitsch.

The story of *Why Change Your Wife?* has an unsentimental ruthlessness, a portrait of a stodgy but handsome man (Thomas Meighan) over whom two women, his first wife, played by Gloria Swanson, and his second, played by Bebe Daniels, struggle with an abandon that would seem coarse even by today's standards. At one stage, in order to prevent Bebe Daniels from visiting her husband in his sickbed, Gloria Swanson seizes a key; Bebe Daniels flings a glass bottle at her head which cuts her and splashes her blood on the wall. Ruefully contemplating the shattered glass, the assailant remarks, "Seven years' bad luck." The two women lock in a mortal fight, wrecking the room, or compete with savage thrusts of wit, while the husband, helpless and passive, looks astounded at this competition over his humdrum flesh.

The importance of this film and its successors—*Don't Change Your Husband* (1919), *Forbidden Fruit* (1921), and the marvelous hand-tinted *Affairs of Anatol* (1921)—cannot be sufficiently emphasized. De Mille was responsible for Chaplin's temporary abandonment of his Griffithian mode for the stylized comedy of *A Woman of Paris* (1923). With his characteristic eye for detail, Chaplin emphasized objects— jewels, shoes, movements of hands—in a way that surpassed De Mille's own use of significant objects, though his direction lacked De Mille's energy. Both men influenced Ernst Lubitsch, the brilliant young director who had just arrived from Europe, and who was overwhelmed by *A Woman of Paris*. And it was Lubitsch who was destined to lay the whole basis of sophisticated comedy when talkies came along.

■ ■ ■ ■ ■ ■ ■ ■ ■ ■ ■ ■ ■ ■ ■ ■ ■ ■ ■ ■ ■ ■ ■ ■ ■ ■ ■ ■ ■ ■

# 7. Lubitsch and Other Europeans

■ ■ ■ ■ ■ ■ ■ ■ ■ ■ ■ ■ ■ ■ ■ ■ ■ ■ ■ ■ ■ ■ ■ ■ ■ ■ ■ ■ ■

Of all the Twenties sophisticates who made the motion picture their medium, none was more important than the great Ernst Lubitsch. Born in Berlin, he began his career as an actor at UFA and on the stage with Max Reinhardt's company. His earliest major features were made for Pola Negri. He became known as a master of spectable, of sumptuous historical reconstructions. He never shook off the influence of the stage: his films are chiefly of interest for their social commentary and for their acting performances, handled with a genial, entirely ruthless German sophistication. Lubitsch's camera setups, even at the end of his career in the 1940s, remained geared to the concept of the proscenium arch, with exits and entrances right and left, and performers playing "to" the audience. While a Griffith or an Ince strove for a degree of realism, Lubitsch and his imitators sought to capture for Americans the experience of seeing a polished European theatrical production. Critics of the time commented upon his skill in singling out details of gesture and expression by means of spatially interesting shots. In particular, he liked to begin a film by focusing on an action which said something revealing about the central character. It was as though someone had focused an opera glass on a point of detail, and we were being made to share that revelation.

But Lubitsch moved beyond theater as he progressed, to a complete and perhaps unequaled sense of pacing, of timing scenes strictly to the dictates of sophisticated taste. His genius flourished in an artificial world of cuckolded husbands, erring wives, ambitious mothers, and class-conscious military men, a world as formalized as Schnitzler's, though Lubitsch's feelings were perhaps closer to the bourgeois sentiments of a Molnár. Alongside him was the great writer Hans Kräly, a genius of equal caliber, whose mercurial wit, superb constructional powers, and mastery of the use of titles made his films with Lubitsch stand head and shoulders above most of the period's works in terms of enlightened intelligence.

Brought to Hollywood for a project that did not materialize—Mary Pickford's *Dorothy Vernon of Haddon Hall*—Lubitsch began his American career with a routine proof of his ability to make a commercial film: *Rosita* (1923) starring Mary Pickford. He followed it with *The Marriage Circle* (1924), a much more congenial subject. Based by Kräly on Schmidt's *Nur Ein Traum,* photographed most elegantly by Charles Van Enger (who became Lubitsch's associate on several films), the film presents in a manner that refreshed or shocked American audiences of the time the precise antithesis of the Victorian sentimentality about "love."

The setting of *The Marriage Circle* is that unreal Vienna which the cinema made convincing to untraveled Americans in the Twenties. The elegant melancholy of the real place did not make itself felt save in rare imported works later on in the sound period—films like Forst's *Maskerade* or Ophuls' *Liebelei.* Lubitsch was taken to be the epitome of Viennese charm—odd in view of his own hard Berlin wit—and *The Marriage Circle* as the nonpareil of Viennese humor and culture. Casually, insolently, from its opening shot of the cynical Professor played by Adolphe Menjou drawing on an expensive black silk sock with a hole in it, the film portrays a Schnitzler-like pattern of deceit. Adultery is commonplace in a world in which love is merely a word. The practiced playing of Dr. Braun by Monte Blue, his wife Charlotte by Florence Vidor, Dr. Muller by Creighton Hale and Professor Stock by Menjou, became the standard for film acting in the genre; mocking, astute, seemingly throwaway. A conversation between two bitchy women provided the one touch of "cinema" in the work: they dissolve over each other as they talk relentlessly, the one indistinguishable in her loquacity from the other.

Touches of this kind were associated with Lubitsch and he became a celebrity in America almost overnight. His next film, *Three Women* (1924) shows an increased refinement and a more deadly wit: the

*Ernst Lubitsch* directs *Pauline Frederick* in THREE WOMEN

central portrait of the aging, jealous mother is quite unsparing. Made
only two years after the William Desmond Taylor murder case, the
story echoed one popular interpretation in the account of a woman
(Pauline Frederick) who covets her daughter's lover: some believed
that the mother of Mary Miles Minter, a star questioned in connection
with the director's killing, had destroyed him because he had rejected
her in favor of her daughter. The opening carefully establishes the older
woman's terror of age: the exceptional Miss Frederick exposes in a
few quiet strokes the horror of the American woman's attempts to
preserve her youth: a pair of greedy hands running over a scale, a

dressing gown slipped on no longer youthful arms, a face growing flabby, primped and patted into shape in a mirror, a silver turban tied to her head as she goes out to face the world. She emerges at an opulently staged *thé dansant,* introduced with a shower of balloons as guests—one fat man stuck—sliding down a chute into the crowd, she arriving with a fatuous smile on a young man's arm. The mother's impatience and the desperation with which she conducts an affair are pitilessly observed; Miss Frederick is splendid in the sequence in which she cynically assesses her lover's moneygrubbing intentions, or tricks out her fading charms as she heads for the Monkey Cafe, where monkeys are dangled from the ceiling for the guests to catch, and—a practiced Lubitsch effect—the dark frameline rolls up like a blind to show a man fondling a woman's silvered leg.

Unfortunately, Lubitsch's equally celebrated *Forbidden Paradise* (1924) now seems mediocre, as well as peculiar. Ostensibly based on the life of Catherine the Great, drawn from a Lajos Biró/Melchior Lengyel play of 1913, it is given a Ruritanian setting of the Twenties. It features a World War I vintage car and a court chamberlain (Adolphe Menjou) in contemporary evening dress, while Catherine is gowned in a confusion of styles which would have infuriated Molyneux. Directed in an interminable series of stagy medium shots, the film does not even succeed as theater, and Pola Negri, despite her exotic beauty, makes little impression as Catherine. Opposite her as Count Alexei, Rod la Rocque is miserably "off" both in period and class, and he plays with a wooden inexpressiveness throughout.

*Lady Windermere's Fan* (1925), extremely well-shot by Van Enger, was far more successful. The adapter Julien Josephson converts Wilde's feline complexities into a simple story of a scandalous woman with a heart of gold. Despite the compromises involved, Lubitsch's handling is excellent and his observation of English society—the play has been updated to the period in which the film was made—nicely sharp. It begins with a lighthearted title: "Lady Windermere had a problem—seating her dinner guests," and the note of delicate banter is sustained throughout as the infamous Mrs. Erlynne, secret mother of Lady Windermere, resorts to blackmail and enforced marriage before showing a brief twinge of genuine feeling at the finale.

It would be impossible to improve on such scenes as that in which Mrs. Erlynne—played with a delicious sense of ironical wit by Irene Rich—observes Lord Windermere writing her a blackmail check that grows larger at every lift of her eyebrow; the visit to Ascot, rich dowagers commenting on her advance toward middle age; the use of a racecourse sign—a private reference to Ronald Colman, who plays Lord Darlington—advertising Colman's Mustard; or Mrs. Erlynne's crashing of the Windermeres' party, observed by a series of aggrieved faces popping up against a tapestry from the lower edge of the frame.

After *Lady Windermere's Fan, So This Is Paris* (1926) was a distinct letdown, a tired reworking of the comedy of adultery which gave *The Marriage Circle* its impetus. The star playing by Monte Blue as a philanderer was strained and obvious, the direction full of tired borrowings from Jacques Feyder, and only one sequence—a Charleston at an Arts Ball, with the winning couple's success so announced on the radio to shock the male half's deceived wife—was interesting. The use of prism lenses and multiple dissolves, executed by the cameraman, John Mescall, created a hallucinatory quality that still looks effective.

Lubitsch's next silent film was *The Student Prince in Old Heidelberg* (1928). The first reel is very spirited: King Karl of Karlsburg is dying, but the streets are full of enthusiastic citizens, and a sea of top hats appears, removed first by the dozen, then by the score. As the young heir to the throne arrives by train, a cannonade of welcome goes off, startling him so violently he retreats into his carriage. The crowd greets him upon his succession to the throne, its huzzahs intercut with a shot of him crouched miserably behind the barred palace gates. He watches children playing with a ball, forced to toss his own ball mechanically to a trio of stiff-necked retainers. Shrewd, witty, and of a fairy tale completeness, the opening passages show Lubitsch at his best. But with the Prince's adulthood, the film steadily declines: Lubitsch's proscenium arch direction, Ramon Novarro's anemic young king, Norma Shearer's somewhat coarse and overblown portrait of young love (her anguished farewells are particularly amateurish) make much of the film quite flaccid, and John M. Stahl was engaged to reshoot several sequences.

Lubitsch's last two silent films were *The Patriot* (1928), with Emil Jannings, an elaborate historical work, and the rarely seen, fascinating *Eternal Love* (1929). *Eternal Love* is a magnificent piece of theatrical craftsmanship, perhaps Lubitsch's most Germanic American film. Set entirely in a mountain village in Switzerland in the early nineteenth century, the story, based by Kräly on a novel by Jakob Heer, concerns a patriot (John Barrymore) who refuses to lay down arms when the French set up a local military garrison. Torn between two women, he kills the husband of the girl he passionately loves (Camilla Horn) and deliberately walks with her into an avalanche to be united with her in death. As their bodies vanish in snow, the sun blazes against a white sky, filling the entire screen in an unforgettable final image. Photographed in glittering high key by Oliver T. Marsh, the film is persuasive as a portrait of Middle Europe, and Lubitsch's narrative style has seldom been as compelling. The snug, tight little rooms lanced with sunlight, the change from high summer to snow, the blizzard in the last reels, and the meaningful analysis of mob psychology, are all extremely exciting. The film was a financial disaster, but it remains Lubitsch's best-made work of the silent period.

Lubitsch had a flock of imitators, most notably Mal St. Clair, whose *The Show Off* (1926) was a pleasant reflection of the master, and the more skilled Harry D'Abbadie D'Arrast, who had a delicate feeling for comedy more clearly exemplified in his supremely elegant talkies *Laughter* and *Topaze*. The Russian Lewis Milestone's comedy *Garden of Eden* (1928) was based on a script by Hans Kräly replete with the witty situations that had provided a field day for Lubitsch. A young and beautiful girl (captivatingly played by Corinne Griffith) flees her family in Vienna, announcing that she is going to Budapest to commence an operatic career. A letter from what she has assumed to be an opera house promises her work as a result of her diploma. On arriving, she finds a charwoman sweeping the steps of a seedy dance palais presided over by a lesbian (the incomparable Maude George) who commands her to show her legs instead of sing. After refusing to make love either to her employer or to an important client, the innocent is dismissed with the wardrobe mistress, who turns out to be a countess in disguise. They leave for Monte Carlo together. Deliciously absurd, this effervescent, utterly charming film is one of the best comedies ever made. It proved Milestone's command of expressive acting, of brilliant cutting, to be at least the equal of Lubitsch's. Not even the master could have improved on the direction of Kräly's final scene when Cinderella and Prince Charming are married literally in bed by an astonished preacher, or the evocation—aided by William Cameron Menzies' sets—of the Budapest de Paris and the Hotel Eden at Monte Carlo.

In the wake of Lubitsch, several German directors and others from France, Sweden, and Denmark were lured to Hollywood, many of them

by the European Carl Laemmle, who ran Universal. Few were entirely
at ease in their new environment, missing the freedom and the unbridled
power they were used to exercising in Europe, and the extremely long
periods allowed for rehearsal and preparation.

The majority of the European imports to Hollywood were preoccupied, not with the foibles and absurdities of the very rich, but with
the sensational, the weird, and the bizarre; only a few tried, with de-
cidedly mixed success, to abandon the artificialities of the UFA studios
and come to grips with the realities of the American poor. When they
did so, they succeeded only in producing hybrid works, awkwardly combining German, American, and even Russian techniques, as the last
reel of Murnau's *Sunrise* proves. Their artiness impressed American
critics, who mistook many of their excesses as evidences of fully trans-
planted native genius. The wisest of the group was Paul Leni, who
obtained Carl Laemmle's approval to make at least one film replete
with uncompromised UFA-esque horrors, in *The Man Who Laughs*.

Just as in 1915 Griffith had created a revolution in the American
film by welding its techniques into a viable form for the feature film,
and just as Lubitsch in 1924 had refined De Mille's and Chaplin's approach to comedy to provide the basis for a native screen comedy of
manners, so in 1927 this group of European invaders changed the face
of the Hollywood product. The impact of the great UFA films of the
mid-1920s cannot be overestimated: *The Last Laugh, Variety,* and
films by Lang and Lupu Pick astonished studio chiefs by showing not
only the rich potential in low-key photography, using the recently developed panchromatic stock, but, most importantly of all, how the camera
could be moved to tell a story. Fox imported Murnau, Universal imported Leni and Féjos. Universal films in fact became by-products of
their European associates UFA, and well into the sound period Universal continued to make bizarre horror stories lit with all the stylized
grimness and designed with all the surrealist angularity of the German
cinema. Unhappily, though, the influence did not work very satisfactorily against the grain of the native film. Applied to a routine melodrama like *The Last Warning,* the intricate shadows and labored humors
of a Leni seem preposterous. Except for Universal, Hollywood abandoned the UFA/Gothic after a few years; it was not until Welles created that amalgam of many movie styles, *Citizen Kane,* that the mode
came back to influence the films of Warner Brothers and—again—
Universal in the 1940s.

F. W. Murnau was a dilettante with a passion for decoration; his films suffered from a slow pace, an extreme artificiality of approach to character, and a kitsch lyricism masquerading as poetic romanticism. *Sunrise—A Song of Two Humans,* his first American film (for William Fox), has been extravagantly admired, and is in itself an extravagance of camerawork, lighting and décor, a travesty by Carl Meyer of the harsh and bitter Hermann Sudermann story on which it is based (*Die Reise nach Tilsit,* 1917).

The intention here—odd in Murnau's case—is to sing a sentimental hymn to married love. The treatment is heavily vulgar, laden with the worst excesses of German expressionism. The pace is portentous, the acting rudimentary. A secondary theme—a young man's love of the farm, which a dark-eyed vamp wants him to sell—is no more deeply felt than the primary one. All the director's concentration has been given to the *mise en scène*: the moon over the water—a recurring image in Sudermann—and the winding streets of the Grimm's fairy tale town, the crowded interiors to which UFA had accustomed us. The effect, for all Murnau's flourishes of "cinema," is deeply theatrical. Patches of technique survive: the hero seeing himself adrift in water as the walls of his room appear to dissolve in a dream, the introduction to the dance hall with a close-up of an enormous revolving silver disc, and the skillfully cut pursuit of the lost wife by lantern-lit boat.

*Four Devils* (1928), Murnau's next film (of which a rare print exists in Australia), was set in a circus, a popular scene of films of the period. Four young people are raised as acrobats, their romances and tensions unfeelingly charted through sequences of trapeze and sawdust ring, of the tawdry life behind the big top. At times, as in *Sunrise,* the visual style seems too carefully worked out, too scrupulously "pictorial," extinguishing life, and a vamp played by Mary Duncan is crudely drawn. But at moments the fluency of the visual style recalls the best passages in *The Last Laugh.*

The theme of *City Girl* (1928) is the land: a young farmer meets a waitress in Chicago; he brings her home to meet his overbearing father and the lustful farmhands who covet her. A tacked-on studio ending has the father begging the wife, whom he detests, to forgive him for his enmity and there is a reconciliation of great absurdity, imposed on Murnau and reshot by Buddy Erickson. The film is a companion piece to Sjöström's *The Wind,* dealing with a favorite Twenties theme of the urban woman confronted with an alien environment (also seen in

*Janet Gaynor, George O'Brien,* SUNRISE

William K. Howard's *White Gold,* Mal St. Clair's *The Woman of the World,* and Stiller's *The Temptress*). Unfortunately, Murnau's sophistication endistances him from the subject. Although much of the film was shot on location in the Middle West, it might as well have been made entirely at Movietone City, so slight is Murnau's grasp on rural reality. The film lacks pace, cohesion, and passion; only Ernest Palmer's photography, occasionally suggesting Grant Wood paintings, lends it a touch of visual distinction. After a lush semi-documentary made with Robert Flaherty, *Tabu,* Murnau died tragically in a car crash in 1931.

The German Paul Leni managed more successfully to import a native style to the American film. He emerged as a typical UFA product, presenting a recrudescence of the Gothic tradition; his black vision was fully expressed in America, his sense of film pacing very sure. If Murnau represented the softer, more languorous side of German romanticism, then Leni represented its truly sinister aspect. There is a sense of almost palpable evil in his best films, overlaid with a cool humor.

Admittedly his first Hollywood work, a version of the stage success *The Cat and The Canary* (1927), was very slight, handicapped by a series of trivialities about sliding panels, screaming women, and the inevitable gnarled long-clawed hand of the silent serials touching the heroine's hair. Not as good as Elliott Nugent's remake ten years later, the film is of interest as a curio. *The Chinese Parrot* (1927) and the fatuous *The Last Warning* (1929) combined horror and amusement; but Leni's most important American work is undoubtedly *The Man Who Laughs* (1928), based on the novel by Victor Hugo. The film is a cross between *The Phantom of the Opera, The Hunchback of Notre Dame,* and *Scaramouche,* Germanic and at the same time deeply imitative of the Chaney vehicles. The first reels are very fine: James II, ill in bed, orders the execution of a rebel Scottish nobleman, Lord Clancharlie, by death in the Iron Maiden of Nuremberg, while the child heir to the title is disfigured, his face cut into a permanent smile. The heir's nightmare escape from the palace of James II is brilliantly effective, the equal of anything Grimm or Hoffmann might have conceived: the exhausted tiny figure making footprints in snow, menaced by sinister stone Düreresque faces, corpses dangling from gibbets, a bell announcing the fugitive's arrival at the peasant Ursus' hut. Growing up as Gwynplaine, the Man Who Laughs, the heir to the Clancharlie fortune is exhibited as a freak in a newly established traveling fair, together with a blind girl and a five-legged cow. Leni's introduction of Southwark, where the show first opens, is miraculously achieved: figures carousing in the streets, the camera whirling on an (anachronistic) big wheel, the announcement spreading that Gwynplaine is about to appear. The images hark back, not so much to eighteen-century models as to Brueghel. Against the settings of the show, the court of the gross and corrupt Queene Anne is pitilessly observed: Olga Baclanova as the lascivious Duchess Josiana, accompanied by a black monkey as by an evil familiar or perversely inviting Gwynplaine to her bedroom to torment him with frustrated desire in a scene of great erotic tension, gives a magnificent performance, surpassed only by Conrad Veidt's as Gwynplaine.

At their best, the Europeans achieved a piercing realism, a harsh accuracy about life that went far deeper than any American's. Leni's *The Man Who Laughs* was a masterpiece not alone in this respect. Ludwig Berger, distinguished director of such important German silent films as *Cinderella,* made an extraordinary Jannings picture, The *Sins of the Fathers* (1928). This production had an acute, raw immediacy equivalent to the best work of Fédor Ozèp in Russia and France. The story is set in New York: Jannings is a retired, unhappy former beer garden proprietor, Wilhelm Spengler; he peddles wood alcohol in the midst of the Prohibition era; his beloved son is killed after accidentally drinking it. Jannings' portrait of a decaying expatriate showed a deeply moving grasp of character, and Ruth Chatterton confirmed her Broadway reputation in the role of a call girl.

Also starring Jannings, Lewis Milestone's *Betrayal* (1928) was the work of an even more gifted immigrant. Milestone's knowledge of Europe gave a rich surface to the film, superbly written by Hans Kräly and shot by Henry Gerrard. Jannings played a tragic German burgomaster, deceived by his younger wife with the handsome Gary Cooper; Cooper's siring of an illegitimate child, symbolized by the flaring of a torch outside a room, a horse's hooves beating against snow, was cut in some versions. This magnificently erotic sequence, years ahead of its time, was surpassed by the astonishing episode in which Jannings, insane with sexual frustration, tries to murder his wife's illegitimate child. The film was the essence of truth: it was, like the best of *Greed,* a determined investigation of life, with long, sustained close-ups stabbing the nerve of human suffering. Not surprisingly, it was a box office failure. Milestone stayed on to make films of considerable power in the 1930s and 1940s. Paul Féjos is one curious minor figure whose importance has been exaggerated because of his odd background (he was by train-

*Esther Ralston, Gary Cooper,* BETRAYAL

ing a bacteriologist and after his film career became an anthropologist, dying in New York as recently as 1969). Féjos' best-known film is *The Last Moment* (1928), a surrealist work made, like *The Last Laugh,* virtually without titles, evoking the thoughts of a suicide with subjective camera effects achieved by Leon Shamroy. He also made two uneven films, *Broadway* and *The Last Performance* (both 1929). The better of the two (in its silent version), *Broadway* features some of the most extraordinary crane shots (by Hal Mohr) ever put on film, and some of the largest sets. The massive Art Deco nightclub that forms the center of the action is a vulgar astonishment, and as Mohr's camera sweeps all over it, dizzyingly rushing in to observe an early morning scrubwoman, rising like an eagle to take in the entire set, the effect is very remarkable. Alas, all of the dialogue scenes in the talkie version are poor.

*The Last Performance,* also photographed by Hal Mohr, was a UFA-esque creation typical of its period and its studio, Universal. Similar to Leni's *Last Warning*, staged also on *Phantom of the Opera* sets, it was a starring vehicle for Conrad Veidt, who played the tragic Erick the Great, an illusionist who travels from the Budapest Casino to success in New York but destroys his mistress' lover in the middle of a cabinet act. In a climactic trial scene, he stabs himself to death with the murder knife. Féjos' attempt to emulate Leni—clearly under pressure from his employer, Carl Laemmle—was singularly ill-advised.

In common with Murnau, Féjos, as well as wanting to please his new masters, wished to prove himself a successful immigrant by dealing with the lives of simple Americans. *Lonesome* (1929) is a story (by Mann Page) of young lovers not dissimilar to the couple in *City Girl*. Here Féjos succeeded rather better than his fellow Europeans in capturing the "feel" of American big city life and the texture of existence for the uneducated classes. Despite its merits, though, *Lonesome* is a very slight work, inviting but not sustaining comparison with Vidor's *The Crowd*. Its visual style, initially attractive, becomes a monotonous succession of busy shots, dissolving over each other in a perpetual flurry, punctuated by constantly moving objects. The opening evokes an awakening of New York, whistles and horns blowing (the film had some of the earliest synchronized sound effects). A boy (Glenn Tryon) and a girl (Barbara Kent) wake up in adjoining hotel rooms, go to work—he in a factory, she as a telephonist—come home to an empty loneliness, and leave by separate routes for Coney Island. Archetypes of young love, like the hero and heroine of countless films of the period, they meet for the first time at the fun fair, and are parted when the wheel of the girl's Big Dipper car catches fire. The camera never stops moving, rushing with the elevated, plunging with the hysterical passengers on the big dipper, or hurtling headlong through crowds at Coney Island, which seems improbably to be caught in an endless blizzard of confetti and ticker tape. Hand-tinted sequences occur: blue and pink balloons in a black and white screen, red glitter on the Ferris wheel, figures bathed in pale green. The film's charm is real, and though its realist and surrealist American and European elements fail to coalesce, it is still far ahead of the Griffith school.

The major French director Maurice Tourneur is of great interest as the tutor of Clarence Brown, his pupil and assistant. Tourneur had a rich pictorial sense, providing images of startling force and beauty, but he had little knowledge of dramatic construction. His best films, therefore, are those in which he collaborated most successfully with Brown: *The Last of the Mohicans* (1920) and *Foolish Matrons* (1921). *The Last of the Mohicans,* based on James Fenimore Cooper's celebrated novel, is very carefully paced: ostensibly, it is an account of the journey of a family across the wilderness at the time of the Indian wars, resulting in the death of the older daughter at the hands of an evil Indian. The surface of the film is all brilliance: light and clean air; a magnificence of canyons and fir trees, lakes and mountains in the direct line of Griffith's early Westerns. But underneath, the film's mood is darker, stranger than anything suggested by Cooper's robust boy's book. The darkness wells from the character of the older girl, played by Barbara Bedford. Prim and proper in her demeanor, she is actually seized by virginal longings, consumed with sexual desire for her Indian guide-protector. At a time when women in movies were supposed to be mere wilting violets, this explicit sexual frankness must have been an astonishment, and was in truth quite revolutionary. Looking into Miss Bedford's sly, animal eyes, looking at the movement of her mouth, we are already aware of the director's sophisticated understanding of the medium's potential for sexual expression. In 1920 this understanding, and the equivalent daring of the actress, whose performance is a triumph of subtle technique, were nothing short of miraculous.

Tourneur's rich visual style was never more in evidence than in *Foolish Matrons,* in which he captured vividly the complex texture of life in New York society. A companion piece to De Mille films of the same period in its story of the problems of marriage, it follows the lives of three couples, concentrating in particular on a celebrated actress and a struggling journalist. In content it offers little above the level of popular women's fiction of the period, observing with an air of aghast moral disapproval the goings-on of a corrupt world. In execution, however, it shows Tourneur's vivid command of physical detail, his sumptuous use of *mise en scène.* In deep-focus photography bathed in a succession of hand-tints—pale gray for the New York exteriors, soft gold for the interiors of the luxurious restaurants and salons of the period— Tourneur and Brown provide a fascinating range of dramatic action. In particular, the sequences in an opulent *café dansant* have a sophistication in advance of the period: coquettish demimondaines flirting with rich clients across potted palms; a powerful Lesbian in a caballero's hat chatting intimately with a young girl; the journalist-heroine lured by her patron into a private room overlooking the New York Public

Library, abandoning herself to him before the seafood cocktail is finished or the champagne is cooled in the bucket.

The weaker side of Tourneur's talent was shown in *The Pride of the Clan* (1918), a Mary Pickford vehicle about a young girl whose father's death leaves her in the position of local leader in a Scottish village. Using the famous Scottish village created by Thomas Ince for *Peggy* some three years earlier, Tourneur richly evokes the wind and weather of the little settlement. The interiors, with their roughhewn furniture, bowls of heather, and grandfather clocks are exquisitely apt. Alas, though, the drama is weakly developed, so that the final predicament of Mary—in a sinking ship, crying desperately for help—goes for nothing.

Tourneur's *ouevre* demands a volume to itself. His *Woman* (1918) and *The White Moth* (1924) were typical of the opposing sides of his talent. The first was an elaborate, *Intolerance*-like spectacle about woman through the ages in many guises. *The White Moth* was an intimate study of a particular career: a girl's rise from attempted suicide to the role of a Lulu-like temptress. Tourneur moved in his work from the romantically sweeping to the personal and would-be profound, succeeding none too well in either genre.

*The White Moth* illustrates his virtues and faults. The opening, staged in Paris, loater copied in von Sternberg's *Docks of New York,* is an elegantly shot sequence of a woman, Mona Reid, played by the ill-fated Barbara La Marr, going to the river Seine to drown herself. As trash floats by and lights shimmer in the water, she falls, and Gonzalo Montrez (known to the theatrical profession as El Volcano) snatches her from a watery doom. Under Montrez' tutelage she becomes a great success in casino and on legitimate stage. Her master trains her well, and she emerges ruthless, a destroyer of men.

One sequence well illustrates Tourneur's sense of the fantastic: the curtain rises on Mona's debut stage performance to show her dressed as a moth, struggling in the toils of a gigantic white web, menaced by a leotarded spider-man. Unhappily, though, this episode in more reminiscent of the Ziegfeld Follies than a modernistic Paris jazz ballet circa 1930.

After he was unceremoniously removed from the bizarre *The Mysterious Island* (1926, shelved by M-G-M and later completed by Lucien Hubbard), Tourneur returned to France. His son, Jacques Tourneur, became famous as a director of horror films, including *Cat People* and *Night of the Demon*. Like his father before him, he withdrew to Paris, unable to contend with the demands of Hollywood.

Two Swedish directors—Victor Sjöström and Mauritz Stiller—made a deep impression in the late 1920s. Sjöström's best work, *The Wind* (1928) was based by Frances Marion on the novel by Dorothy Scarborough, with largely pretentious and futile titles by John Colton, author of *The Shanghai Gesture*. A young, tender girl (Lillian Gish) is discovered on a train, heading for a bleak destination in the Middle West. Dust blows through the windows as she tells a predatory passenger, Wirt Roddy (Montagu Love), that she is looking forward to life at the ironically named Sweetwater. Her arrival at the Sweetwater railroad station is powerfully realized: the man sent to greet her trying to hold his lantern high in a howling night wind, a ribbon fluttering loose from her hair, the two figures struggling across a plain to the temporary refuge of a buggy. The journey to the little settlement assumes the quality of nightmare as the girl shrinks back in the buggy seat, seeing a white horse tossed helplessly over, then riding like a phantom steed through the sky. Such sequences as a meal with her new husband, nervous hands sweeping dust from the bread and the arrival of a tornado, with terrified people crowding into a storm cellar, exemplify screen narrative at its best, every image of an extraordinary immediacy. The climax declines into melodrama. Wirt Roddy returns to try and seduce the girl, she kills him, and he appears to return from the grave, his form forcing back the front door.

None of Sjöström's other American films matched the excellence of *The Wind*. His *He Who Gets Slapped* (1924), about the love affair of a clown (Lon Chaney) and a chorus girl, is tender and appealing, but rather low in terms of creative energy. *The Tower of Lies* (1925), from a novel by Sjöström's fellow countrywoman Selma Lagerlöf, has a dry fidelity to the original and a series of monotonously austere images which gradually erode one's sympathetic attention. Much superior to these films is *The Scarlet Letter* (1926), intelligently directed, adapted skillfully by Frances Marion from the novel by Nathaniel Hawthorne. Sjöström brought to the New England ambience a rich Scandinavian sensibility. The opening sequence, photographed in the pure and blazing whites and profound blacks of a Vermeer by the great Hendrik Sartov, carries the spectator from a giant bell down the stone of a sunlit tower to a close-up of an adulterer trapped in a wicker cage. The atmosphere of hatred, suspicion, and superstition is conveyed with a mastery which Hawthorne himself would have acknowledged, and both principals—

*Lillian Gish,* THE WIND

*Lillian Gish, Lars Hanson,* THE WIND

Lillian Gish superb as Hester Prynne and Lars Hanson as her unfortunate cleric-lover—and supporting cast look very authentic. It is unfortunate for the American cinema that, early in the talkie period, Metro wasted Sjöström; he returned in 1930 to a very distinguished career in his native country.

That equally famous—and tragic—Swede Mauritz Stiller was ruined by an unhappy affair with Greta Garbo, his brilliantly talented Galatea. He came to the United States after the triumph of *The Saga of Gösta Berling,* a mannered affair lacking in the Lagerlöf novel's emotional power. Stiller's one American film with Garbo, *The Temptress* (1926), was based by Dorothy Farnum on a novel by Blasco-Ibañez, that favorite of Rex Ingram; but Stiller altogether lacked the ability to wring poetry out of Miss Farnum's version of Blasco-Ibañez. Garbo was not at her best as Blasco-Ibañez's character of a demimondaine driven to the most serious extremes of discomfort when she accompanies her lover to Argentina. Stiller directed at so slow and solemn a pace that Louis B. Mayer removed the film from him and had it partly reshot by Fred Niblo.

*Hotel Imperial* (1926) was more effectively done. We are in Galicia

*James Hall, Pola Negri,* HOTEL IMPERIAL

in 1915, Russia and Austria are at war, and as a line of ragged Austrian cavalry officers moves against the sky, one rider falls off his horse. Exhausted, he makes his way against bare trees to the ruins of the once resplendent Hotel Imperial, where a maid (Pola Negri) is polishing the floor. Risking her life (this is occupied territory) she takes the fugitive in, and their romance is dangerously conducted under the noses of the Russian guards. The opening sequences are powerfully and excitingly built up and Bert Glennon's magnificent shadowy photography is identical in style with his work on von Sternberg's *Last Command*. Even though Jules Furthman's story becomes more and more ridiculous, and Stiller's direction more and more hollow in its visuals as the film goes on, the cinematography remains captivating. Fascinating to watch, Pola Negri is never wholly convincing as a maid of the 1915 period, her hauteur barely concealed behind a pretended look of humility. She never reaches the greatness that she strives for, relying entirely on her exotic beauty and temperament to carry her through the role. Miss Negri next appeared in Stiller's *Woman on Trial* (1927), a now vanished work which would make fascinating comparison with its remake, von Sternberg's *Blonde Venus*. *Street of Sin* (1928), on which Stiller began work, was not completed by him. Like Murnau and Leni, the director died at the dawn of sound.

■ ■ ■ ■ ■ ■ ■ ■ ■ ■ ■ ■ ■ ■ ■ ■ ■ ■ ■ ■ ■ ■ ■ ■

# 8. Von Stroheim, Von Sternberg

■ ■ ■ ■ ■ ■ ■ ■ ■ ■ ■ ■ ■ ■ ■ ■ ■ ■ ■ ■ ■ ■ ■ ■

Two obsessive artists of the jodhpur-and-whip school were Erich von Stroheim and Josef von Sternberg. Neither was in fact a "von" at all. Stroheim was the son of a Prussian soldier and Sternberg was an American; both hid their true identities in a cocoon of legend.

Von Stroheim's career began inconspicuously with *Blind Husbands* (1918), in which he himself appears as a leering seducer, monocled and dressed in officer's uniform, inexplicably succeeding in seducing a frustrated wife in a mountain resort. The film is prentice work, exasperating in its infantile narcissism, its unleashing of the director's wish-fulfillment fantasies. But it launched a career that was soon to emerge as one of the most brilliant in pictures.

*Foolish Wives* (1922), notoriously cut on the orders of Irving Thalberg at Universal, again dealt with a practiced seducer played by the director. "Count Sergius Karamzin, Captain of the 3rd Dragoons in Petrograd" is in fact an adventurer, who with his two sisters disguised as princesses in post-World War I Monte Carlo sets out to milk rich American visitors of their funds. Implacably, von Stroheim limns the milieu: the cafes made for flirtation, the palms that half disguise an erotic suggestion, the slum house house where counterfeit bank notes are made to support a half-witted daughter, the gambling casino where lives are ruined. The *mise en scène* is flawlessly brought off in a California setting, and there is a richness of detail, a sumptuous visual texture, indicating the advent of a master. The shadows that bar the

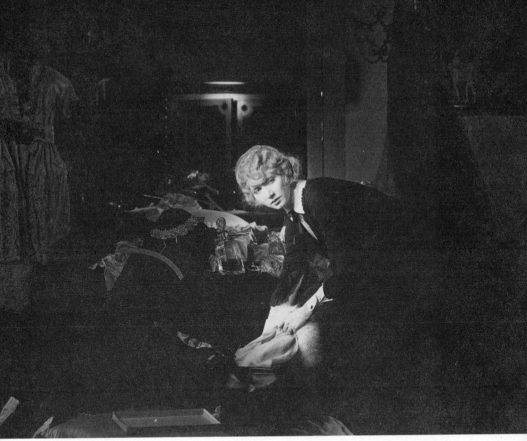

*Mae Busch,* FOOLISH WIVES

counterfeiter's room, the flashing glitter of lamps in an elevator, the suggestion of ocean and promenade—the director's ability to create an ambience, lived in and real, has not been exaggerated. Nor has his pitilessness of observation: the Count fleecing an ugly maid of her life savings, his lewd eyes caught in a mirror as a woman undresses, the cold portrayal of the flirtatious American woman Mrs. Howard Hughes (*sic*), played perfectly by Miss Du Pont, the shot of the Count's corpse being unceremoniously thrust down a manhole.

Von Stroheim's misanthropy was even more spectacularly displayed in his masterpiece, severely cut by Irving Thalberg, *Greed* (1923). Here the clarity of detail, the scenes portraying squalor and corruption are astounding. The director uses an extreme degree of physicality not only to give us the feeling of being thrust into intimacy with the characters but to show us the horror and hopelessness of the human condition. *Greed* is life itself.

*Jean Hersholt*, GREED

Frank Norris' novel provides the story but von Stroheim's artistry surpasses the book's. Even the titles ("Mysterious instincts, as ungovernable as the winds of the heavens, were knitting their lives together") cannot ruin the film.

The plot follows Norris to the letter: a struggling dentist, McTeague (Gibson Gowland), falls in love with his patient Trina (ZaSu Pitts) and wins her. She becomes a miser, and he murders her in a fit of rage, heading out into the desert, where he is confronted by an old friend and later rival, played by Jean Hersholt. From the beginning of the film to its horrifyingly powerful end, the characters are pursued by fate from which there is no escape. Improbable as it seems, we know that the ugly McTeague will somehow persuade the fragile Trina to marry him, that when she wins a $5,000 lottery she will become obsessed with the money, which replaces sexual fulfillment. We know that she must die and McTeague must face his destiny in a setting stripped of humanity and beauty. The symbols in the film are obvious but of a Zolaesque power: wringing hands convey the wife's desire for money, and in a magnificently photographed sequence, a cat waits to pounce on a caged bird as the wife reveals her dangerous inclinations. As it becomes clear she is doomed, we see a drowning hand clutching at an underwater treasure. The successive details of the husband's downfall are unsparing, from his dismissal from a surgical instrument factory, to his death at the end, the camera shooting directly into the sun as McTeague arrives in Death Valley, the black figures against the salt flats, the words "We are dead men" uttered against a light-drenched, blankly indifferent sky. The performances of Gibson Gowland, ZaSu Pitts, and Jean Hersholt are so accurate that we seem to have eavesdropped on real lives. With this one work, von Stroheim proved that theatrical gesture and romantic nonsense were not essential in the silent film. It was a lesson well known to the Russians, but it was new to Hollywood, and it did not take.

Von Stroheim's next film, *The Merry Widow* (1925), was something of a disappointment, partly because of the restrictions imposed by a conventional studio cameraman, Oliver T. Marsh, and partly because of the mediocre stars, John Gilbert and Mae Murray, also foisted on

*Mae Murray, John Gilbert,* **THE MERRY WIDOW**

him by a studio anxious to avoid the commercial disaster of *Greed*. The character of the seducer as played by Gilbert may be more physically attractive than von Stroheim, but he lacks von Stroheim's ferociously sensual personality. This is the director's weakest film since *Blind Husbands*.

*The Wedding March* (1927) is altogether more satisfactory, despite a somewhat dull opening sequence in which Nikki (von Stroheim) flirts with the girl Mitzi (Fay Wray) in the crowd outside the cathedral on Corpus Christi Day. Their mutual attraction is so repetitively built up that it becomes excruciating. Later, von Stroheim evokes a Vienna of amazing realism, equal to his Monte Carlo in *Foolish Wives*. His sense of milieu is matched to his acute observation of a decaying aristocracy. With sly humor and a streak of sadism he delineates the outrageous maneuverings of the Wildeliebe-Rauffenbergs, forcing on their son Nikki the horrible experience of marrying Cecilia, a cripple, played by ZaSu Pitts. Unfortunately, despite the film's many qualities, its portrait of Cecilia is needlessly cruel, and von Stroheim's heartlessness pervades his reptilian performance.

*Queen Kelly* (1928), not completed by von Stroheim, was made for Joseph Kennedy of United Artists, who was then in love with its star, Gloria Swanson; it was abandoned before completion and given a new ending. Something of a patchwork, the film is, once again, interesting for its ugly portrait of the rich and powerful, here symbolized not by a whole family but by the cruel Queen Regina, played by Seena Owen. Once again, too, as in most of von Stroheim's films, the heroine is as dewy-eyed and virginal as any of Griffith's. But against these conventional portraits of character can be placed the extraordinary set pieces, perverse and baroque, that von Stroheim created: the Queen whipping her victim, or walking naked except for the clinging fur of a white cat; the wedding in the brothel; the splendid banquet, a symbol of corruption and decadence. The director did nothing else in the silent period, and his one talkie, *Walking Down Broadway*, was largely reshot by another director.

As autocratic, overpowering, and ruthless as von Stroheim, and influenced by him, Josef von Sternberg's films were marred by his own affectations. His first venture, *The Salvation Hunters* (1925), an account

*Maude George, Erich von Stroheim,* THE WEDDING MARCH

of the lives of people on a dredge, was overburdened with the pretentious symbolism that became his trademark and made with a depressing amateurishness. It is notorious that until he proved himself commercially with *Underworld* (1927) von Sternberg's career in Hollywood was a disaster. His first important features, *The Exquisite Sinner* and *The Masked Bride*, were taken out of his hands and reshot. *The Seagull*—made for Chaplin, who had admired *The Salvation Hunters*— was bundled into a vault and lost. We can see only some of his hand at work in *Children of Divorce*, which he largely reshot when director Frank Lloyd failed to provide Paramount with the film they wanted.

Von Sternberg's *Underworld* fascinates as the precursor of the gangster films of the Thirties, fast-moving and journalistic, based on a conventional adaptation by Charles Furthman of a Ben Hecht story, a work outside the body of the director's *oeuvre*. Dispassionate and superficial, it is interesting chiefly as a piece of machinery, a series of carefully worked-out set pieces punctuated by a novelettish account of the gang moll Feathers (Evelyn Brent, miscast) and her romantic addiction to two men: Bull Weed, the gross, mindless gangster boss (George Bancroft), and the laconic drunk Rolls Royce (Clive Brook). The characters and their interrelationships are stock fiction, drawn from the dime books of the period, and as a portrait of the Capone era, the film falls short of its aims. The opening, with a bank robbery and a casual getaway; the jewel store holdup, neatly and swiftly handled; the flower shop shooting à la Dian O'Banion; the trial, with the judge's shadow looming over the condemned; an attempted prison escape by means of a hearse; the sentimental and carefully handled climax when Bull Weed and his girl are hemmed in by the police, a sequence foreshadowing Hecht's *Scarface*: these slickly directed scenes to some extent compensate for the improbabilities, the "Hollywood" approach which ignores all the psychotic tensions of gangster life and sentimentalizes an already soft script.

Von Sternberg's next film, *The Dragnet* (1928), does not survive; it was a companion piece to *Underworld*, but did not repeat its commercial success. *The Docks of New York* (1928) shows that by this time the director was more interested in pictorial effects than in penetration of character. The story, told in mediocre titles, is typical of the genre which von Sternberg liked: an emptily romantic account of self-sacrifice because of love. A stoker (George Bancroft) rescues a girl from suicide, a theme previously used in Tourneur's *The White Moth*, and suffers constantly on her behalf. Remote from truth, the film is very beautiful to watch, particularly the opening reel with shots of light rippling over the muscles of the stokers, and the pounding machinery of the ship.

*The Last Command* (1927) was far more successful, more deeply engaging von Sternberg's perverse sensibility. Lajos Biró, a Hungarian *émigré* who was at a later stage the closest associate of Korda, wrote the story. It concerns a former Russian Grand Duke, Sergius Alexander (Emil Jannings), who sinks to becoming a Hollywood extra, playing himself in a World War I story directed by his former enemy, the revolutionary Leo Andreyev (William Powell). Directed with cynical skill, photographed in a rich flow of low-key images by Bert Glennon, the film is persuasive as a portrait of the brutality and mercenariness of Hollywood, courageously exposed from the inside and symbolized by the aggressively ignorant crew. It is also a fine picture of revolutionary Russia, shown in low-key flashback within the framing device of Alexander's face in his mirrored makeup box. In the opening shot, von

*William Powell, Evelyn Brent,* THE LAST COMMAND

Sternberg's sophisticated humor is evident: Andreyev egocentrically contemplating a scene, a dozen minions surrounding him with lights for his cigarette. Von Sternberg is also brilliant in his creation of the rebel attack on the train, in which the Grand Duke is humiliated before the crowd; in the obsessive tracking shots along lines of extras humiliatingly equipped with uniforms or snarled at by the assistant director; and in the magnificent final sequence when the Grand Duke crawls into the artificial studio trench, relives his past at the sound of the Czarist Russian Anthem, and shrieks a battle cry before dying of a fatal heart attack. Here the editing and lighting, the incisive playing of William Powell, and Jannings' classic portrayal of defeat and madness are unforgettable.

*The Last Command* remains the greatest of the late silent films, more sophisticated, daring, and pitiless than any other save *Greed*. And more than any other silent film, it pointed the way to the new harshness, the New York-inspired realism that was to come with the talkies like a stinging Atlantic breeze.

# PART TWO
## The Talkies

■ ■ ■ ■ ■ ■ ■ ■ ■ ■ ■ ■ ■ ■ ■ ■ ■ ■ ■ ■ ■ ■ ■ ■ ■ ■ ■

# 1. Into the Sound Era

■ ■ ■ ■ ■ ■ ■ ■ ■ ■ ■ ■ ■ ■ ■ ■ ■ ■ ■ ■ ■ ■ ■ ■ ■ ■

At the end of the silent period, Hollywood film-makers, even the greatest, were still concerned first and foremost with making money, sec-
ondly with providing an object of harmony, balance, and beauty of
which they could be proud. Alongside the tissue of compromises which
composed the successful West End or Broadway play, the theater could
still support a wide degree of experimentation. Hollywood provided
almost no room for experiment. The sentimental sagas of Griffith and
his followers, the spectacular Belasco-like exercises of De Mille, even
the polished comedy of Lubitsch and the Scandinavian or German
theatrical modes of other imported directors all were dictated by the
tastes of the masses of people, and the rare realistic film made in defiance
of those tastes—*Greed,* as an example—was almost invariably a failure.
Lighting was conceived as a cosmetic device, portrait close-ups resembled those faces of the kings which loyal court painters provided
flatteringly to protect their own employment. Even Lubitsch was
visually kind to his feckless central figures. Only very rare figures,
among them Leni, Ingram, and Sjöström, or Chaney's directors, used
close-ups to paint pictures of a soul.

Critics, attempting to come to grips with the medium at the outset of
the 1930s, often claimed that photography was superior to the eye's
view of the world. In fact, the camera could not fully encompass reality,
and the eye saw less in a composed shot than it could see while moving
freely around a stage, or looking at the beauties of nature. Photography

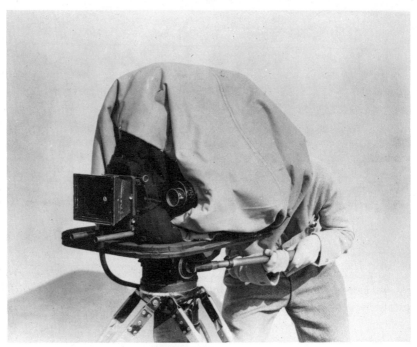

Early talkie camera

provided a selection from reality which the director could make at will. The screenplay was the equivalent of a blueprint from which the director, the cinematographer, and the art director constructed an intricate peep show, a funnel of darkness at the end of which brilliant images moved.

It became obvious from the examples of De Mille, Lubitsch, and the comedians that the greatest silent films were those in which the director provided a heightened, almost surrealist vision of reality informed by his own vision and which used the actors, together with the decor, in an original and untheatrical way. The best passage in the whole of Lubitsch, as we have seen, was the opening of *The Student Prince in Old Heidelberg*, which owed absolutely nothing to the theater. Unfortunately, the advent of the sound film resulted in a reversal to almost uniformly theatrical techniques.

By the outset of the 1930s it had become obvious that the chief aesthetic qualities of the American film still lay in its visual beauty. Its "ideas" were still depressingly banal. Hollywood perpetuated the ro-

mantic lies of the dime novels which were widely sold in the period
between 1910 and 1929. The intelligent were found taking seriously
ideas they would have ignored on the printed page. The moralistic conventions were ruinously perpetuated in the silent film. Adultery was
evil and punishable by extreme anguish; men and women must be vir-
gins until they were married; businessmen who were ruthless were inevitably punished; a dear little girl with long curly hair could melt the
heart of an evildoer in the space of two hundred frames.

During the late 1920s the public started to tire of silent films. It grew
weary of the conventions of staunch heroes and wilting heroines, of
broadly characterized villains, simple-minded stories of action and
crude comedies which formed the basis of many of the silent scenarios.
It was growing more sophisticated. Though film-makers provided the
Lubitsch wit and the flapper comedies and thrillers in which the brilliantly amusing Clara Bow and Bebe Daniels excelled, the public was
greedy for a new approach to deal with the new America that was
emerging. Radio's enormous success had provided competition for
some time, and audiences wanted to hear the voices of their idols (once
they did hear them, they were frequently disappointed). The masses
also wanted to hear the voices of the great Broadway stars, who were
mainly legends outside of New York. They were tired of the tedious
versions of Broadway plays without dialogue or with laborious titles
that interrupted dramatic scenes.

Griffith was among the first to see that there might be potential in
talkies. In May 1921 he demonstrated scenes of talk in his film *Dream
Street* at the New York Town Hall, but the screening was not a success.
An inventor named Lee De Forest made a number of short talkie films
and a synchronized track for some scenes of *The Covered Wagon*.
Among those appearing in De Forest's electioneering talkies was Calvin
Coolidge.

The Warner brothers were the first to develop the medium with
any degree of enthusiasm. In 1925 they had become interested in radio,
and on March 3 of that year began their first radio broadcasts in Los
Angeles. They worked in collaboration with the Bell Laboratories to
provide synchronized sound for the feature *Don Juan* (1926), directed
by Alan Crosland. The screenings were a major success, the sound recorded on discs which were played in and relayed from the projection
booth. William Fox of the Fox studios competed successfully with sound
on film, achieving his first triumph by giving an audience at the Roxy

Theatre in New York the excitement of hearing Lindy's motors roar before he took off for Paris.

The synchronized Fox newsreel were very mechanized. Warners *The Jazz Singer*—also directed by Crosland—was a cleverly promoted introduction for sound on disc, previewed on August 7, 1927, rivalled by Fox's sound-on-film *Fox Movietone Follies*. Talkies obviously had come to stay.

The problems of making early talkies were many. Several studios were so nervous of the new medium that they delayed as long as possible, and then made talkie and silent versions of their films. Once the box office results of several new films proved that *The Jazz Singer* was not merely a flash in the pan, the entire industry rushed to climb onto the bandwagon. Foreign silent stars like Pola Negri and Renée Adorée were swept away. The earliest talkies were often ungainly, though, and those

*May McAvoy, Al Jolson,* THE JAZZ SINGER

films which featured some talk amid long stretches of silence were very aggravating. The earliest microphones—used in such films as Bryan Foy's lamentable first all-talkie *The Lights of New York* (1929)— were so primitive that they made the fingering of beads sound like hailstones. If a performer looked away from the microphone, his voice could be "lost." Fortunately, a number of technicians headed by Douglas Shearer at M-G-M introduced the fishing pole, and later the boom, as a means of moving the microphone, and directors like Curtiz, Tay Garnett, and Mamoulian developed the use of two soundtracks. They and others managed to move the cameras, formerly connected in telephone box-sized blimps.

The character of the star system changed in the sound era. In the silent period, the great stars were those who could captivate millions by sheer force of personality, through gift with exaggerated mime, and in their ability to personify certain fixed ideals, ranging from the girl-woman to the Continental charmer, the husky athlete to the glorified lounge lizard. Gloria Swanson, Mary Pickford, Pola Negri, Garbo, and the other great female stars somewhat dominated the males in terms of popularity, releasing the fantasies of women still largely under the thumb of men. The greatest silent idols of women, Valentino and Gilbert, had a softness under their muscular exteriors that fascinated the public. Fairbanks and Mix were more the idols of men. Few were really good performers, though all were superb and overpowering stars.

In the talkie era the very character of acting changed. Broadway became the exemplar and the supplier. True, an actress like Katharine Hepburn could remain as prone to striking dramatic attitudes as a silent star. True also that Garbo remained essentially a silent actress, "behaving" beautifully at moments when a painful realism was called for. Joan Crawford was always a star before she was an actress. But along with these major female figures, and inheritors of the mantle of silent stars' broad-chested virility like Clark Gable, there were the actresses and actors who really understood the need for sophistication in their playing, among them Bette Davis, Spencer Tracy, Edward G. Robinson, Humphrey Bogart, and James Cagney. Most worked for Warners, a studio which can be said to have laid the foundations for contemporary acting as we understand it today.

Except for Hans Kräly, Jules Furthman, and a handful of others, sophisticated writers had avoided working in the silent film; Ben Hecht was among those who was disgusted by the sentimentalization and falsification of his screenplays by silent directors. Good writers had preferred to express themselves without interference through the medium of their books or plays; and screenwriting was widely felt to be a corrupted form of work, based on a variety of considerations which would force a specialized writer to descend to the able foolishness of a Fannie Hurst or an Olive Higgins Prouty. The talkies provided more allure, because directors were so busy trying to surmount the problems of the sound-track that scripts were not as frequently interfered with (except at Metro). In the early days of talkies, before the onset of censorship and the panic that followed the collapse of the film market in 1933, scripts became racy, funny, and insolent; at their best, the screenplays of such figures as Samson Raphaelson, Ernest Vajda, S. J. Perelman, S. N. Behrman, and Dorothy Parker achieved the hard-bitten wit of the best of Broadway and of *New Yorker* writing. The Marx Brothers, Mae West, and W. C. Fields worked very closely on their scripts themselves, adding a raucous irreverence to the writers' already iconoclastic lines. Many took their approach from Hans Kräly/Ernst Lubitsch, parodying the absurdities of Graustarkian ritual, using petty invented republics as analogues of America itself.

At the outset of the talkies, only a few great directors continued to carry on the major legacies of the silent film. The majority for many years turned their attention exclusively to presenting as clearly and as simply as possible stage actors speaking slightly above normal theater volume in adaptations of Broadway or action successes. Early talkies bear a striking resemblance to television, presented chiefly in medium shots and in sustained takes. The important differences are that producers then could call upon the refined talents of great stage stars and that the films were sometimes written by men of wit and refinement.

The musical was simply an extension of the typical Broadway production in a Hollywood setting, with the Astaire/Rogers and Busby Berkeley films, for all their directors' nimble techniques, essentially developments of the Ziegfeldian theatrical tradition. The crime film was in essence an extension also of Broadway hits like *The Racket,* and the mode's chief histrionic exponent, Edward G. Robinson, had in fact played in Broadway melodramas. Here again the camera remained largely fixed, the urban environment achieved largely in a studio in stagy sets against obvious backdrops. In the field of the horror film could be seen an extension of the UFA tradition—but that in itself was deeply theatrical.

*Mae West* and cameraman *Karl Struss* on set of BELLE OF THE
NINETIES

The most successful directors were those who discreetly opened the boundaries of purely theatrical film to show the possibilities inherent in selectively filmed dialogue scenes, among them the very distinguished Lewis Milestone, William Wyler and George Cukor. It was not until the 1940s that these and other directors managed to give a rich and various surface to their films, combining the freedom and fluency of the silents with the intelligence and acuity of the dialogue film. Deep focus, not seen since the heyday of Griffith, Murnau, and Féjos, and ceilinged sets returned through the medium of Orson Welles, a director who advanced the art of film by wedding radio techniques to the others which the cinema's major figures had succeeded in mastering. By the 1940s the cinema had regained the sumptuous beauty of the late silent films. At the same time it developed a rich new range of aural and visual possibilities and achieved, as most Thirties films had not, a proper extension of mechanical techniques. It was not until as late as the 1960s, though, that film music matured, substituting for the crashing Wagnerian or Brahmsian chords of Erich Wolfgang Korngold or Franz Waxman the subtlety of a Jerry Goldsmith or an Elmer Bernstein. Up to that time examples of good film music were rare—music which discreetly underlined the dialogue or enhanced a romantic mood rather than striving to dominate everything. Generally speaking, film music was the laughingstock of the musical world, just as post-code film dialogue was the laughingstock of the theater.

During the silent period the production of film in Hollywood had offered a scattered and confused scene. Numerous small studios were situated among the alfalfa and mustard fields, the sand dunes, and the orange groves that occupied what is now a grotesque urban environment. With the decline of the silent film's fortunes, the smaller studios went under or were absorbed. Warners narrowly escaped this fate by developing sound. By the outset of talkies the big studios had become consolidated and by the spring of 1934 largely absorbed by banks, though their executive operation was marked by all the reckless extravagance of the previous decade.

The most powerful single studio was Metro-Goldwyn-Mayer. Nicholas Schenck, a former druggist and amusement park owner, had developed the company with the aid of Marcus Loew in the 1920s. It was run from New York by Schenck's parent firm, Loew's Incorporated. Louis B. Mayer was in charge on the Coast. Under Schenck's supervision, he managed to give the studio something of the quality of his personality:

opulent, vulgar, ostentatious. M-G-M, hypocritically moralistic, was the studio which became famous for portraying riches. The films in which Garbo and Gilbert, Eleanor Boardman, Norma Shearer, Joan Crawford, and the other M-G-M stars appeared often displayed magnificent sets designed by Cedric Gibbons, the studio's art director, who created an M-G-M image for the world. The M-G-M cameramen, led by Oliver T. Marsh, made sure that high-key lighting showed every detail of these sets. Herbert Stothart, head of music at the studio from the early Thirties on, provided Palm Court violins which added to the sense of vicariously enjoyed luxury for the Depression masses.

Irving Thalberg was, of course, the dominant figure at Metro with Schenck and Mayer, an obsessed moviemaker who constantly ordered retakes to improve certain scenes. Widely regarded even to this day as a "genius," Thalberg was in fact a shrewd businessman, "square" and rearguard in his views, an old-fashioned grandma among production chiefs. He preserved and bequeathed after his death the moral fervor, the Bostonian conservatism that made M-G-M a bad word among intellectuals. The studio was staunchly upright, condescendingly liberal-minded to such unfortunates as Chinese peasants or French revolutionaries. Some comedies aside, M-G-M scripts were almost invariably dull and worthy, high-toned moral tales from some nineteenth-century volume.

Paramount was by contrast an immensely sophisticated studio. Instead of the cold and calculating propriety of a Thalberg it boasted the wit and intelligence of such successive production heads as Lubitsch himself, B. P. Schulberg, Buddy De Sylva, and Y. Frank Freeman. Paramount pictures were, like Metro's, lit to show details of the elegant sets designed there as simulacra of high life by the gifted Hans Dreier, rival of Gibbons. Paramount scripts had much of the variety and degrees of shading the studio's lighting style lacked. Paramount films were the ones the New York intellectuals who liked the movies could point to as proof that Hollywood was not entirely a mindless provincial settlement. At Paramount, De Mille, Lubitsch, Mamoulian, and Mitchell Leisen had a sophisticated command of the medium, their films frequently *risqué* to an extent that a Thalberg or a Mayer would have thought indecent.

Warners was the studio of low life, of the murky melodrama set among poor people, the stories of prostitutes, criminals, and crooked politicians. Warners showed America as it really was: down on its luck, half-starved, desperate, greedy. At first it eschewed music, then developed the rich, baroque rhythms of Max Steiner and Erich Wolfgang Korngold in the late 1930s. Twentieth Century-Fox was a studio that specialized in a hard, glittering, and glossy surface look, its screenplays unfortunately somewhat bloodless and soft-centered and its stars— Tyrone Power and Alice Faye among them—seldom particularly gifted. The head of the music department, Alfred Newman, an uneven composer, was a brilliant arranger, as many of his Forties films proved. The "big" pictures always had fine production qualities equal to the best of Metro's; Frank Lloyd's *Cavalcade* and *Berkeley Square* were handsome prototypes of the studio's style. Universal specialized in importing figures from Germany and Britain, its starring directors James Whale and John M. Stahl. Later in the Thirties, the European expatriates Henry Koster and Joe Pasternak presented Universal's enormously successful Deanna Durbin comedies. Columbia under Harry Cohn was chiefly notable for the comedies of Frank Capra and the accomplished talent of Jean Arthur, its major star until the advent of Rita Hayworth. RKO was a studio run on an equally modest scale, but offering entertainment of some taste and refinement: most notably the Fred Astaire/ Ginger Rogers musicals and Garson Kanin's pleasing light comedies starring Ginger Rogers. The studios engaged directors, stars, writers, cinematograpers, art directors, and editors on long-term contracts, insisting on a "studio look" to which all but the greatest had to conform.

Conformism remained, in fact, the bane of the American film as late as 1940. No sooner did an original idea emerge than it became a fashion. Even the wit I have remarked on in the scripts of the early 1930s became stereotyped, so that one always knew the girl reporter would have a heart of gold and that her editor would fire and reinstate and perhaps marry her in the final reels, that heiresses were madcap and their suitors dashingly tailored. The tight conservatism of the studios made its own strait-jacketing rules, as major novelists whose works were adapted for the screen so frequently discovered.

As an entertainment form, whatever its serious shortcomings as art, the American film reached a high point in the Thirties. And a few great artists of the silent film did succeed, in those years of the Depression, in following their romantic vision unchecked.

# 2. The Masters Respond to Sound

The talkie revolution firmly closed an era for many figures. By the time it came along, Leni, Ince, and Stiller were dead, and Murnau barely survived it. Sjöström, as we have seen, made halfhearted efforts to cope with it, then returned to Sweden. Herbert Brenon and James Cruze never made another interesting picture. Clarence Badger, creator of Clara Bow's enchanting *It,* was similarly affected by the change-over. Rowland V. Lee, except sporadically in such films as *Zoo in Budapest* and *I Am Suzanne,* never fulfilled his early promise. The silent comedians suffered severely. Keaton and Langdon struggled on; Chaplin defiantly —and intelligently—went on making silents for years, using occasional sound effects and preserving a broad Griffithian sentiment in his portraits of heroines. Of all the great directors of the silent screen only a handful —among them Henry King, King Vidor, William Wellman, Clarence Brown, De Mille, Lubitsch, and von Sternberg—survived.

Henry King never recaptured the greatness of *Stella Dallas,* although many of his talking films had moments of physical beauty; he preserved the Griffithian virtues where possible, though his style remained a trifle stolid. He continued as a silent director insofar as his handling of dialogue scenes often had a stiffness and lack of fluency, while his pastoral sequences were uniformly good. *State Fair* (1933) had a vigor, freshness, and sympathy in its admittedly idealized fantasy treatment of small-town life, and it showed that King had lost little of his skill. His remake of *Way Down East* (1935) did not quite disgrace the memory of the original. *Ramona* (1936) was a moving account of the life of a half-Indian girl, distinguished by William V. Skall's Madonna-esque close-ups of Loretta Young and (again) by a strong rural feeling. *In Old Chicago* (1938), the story of the O'Learys whose cow started the Chicago fire, had an impressive dramatic sweep. All of King's Griffithian mastery of detail was shown in the first great crossing of the Illinois plain by Mrs. O'Leary and her family, the evocation of the muddy wooden nineteenth-century city, the tensions of its newly rich citizens, and the fire itself, staged with a verve that recalled Griffith's fall of Babylon sequence in *Intolerance*. These last sequences were bathed in the crimson glow of flames, which startlingly interrupted an otherwise black and white film. The figures of the refugees going into a river seemingly made of molten steel had a Dantesque quality.

King's *Jesse James* (1939) alternated lovely country scenes with slow-moving dialogue-laden interiors; and all through his work of the 1940s and 1950s King kept returning to the American landscape with a lover's warmth. *Chad Hanna* (1940) had many of the tender qualities of *State Fair*. *Wilson* (1944) was as solid and affectionately patriotic as the *America* which influenced it. *Margie* (1946) was an apt evocation of the life of young people in the 1920s, probably his most consistently

*Alice Brady, Tyrone Power,* IN OLD CHICAGO

*Courtesy of Twentieth Century-Fox.*

*Jean Parker, Gregory Peck, Millard Mitchell,* THE GUNFIGHTER

appealing film since *Stella Dallas.* The high school debate, an iridescent ice-skating scene, and the lovely snow sequences had a purity seldom seen since the silent period. And in his last major work, *The Gunfighter* (1949), King paid a splendid homage to Griffith. The daguerreotype images of the cameraman Arthur Miller were deliberately modeled on those of the master Billy Bitzer in this realistic story of a gunman in a small western town.

King Vidor emerged as an even more impressive figure of the talkies; unlike King, he gained enormously in technical sophistication in the new medium, while sharing King's—and Griffith's—love of the wild. Vidor's career was one of the few to help disprove that talkies destroyed the art of motion pictures. He showed that natural sounds and a rich orchestration of human voices could add immeasurably to any drama.

Like King, and like his master Griffith, he was always at his best in scenes of action, weakest when dealing with intimacies of human nature. He continued to share those directors' passion for the soil, and his exteriors reflect his preference.

His first talkie, *Hallelujah* (1929), courageously made with an all-black cast, excellently utilizes sound techniques. Based on Vidor's memories of black religious meetings and mass baptisms in Texas and Arkansas, the film was shot silent and dubbed later; a difficult task in a period before moviolas. Vidor's purpose was to explore the neurotically intense, hypersensitive creative character of the black people at a time when most studios showed them only as grinning servants. With warm and direct honesty he evoked the woods, the rolling hills, and the shabby cabin settlements of the South.

The chief protagonist, a young revivalist minister tormented with religious mania, falls in love with a foolish, fickle girl. Their relationship ends in betrayal and murder. The mass baptism is excellently staged: the postulants rushing into the river like white geese, bathing as though in the blood of Christ. Here the good-time girl becomes seized with convulsions, which the preacher on a pretext of curing brings to an end with a sudden seduction in his hut. The revivalist meeting, too, with its preacher's "cannon ball to hell" sermon delivered in a complex of shadows, is very fine; but it is the last sequence that is really surpassing. As the preacher returns home to his community, he sits on top of a boxcar, singing "Goin' Home." Behind him the landscape rolls away to the horizon, with its copses, low hills, and clumps of scrub. The sun is shining, and for a few minutes he feels an animal contentment, a quiet acceptance of freedom.

*Billy the Kid* (1930) is almost equally moving. Billy, as played by Johnny Mack Brown, becomes in this version a Robin Hood figure, infuriated by the depredations of the New Mexico vigilantes. As in *Hallelujah,* the realism is extraordinary: Vidor shows us the true West —seedy, shabby towns in the middle of gray plains, rolling scrub, gloomy hills against the horizon. Bandits and vigilantes are shown as the mean, petty and crude men they really are, and Billy the Kid, as played here, is a lean, slow-speaking, underprivileged youth.

In *Cynara* (1931) Vidor moved to an English setting: a London barrister (Ronald Colman) confesses to his wife (Kay Francis) in a Naples hotel that he has fallen from grace with a shopgirl. The film is framed within his confession. Vidor's sympathy raises the script (by

*William Fountaine, Nina Mae McKinney,* HALLELUJAH

*King Vidor* on location for BILLY THE KID

Frances Marion and Lynn Starling) to a work of art. Shot in a romantic glow by Ray June, the lovers' idyll influenced von Sternberg's *An American Tragedy*: punting on a lake, as the camera explores a line of weeping willows; or a night in a candlelit inn, the girl terrified of darkness and storm, feeling a premonition of her own death. Here is screen narrative as fluent as any in the silent film.

In *The Stranger's Return* (1933) Vidor yet again focused with Griffithian warmth upon the American rural scene. Louise Storr (Miriam Hopkins) returns home from New York to stay with her family, a troubled landowning clan. The countryside is delicately evoked. We see a garden full of butterflies and spring flowers, figures in doorways like Grant Wood primitives. A rural church service is impeccably observed, from the introductory shot of a porch, a dog wandering into the aisle, to a slow pan across a choir as the parson drones through a passage from Corinthians while Grandpa Storr nods asleep and Louise watches him with a gentle smile. The last images of the grandfather dying, the girl walking behind the plow, the plow breaking the earth for the harvest are quintessential Vidor, asserting his belief in the supremacy of nature.

*Our Daily Bread* (1934), rather stiffly made on a small budget, is another subject close to Vidor's heart: the story of a cooperative farming community. The last sequence of an attempt to bring water to the struggling farmers by means of an irrigation ditch is a trifle too academic in its Russian cutting, too calculated to be moving.

*The Wedding Night,* made in the same year, continued Vidor's explorations of rural life, although this time the script (by Edith Fitzgerald) restricted his range. The story again concerns the attempts made by city dwellers to enjoy a life of rural simplicity. A novelist (Gary Cooper) settles down on a Connecticut farm to write a novel which he hopes will benefit from a more relaxed and generous environment. His last works have all had urban settings and have been failures. His wife can no longer tolerate the life he is leading and returns to the city; we are made to share her sense of guilt and of pain at the need for urban excitement. He falls in love with Manya (Anna Sten), the daughter of a stern Polish paterfamilias (Sig Rumann) who marries her off to a stalwart scion of another Polish clan. On the wedding night her husband comes drunken to her room; Manya runs out into the blizzard-swept night to the novelist's house, falls down stairs during a subsequent quarrel, and dies. One assumes Goldwyn was responsible for the final image, presaging his own *Wuthering Heights*. As the anguished lover peers out into the snow, Manya's ghost stands on the hill and turns back to wave to him a last farewell.

The script is an example of Thirties kitsch, and its first half weighs the director down. But gradually his intelligence and pastoral feeling take over. The re-creation of the Polish community life, the feasts and ceremonies, the shots of wooden houses in the snow, all have a recognizable poetic flavor. Anna Sten's at first cold but later touching performance is always worth watching, even if Gary Cooper is miscast as the novelist and the excerpts from his work in progress scarcely encouraging.

*The Wedding Night* wore out King Vidor's creative resources; it was twelve years before he was again able to make a personal film. A long succession of box office contrivances followed the financial failure of *Our Daily Bread* (which deeply embittered him) and the obvious compromises with Goldwyn over *The Wedding Night*. *The Texas Rangers* (1936) was a routine Western about two bandits who disguise themselves as members of the Rangers to spy on behalf of a third; they are finally, in a Ford-like sentimental conversion, made to see the error of their ways. *So Red the Rose* (1935), though ravishingly shot by Victor Milner, was a poor man's *Gone With the Wind*, *Stella Dallas* (1937) a crude tearjerker (with the diamond-hard Barbara Stanwyck miscast in the sentimental role Belle Bennett so exquisitely created in the silent version). *The Citadel* (1938) was a commonplace version of Cronin; *Comrade X* (1940) an impersonal entertainment along the lines of *Ninotchka*. There was also a version of Marquand's *H. M. Pulham Esquire* (1941). None of these was out of the ordinary. Only in *Northwest Passage* (1939), from a story about Rogers' Rangers and their crossing of the American wilderness during pioneer days, could one sense a response to the material. The evocation of forests and lakes was affectionate, and at least one sequence—when the younger boy attached to the regiment wakes up and sees as in a dream the redcoats marching over the hill—had the fullness of response one looks for in the best of Vidor.

In 1946, after several failures, including *An American Romance* (1944), an ill-advised attempt to betray his rural longings and create a hymn to machinery, Vidor found a congenial subject, *Duel in the Sun*. Adapted by David O. Selznick from a novel by Niven Busch as a spectacle to match his own *Gone With the Wind*, this was a diffuse and tiresome script, chiefly concerned with the relationship between a tempestuous half-breed, Pearl Chavez (Jennifer Jones), and two Texan brothers; a subplot far more appealing to Vidor—he may have had a hand in it himself—showed a land baron (significantly played by Lionel Barrymore, repeating his role in *The Stranger's Return*) fighting the intrusions of commerce in the form of the railroad, which threatens to carve across his territory and bring his ancestral land within the bounds of civilization.

*Duel in the Sun* owed more to Selznick, than to Vidor, its opulent vulgarity and studio exteriors constantly jarring. Many of the best scenes were directed by second-unit men, experts like Otto Brower and Reeves Eason, or handled by other craftsmen (Dieterle, von Sternberg). Vidor's touch was displayed, though, in two splendid baroque sequences based on Griffith's editing principles: the summoning of the ranch hands to the railroad, in part directed by Brower, and the final ride of Pearl Chavez into the sun, Gila monsters and lizards writhing from under her horse's

*Franchot Tone, Miriam Hopkins, Lionel Barrymore,* THE STRANGER'S
RETURN

hooves, accompanied by the powerful score of Dimitri Tiomkin, based on Indian tribal themes.

Throughout this Wagnerian horse opera, Vidor's love of landscape (his native Texas) often emerged very fully.

In *The Fountainhead* (1949) he also showed strong feelings—for the world of New York, observed with much of the flair he had shown in *The Crowd*. As in the earlier film, he opted for a surrealist style in this Ayn Rand story of an architect (Gary Cooper) who is prepared to destroy anyone or anything for his obsession. Vidor's bold use of space and deployment of figures had not been lost. The best sequence shows a rich girl (Patricia Neal) in love with the architect watching him drive a phallic drill into the face of a cliff, her skirt with its knife-blade pleats resisting his gaze.

Vidor the same year attacked another overblown work, a novel, *Beyond the Forest,* by Stuart Engstrand (who lived entirely up to his own romantic prose by walking into a lake and drowning after the book was finished). Rosa Moline (Bette Davis) is a hick-town Madame Bovary; in Loyalton, Wisconsin, she aches to go to the Big City, Chicago, to escape her provincial origins, her dull, good, worthy husband, and his dreary suburban home. Against the bedroom windows, she broods against a skyline of powerhouses ("If I stay in Loyalton, I'll die!"). Desperately she seduces a Chicago industrialist (David Brian), in a log cabin the size of the Beverly Hilton. When she goes to Chicago to plead with him to take her away from her small-town life, he refuses to see her. Later, he returns and decides to marry her after all, but the plan to elope is overheard, and on a hunting trip, Rosa shoots the eavesdropper dead. She is acquitted at the subsequent trial, but discovers she is pregnant. Now that the industrialist, afraid of scandal, has again deserted her, she struggles out of bed, totters peritonitis-stricken to the railroad tracks, and, still firmly on the wrong side of them, dies while the engine carries its load to the Windy City.

Given this farrago, Vidor seizes what he can. The trial scene, with Rosa racing down the mean Loyalton streets to burst in and announce her innocence, is brilliantly staged. So too is the whole of her visit to Chicago, for which she wears a sinister black hat, pacing round her lover's office in an agony of frustration, brushed off by a snooty secretary, and finally running out into the rain for a last-minute plea with him. Through the murk, Vidor's passion for the countryside is again clear: the hunt sequence is at once realistic and responsive to the woods

*Bette Davis, Joseph Cotten,* BEYOND THE FOREST

and hills of the setting, and Rosa's final walk to the railroad has an authentic power, greatly aided (like the rest of the film) by Max Steiner's brilliant score.

Since *Beyond the Forest,* Vidor has done little of interest. *Ruby Gentry* (1952), a story about a vengeful girl from the wrong side of the tracks who destroys her enemies in a small town when she inherits a fortune, seems to have left his interest unengaged, except in one brief scene—inspired by an incident in Vidor's Texas youth—when Ruby and her lover drive into the sea, leaving the car to drift away into the surf. *Man Without a Star* (1955) was a straightforward Western, and *War and Peace* (1956) a stolid version of Tolstoy. *Solomon and Sheba* (1959), despite some fine early sequences of cavalry skirmishes reminiscent of *Duel in the Sun,* was for the most part a pale imitation of De Mille. No subject has since emerged to attract this great director. Characteristically, he has refused offers of more spectacles, hoping finally to raise money to make a 16mm. film about young people. One hopes he can, and that it will be set in the fields, forests, and rivers of that forgotten America he knows and loves so well.

Unlike those directors previously discussed, the Griffithian John Ford did not direct major films in the silent period, but rather a series of minor works reflecting the master's principles. His silent films, including *The Iron Horse* (1924) and *Four Sons* (1928), were not very interesting, alternately labored and stodgy, boisterous or perfunctory. But as he progressed, Ford emerged as a fully fledged Griffithian in scenes of action, in the evocation of the American landscape. Just as Griffith portrayed the South in false colors in *The Birth of a Nation,* so Ford distorted the history of the West for generations of young people, failing to convey its Spartan crudity, its dryness, its competitiveness under the shadows of the mesas. In his world, as in Griffith's, men were staunch and powerful, women were bony pioneers or melting frails; his Irishness suffused his portraits of the figures of the past, giving his work at best the feel of an O'Casey, at worst a boisterous militancy. His range was wide—all the way from expressionist melodrama (*The Informer*) to historical pageantry (*Mary of Scotland*) and even the *roman policier* (*Gideon's Day*). But it is for his Westerns that Ford chiefly deserves to be remembered.

At the outset of sound, Ford had established a strong visual style based on American primitive painters, and when he worked at Fox studios, collaborating with the writer Dudley Nichols, his military or bucolic themes were combined with a simple, unsophisticated approach to an audience. *Men Without Women* (1930) was a story about fourteen men trapped in a submarine, based on a famous incident of the Twenties, full of the rough humors that marked much of Ford's work. *Born Reckless* (1930) was one of the earlier talkie crime films, unremarkable in every way. *Arrowsmith* (1931) and *Doctor Bull* (1933) showed Ford's talent at its best. *Arrowsmith* is in fact Ford's finest film of the early sound era, like *Doctor Bull* an account of the life of a general practitioner in a time when warmth, personal attentiveness, and house calls were still possible. Ford's frame houses, white fences, and dusty shady streets still have the look of Griffith's, based on Mathew Brady and Grant Wood. Ronald Colman as Martin Arrowsmith is a trifle cool and smug, and Helen Hayes as actressy as usual, but Myrna Loy is excellent as Joyce Lanyon, the renounced Other Woman, and the narrative, in Sidney Howard's script, admirably simple. Two gentle and beautiful Will Rogers vehicles, *Judge Priest* and *Steamboat Round the Bend,* were in strong contrast with Ford's hymns to men of action —such epics as *Flesh* (1932), and *Air Mail* (1932).

*The Informer* (1935) was a complete departure for Ford, an expressionist version of Liam O'Flaherty's novel. The realism of *Judge Priest,* the heroics of *Air Mail* are replaced with a Germanic, moonlight-and-fog approach that recalled the worst of Murnau or Robison. Not since *Sunrise* had audiences seen so many painfully artificial streets, overpolished cobbles, heavy cliché symbols and "significant" decors. As Gypo, the very summation of brute stupidity, Victor McLaglen gives a powerful if overindulged and overemphatic performance.

*The Prisoner of Shark Island* (1936), Nunnally Johnson's screenplay about Dr. Samuel Mudd, who repaired John Wilkes Booth's leg and was punished by exile to the Tortugas, is much better directed, with an equally Germanic visual style more functionally and effectively used. The line of captured suspects dragged hastily before a tribunal in chains; the evocation of the Tortugas prison settlement dominated by a sadistic and skeletal warden (John Carradine); the sequence in which a black prisoner is thrown into a punishment pit, watched by the light of torches —all of these are scenes of some power. Ford's dynamic narrative skill, immeasurably aided by Bert Glennon's camerawork, makes this the director's best work of the Thirties. *Mary of Scotland* (1936) was less satisfactory, despite its set and costume design capturing the look of contemporary drawings. The casting was poor: Katharine Hepburn was too American as Mary, Fredric March an awkwardly self-conscious Bothwell; and the portrait of Darnley as a homosexual fop was a caricature. With the exception of a vivid John Knox sermon the film appears to have left Ford quite disinterested.

Throughout that decade, Ford became more and more eclectic. *The Hurricane* (1937) was an unbridled example of hokum, with several extraordinary set pieces, one of which was among the most beautiful episodes ever put on a screen: the escape of the Apollo-like South Sea Islander (Jon Hall) from prison, diving into a glittering ocean, a symbol of the beauty and freedom of the Polynesian people. The final hurricane was stunningly staged by James Basevi, but another virtuoso sequence surpassed it: the bamboo and fern evocation of the South Sea nightclub

*Courtesy of Twentieth Century-Fox.*

*Tom Brown, Anita Louise,* JUDGE PRIEST

*Courtesy of Twentieth Century-Fox.*

*John Carradine, Warner Baxter,* THE PRISONER OF SHARK ISLAND

*J. M. Kerrigan, Victor McLaglen,* THE iNFORMER

and bar, full of whirling fans and distorted figures dabbing their sweaty faces.

In 1939 Ford returned to Griffithian principles with *Stagecoach,* a fluent, almost bare work written by Dudley Nichols, devoid of the lushness of the director's films of the late 1930s and setting the Spartan tone which he has retained in his films since that time. Stripped to the muscle and sinew of pure screen narrative, the film seems today a trifle flat—lacking the energy which made so electrifying an experience of *The Hurricane.* The great chase across the salt flats, with a mousy Donald Meek clinging to his Bible and Claire Trevor as the *Boule de Suif*-like prostitute opening her lovely eyes in fright, is exhilarating, coming as a relief after a maundering de Maupassant-like narrative. *Drums Along the Mohawk* (1939), as scripted by Lamar Trotti and Sonya Levien, is a better and more moving work. Once again it shows a contrast between Ford's marvelous feeling for long shots, for men moving in action, and his somewhat stilted approach to dialogue scenes.

*The Young Mr. Lincoln* (1939), with a screenplay by Lamar Trotti,

*John Carradine, Katharine Hepburn,* MARY OF SCOTLAND

photographed by Bert Glennon, was introduced with a poem of Rose-
mary Benét's about Lincoln's mother. The film begins in New Salem,
Illinois, in 1832, Lincoln lying under a tree studying law, wandering
along a riverside with Ann Rutledge. Ripples of water from a tossed
stone change to a shot of ice as winter settles down on New Salem, and
we see that Ann has died. Kneeling by her grave, Abe decides to pursue
his legal career. Stovepipe-hatted, he rides into Springfield for his work
as counselor-at-law, meets Mary Todd, and enjoys the Independence
Day celebrations. The period details are lovingly sketched in: a log-
splitting contest, a tug of war, a tar-barrel-rolling match. The film re-
sembles a Griffith film throughout, particularly in the sequence in which
two boys accidentally kill an older man. We see the softly moonlit clear-
ing, the struggling figures, the anguished mother standing watching at
the property fence, and are taken all the way back to a Griffith short
film made before *The Birth of a Nation* called *A Corner in Wheat*.
Abe arranges to defend the supposed murderers, and the trial forms the
centerpiece of the action. Unfortunately, the film is marred by artificiality
in the second half, except in the vivid scene when the mob storms the
jail in an attempt to lynch the youngsters. Here Ford's direction and

*Pauline Moore, Henry Fonda,* YOUNG MR. LINCOLN

*Courtesy of Twentieth Century-Fox.*

Fonda's playing (despite the serious handicap of his makeup) are at their best. *Drums Along the Mohawk* also suffers from artificiality, the scenes of the setting up of the camp in the Mohawk Valley to some extent offsetting the absurdity of Claudette Colbert, with plucked eyebrows and powder, and Edna May Oliver, complete with phony "country" accent, as pioneer women.

In the 1940s John Ford developed considerably as a technician while retaining his traditional themes. His narrative style—based on the still camera and fluid cutting of Griffith—achieved an additional visual richness because of the major improvements in film stock and lighting equipment in the new decade. He had shaken off the kitsch of the Thirties films and had learned to deepen and enrich the story methods which made *Stagecoach* move along so capably. *The Grapes of Wrath* (1940) was a faithful realization of Nunnally Johnson's version of Steinbeck's novel, about the Okie emigrants from the dust bowl region in the 1930s. The film is decent, austere, and beautifully photographed by Gregg Toland. It is especially well shot in such scenes as Ma Joad's burning of the family souvenirs; the arrival, in subjective camera, at the strange and menacing transit camp; and the emergence on the edge of

Scene from THE GRAPES OF WRATH

*Courtesy of Twentieth Century-Fox.*

the Promised Land of California. Granted that the characters spoke with an improbable poetic loquacity and that Henry Fonda and John Carradine among the cast seemed uncomfortably citified; the film is still an honorable achievement and Jane Darwell's Ma is among the cinema's monumental performances.

*How Green Was My Valley* (1941) suffered from a sentimental Alfred Newman score, a pedestrian screenplay (by Philip Dunne) that constantly erred in the direction of naïveté, and a mixed cast of Irish, American, and British players trying to be Welshmen. Supported by the Griffithian lighting, Ford surmounted these obstacles to provide a magnificently made picture, evoking an admittedly ersatz but still gripping acount of life in a Welsh mining community. A realistically staged mining disaster, labor meetings, and family scenes had a charged vitality; and the Fox craftsmanship was at its best.

His *My Darling Clementine* (1946), beautifully written by Samuel C. Engel and Winston Miller, was a work which may have idealized and romanticized the West just as *How Green Was My Valley* romanticized Wales, but it offered equally superior craftsmanship. Wyatt Earp vs. the Clanton gang is not an unfamiliar theme, yet the playing of Henry Fonda—as Earp—and Walter Brennan, the embodiment of evil as Old Man Clanton, has a classic authority. The dedication of the Tombstone Church is the finest sequence in the picture. Here we see a square dance, bells ringing, stars and stripes fluttering, the sky washed out with light. It is a legendary archetypal scene of moving grandeur.

As Ford moved away from 20th Century-Fox in the late 1940s his shortcomings became apparent: his dependence on his writers and, in particular, his cinematographers. *The Quiet Man* (1952) and a string of famous Westerns from *Fort Apache* (1948) to *The Sun Shines Bright* (1954) were not uniformly impressive, though all had patches of affectionate observation or strong technique. In *The Quiet Man,* set in Ireland, a Donnybrook and the tender love scenes between Maureen O'Hara and John Wayne were still recognizably the work of a great director. Except for *The Searchers* (1956), an excellent VistaVision Western, Ford has rested on his laurels in recent years.

Clarence Brown was for many years immured in the plushly claustrophobic Greta Garbo vehicles—travesties of the classics (*Anna Karenina*) or history (*Marie Walewska*) made with a dead marmorial smoothness. In *Ah, Wilderness!* (1935) and *Of Human Hearts* (1938)

*Courtesy of Twentieth Century-Fox.*

Scene from HOW GREEN WAS MY VALLEY

*Courtesy of Twentieth Century-Fox.*

*Henry Fonda, Jane Darwell, Roy Roberts,* MY DARLING CLEMENTINE

his Griffithian character emerged: the first a fine version of the O'Neill play, the second a moving account of the growth of a poor boy in Ohio before and during the Civil War. Bradbury Foote's superb screenplay *Of Human Hearts* was the best Clarence Brown had worked with up to that time, quite distinct from the depressing artifices of Benjamin Glazer's version of Sudermann in *Flesh and the Devil*. The finest sequence in this story of a clash between father (Walter Huston) and son (James Stewart) is the father's taming of a white stallion, symbol of his desire to control life and to mold it in his own image. The film is enormously persuasive as the portrait of an era, equal to the best of Ford, superior to the more famous *Gone With the Wind* in its evocation of the 1860s.

Finer still—indeed Brown's most satisfying movie of the 1930s—was *The Rains Came* (1939), set in India during a flood, in which he moved temporarily from M-G-M, welcoming the finer technical skill of 20th Century-Fox's special effects department. Aided by Arthur Miller's hard and glittering cinematography, he greatly improved on the vapid screenplay (by Philip Dunne) drawn from a novel by Louis Bromfield. Brown's direction of players like Myrna Loy and George Brent is especially noteworthy. It would be difficult to improve on the direction of sequences like the outbreak of the monsoon, a curtain billowing in the breeze, a lamp casting the shadow of a latticework against white silk, servants scattering for cover; the death of the Maharajah; or the earthquake, a crystal chandelier swaying as a pampered courtier (Joseph Schildkraut) shrinks back among his friends. Although the film was made entirely in Hollywood, Brown gave a convincing account of life among the sahibs.

*The Rains Came* owed almost as much to Darryl F. Zanuck and the "Fox look" as to Brown. If there were any doubts left about Brown's greatness they were settled by his three major films of the 1940s, *National Velvet* (1944), *The Yearling* (1946), and *Intruder in the Dust* (1949). With the sumptuous quality of three-color Technicolor at its height, his genius could express itself magnificently. *National Velvet,* based on the novel by Enid Bagnold, was a triumph of craftsmanship, its studio "England" flawlessly re-created, its photography by Leonard Smith ravishing, its story of horse-training, leading to a stunningly shot finale of the Grand National, virtually a model of rhythmical screen narrative. *The Yearling* (1946) was an almost equally marvelous example of Brown's skill. True, Marjorie Kinnan Rawlings' novel of Florida swamp life was somewhat compromised by Paul Osborn's script,

*Gregory Peck, Claude Jarman, Jr.,* THE YEARLING

and the "country folks" (Gregory Peck, Jane Wyman, and Claude
Jarman, Jr.) were too much city people. Nevertheless, in many sequences, Brown gave a moving picture of the life in the Florida swamp
country. With the great cameraman Charles Rosher and (once again)
the even greater Leonard Smith, Brown magically captured the Everglades, the dark waterways and undergrowth of the state, the tight little
compound where the fawn is raised, and the sudden heartbreaking ruin-
ing of the crops.

*Intruder in the Dust* was equally alive with Brown's sympathetic response to nature and to simple, uncultivated human beings. Drawn from Faulkner's novel, with a skillful screenplay by Ben Maddow, the film focuses on the events of two days during which the black Lucas Beauchamp (Juano Fernandez) is held on suspicion of murdering a white man. Characteristically, Brown shot the entire feature on location in Faulkner's home town of Oxford, Mississippi. In its sympathetic, uncondescending treatment of blacks it was well ahead of its time.

William Wellman, alas, never again recaptured the poetic intensity of *Beggars of Life*. At the outset of talkies he became a Warners journalistic director, a vigorous exponent of the "headlines" school of filmmaking. *Public Enemy* (1931) and such films as *Night Nurse* (1931), *Hatchet Man* (1932) and *Frisco Jenny* (1933) could have been directed by anyone, and were, strictly speaking, studio creations of Darryl F. Zanuck or Hal Wallis. Even the admirable *Heroes For Sale* (1933) was an obedient development of a studio-manufactured script. Later in the Thirties, Wellman simply followed the clever scenarios of *A Star Is Born* (1937) and the Hecht-MacArthur *Nothing Sacred* (1937), and remade Brenon's *Beau Geste* (1939) with little of the skill and much of the sadism of the original.

Cecil B. De Mille entered the talkies with immense *élan*. His first sound film was *Dynamite* (1929), a surrealist melodrama about a wealthy society beauty (Kay Johnson) who marries a condemned prisoner (Charles Bickford) in order to inherit a fortune. Exuberant, wonderfully vigorous, the film skillfully evokes the look and character of the Jazz Age: the socialite's parties dissolving into drunkenness and hardbitten jokes; the hoop race with pretty girls revolving inside the hoops; the squabbles in the Art Deco house, a structure superbly realized by the designer Mitchell Leisen. In the jail scene, Russ Columbo, that lost singer of the change-over period, movingly sings a Dorothy Parker song, "How Are We to Know?" symbolizing with almost unbearable accuracy the feeling of forgotten men. It is typical of De Mille's invention that he should use a guitar accompaniment, which makes the whole sequence seem startlingly contemporary today. De Mille's genius again flourished in the final sequence of the otherwise feeble *Madam Satan* (1930), a daring, even outrageous symbolic evocation of the death of the Jazz Age in the Wall Street crash. Guests file into a Zeppelin moored outside New York. A weird version of a Ballet Mécanique staged by LeRoy Prinz is performed during the airship's voyage, includ-

Scene from MADAM SATAN

ing Germanic girls dressed as spanners, nuts, and bolts cavorting in the drunken crowd. Lightning strikes and the Zeppelin breaks in two, spilling its occupants in parachutes.

Almost equally skillful, *The Sign of the Cross* (1932), false though its "religious" elements are, portrays Nero's Rome with a fine erotic abandon. Shot in shimmering soft focus by Karl Struss, this is a beautiful film to watch. Its detail is ferocious in such scenes as when we see a grotesque face orgasmically spouting milk into the Empress Poppaea's pool, or the lesbian occupant inviting a handmaiden to strip and join her. The arena scenes are very well shot, from the first line-up of gladiators, the Emperor accompanied by a naked male slave, to the horror of dismemberment, the tragic banality of Christian self-sacrifice. Charles Laughton's Nero—a psychotic baby, hairless and effeminate—is a vividly observed portrait, almost matched by Claudette Colbert's lascivious and perverse Poppaea.

*Charles Laughton,* **THE SIGN OF THE CROSS**

*Ray Milland, John Wayne,* **REAP THE WILD WIND**

The film was a triumph of popular art, and De Mille rushed ahead—into the extraordinary *Cleopatra* (1934). The film defied the newly formed Hays office with its explicitly cruel sensuality, even daring to include a sequence of bestiality; and the use of drums to suggest the male orgasm in a seduction scene between Marc Antony and Cleopatra was enjoyably audacious. De Mille's mastery of spectacle continued unimpaired in such pictures as *The Crusades* (1935), *The Plainsman* (1937), and the energetic *Union Pacific* (1939). With the advent of color and the 1940s, he became even more vigorous, shooting such exhilarating spectacles as *Reap the Wild Wind* (1942) and *Unconquered* (1947). To the end of his career despite an excess of dullness, he could bring off masterstrokes of technique: the realistic aerial attack in *The Story of Dr. Wassell* (1944), citizens mown down on a ship's deck by Japanese fighters, was brilliant propaganda; the raising of the big top—up, up against blue—in *The Greatest Show on Earth* (1952).

Of the other great survivors of the talkie revolution, Joseph von

*Claudette Colbert*, CLEOPATRA

*Cecil B. De Mille* and cameraman *Victor Milner* on set of CLEOPATRA

Sternberg preserved his sumptuous visual and aural imagination virtually intact, and lived long enough to find himself taken seriously as an artist, a role he contemptuously disdained. A painter *manqué*, he continued to despise characterization, writing, music, and every element in motion pictures except the visual. It was his own expressed wish that his films would be taken seriously as sequences of more or less lascivious photographs. In every respect other than the visual, his films are noveletish—poorly written by Jules Furthman and others, childish, sickly, and banal. The personality of Dietrich—androgynous, laconic, wry—despite indifferent acting ability still gives the films of von Sternberg in which she appears their electricity. She figured in exotic compositions which at times carry a potent charge: in *Morocco* (1930) the shadows snaking over burnouses in the alleys of von Sternberg's imaginary city, and the shots of the star's face as she hears the drums of her lover's regiment; in *Dishonored* (1931) the light of the death cell where the spy waits to die; in *Blonde Venus* (1932) the monkey dance in which Dietrich gyrates before a chorus of Fuzzy-Wuzzies; the Mardi gras in *The Devil Is a Woman* (1935). Von Sternberg's most bizarre film of the period is *The Scarlet Empress* (1934). It was a travesty of the life of Catherine the Great, in which Dietrich was compelled to act inanely. The images of the film—wonderfully photographed by Bert Glennon—often achieved a startling force. The wedding scene has a sharp eroticism, reminiscent of the best of von Stroheim (whose influence on von Sternberg has not been adequately assessed). The candle flame flutters as a symbol of the Empress' spinsterhood, while her lover broods in black near a phallic candle and diffused lights glitter on the cope, the rings, and the heavy sumptuous brocades of the ritual.

It was in 1931 that von Sternberg made *An American Tragedy*, aside from the Dietrich films his most famous work. In 1930 Paramount had offered the novel to Sergei Eisenstein and Ivor Montagu as the subject of a film. The great Russian director conceived the film as an attack on the whole structure of American society: its greed and acquisitiveness, and the way in which avarice can destroy an innocent young man. B. P. Schulberg and Jesse Lasky at Paramount decided that the script was too strong, and it became clear to Eisenstein that they had not read the novel. Finally, the scenario was turned down, officially for budget rea-

*Marlene Dietrich,* MOROCCO

*Gary Cooper, Marlene Dietrich, Adolphe Menjou,* MOROCCO

sons, but actually because it was too realistic. In December 1930 von Sternberg was signed to direct the film, with Samuel Hoffenstein writing the screenplay. It was a rare opportunity for von Sternberg to escape the pretentious flummery of the Dietrich films, but it did not work out well.

Hoffenstein's script was written in a bare five weeks and concentrated almost entirely on the second part of the novel, eliminating all of its social comment and reducing it to a story of a poor boy who meets a pretty rich girl; a poor girl stands in the way so he murders her. Dreiser wrote to Hoffenstein that "it [the screenplay] is nothing less than an insult to the book," and he was right: Hoffenstein's script was a travesty, and von Sternberg's direction of it ridiculously inept. The technical style was fluent, and in one scene—the singing of "Some of These Days" as the boy Clyde, boating along a lake, discovers the pleasures of the rich—rather more than that. The film was followed by a case of great importance: Dreiser tried to place an injunction for-

*Louise Dresser*, THE SCARLET EMPRESS

bidding the studio to release the film, on the justified grounds that it was a trivialization of the book. Judge Graham Wittchief dismissed the suit on the basis that "In the preparation of the picture the producer must give consideration to the fact that the great majority of people composing the audience . . . will be more interested that justice prevail than that the inevitably of Clyde's end clearly appear." The statement made it clear that the law—in common with Hollywood— understood that the public did not want a revelation of the inevitability of truth, but, as always, a moralistic judgment on life.

Von Sternberg's separation from Dietrich by Paramount in 1936 and the end of their famous love affair meant the destruction of his talent, and his last films—*The Shanghai Gesture* (1940) and *The Saga of Anathan* (1951) among them—were almost devoid of any dramatic skill.

Lubitsch seldom equaled the greatness of *Lady Windermere's Fan* or *Three Women* in the sound period. His essentially theatrical technique was exposed when he was faced with the need to have the characters talk. He scarcely varied the motionless medium shots of which he was so fond, and almost never risked the excursions into pure technique of the first twenty minutes of *The Student Prince in Old Heidelberg*. His genius continued to be revealed in the handling of the players, in the seemingly effortless skill with which he timed dialogue and details of personal reaction. In *The Love Parade* (1929) he showed a grasp of the new medium's potentialities, creating the sparkling *mise en scène* for an Ernst Vajda—Guy Bolton operetta, deeply influencing Mamoulian in *Love Me Tonight*. The film amusingly distorts Graustarkian situations: a cannon goes off constantly on a Prince's wedding night, interrupting the consummation of his marriage; servants wittily ape their superiors behind gilded doors. The film introduced Chevalier to the American screen, as did a simultaneously released Robert Florey short about Chevalier's arrival in New York.

Lubitsch's next film, *Monte Carlo* (1930), was lame by comparison, a heavy series of jokes relieved only by the famous "Beyond the Blue Horizon" scene in which Jeanette MacDonald sets out in a train for the South of France to join her lover; here the editing, the gathering momentum of the journey, and the accompanying song brilliantly echo her sexual anticipation. *The Smiling Lieutenant* (1932) is a reworking of familiar themes, *The Man I Killed* (*Broken Lullaby*) (1932) an awkward venture into "serious" drama about World War I. The director (with George Cukor shooting several scenes) recovered with *One Hour with You* (1932), a new version of *The Marriage Circle* which markedly improved on the original. The music of Oscar Straus and Richard Whiting, and Leo Robin's delicious lyrics had an effervescent charm, and the playing of Maurice Chevalier and Jeanette MacDonald was exquisitely skilled.

Lubitsch's masterpiece of the talkies was *Trouble in Paradise* (1932). Samson Raphaelson's script for this film equaled the best of Hans Kräly while adapting many silent film devices. Two jewel thieves and swindlers (Herbert Marshall and Miriam Hopkins) become romantically involved in Venice and decide to deprive a rich American woman (Kay Francis) of her money by posing as servants in her household. At first, it seems that the male half of the team is going to soften, overcome by attraction to his employer. But in the end the thieves leave together, to enjoy their spoils in perfect marital comfort. From the famous opening in Venice, a gondola gliding through a filthy canal, to the climax of crime triumphant, the film is a bitterly amusing satire, each scene orchestrated with a subtlety and intelligence beyond compare.

All through the Depression, Lubitsch continued to provide delicious escapist entertainment for the masses. *Design for Living* (1933) kept as little of Coward as *Lady Windermere's Fan* had kept of Wilde, but proved again to be as witty as the original. *The Merry Widow* (1934), *Angel* (1937), and two films scripted by the new team of Billy Wilder and Charles Brackett, *Bluebeard's Eighth Wife* (1938) and *Ninotchka* (1939), were all civilized pleasures. *Ninotchka* shows Lubitsch at his best guiding three superb performances: Melvyn Douglas effortlessly polished as the man of the world enjoying the capitalist delights of Paris; Ina Claire, greatest stage comedienne of her generation, delicious as the Grand Duchess Swana; and of course, Garbo as the Russian commissar, more human, less posturing, than in any other film. *The Shop Around the Corner* (1940) is an agreeably bittersweet example of light entertainment; *To Be or Not to Be* (1942) as effective an example of comic propaganda as Chaplin's *The Great Dictator,* and far better directed. Jack Benny was inspired as the Polish clown Joseph Tura playing Hamlet for the Germans in occupied Warsaw, forced to Sieg Heil to the orders of the Nazi commandant Sig Rumann. Up to the time of his death in the late 1940s, Lubitsch continued to make witty and sophisticated films.

■ ■ ■ ■ ■ ■ ■ ■ ■ ■ ■ ■ ■ ■ ■ ■ ■ ■ ■ ■ ■ ■ ■ ■ ■ ■ ■

# 3. Major Figures of the Talkies

■ ■ ■ ■ ■ ■ ■ ■ ■ ■ ■ ■ ■ ■ ■ ■ ■ ■ ■ ■ ■ ■ ■ ■ ■ ■

Foremost among the artists of the sound era, Lewis Milestone is a
director of marked individuality, a warm poetic sensibility and strength
which recall his Slavic origins. His best-known silent film was *The New
Klondike* (1926), which dealt persuasively with the theme of the
Florida land rush, especially in one scene when the arrivals in the
Promised Land watch while a real estate man glowingly describes a
new lot, and an alligator slithers across the path behind them. That
Lubitschian masterpiece *The Garden of Eden* (1928) has already been
discussed. Milestone swept into the sound period with tremendous *élan*.
*The Racket* (1928) was a brilliantly sustained crime film, superior to
*Underworld* or *Scarface*. *New York Nights* (1929), an account of the
nightclub era, with many dizzying shots of orgiastic scenes, was made
in defiance of talkie limitations. Corinne Griffith gave as vivid a performance as in *The Garden of Eden,* correcting claims that she was
ruined by sound. Few were surprised when Milestone made the halting,
awkward, but truly eloquent pacifist film *All Quiet on the Western Front*
(1930), a faithful version of Remarque's novel which stood the so-called
"values" of the Hawks/Ford/Wellman military films on their heads.

Because of its simplicity and decency, the picture is preferable to,
say, *Dawn Patrol*, though it also suffers from the general limitations of
early talkies. Overlong and static dialogue-ridden schoolroom scenes
at the outset fail to give a convincing picture of Germany before World
War I, and there are bad and in fact embarrassing sequences between

*Lew Ayres, Louis Wolheim,* ALL QUIET ON THE WESTERN FRONT

the young soldier and his whining mother, Beryl Mercer. Lew Ayres' performance as the novice is touching, partly because of his inexperience. But the scenes in the trenches, the first anguished night advance with the new recruits whimpering like children in the dark, the use of sound to convey the aural horror that accompanied the visual—these are the work of a master.

*The Front Page* (1931) surpasses *All Quiet* in being wholly a masterpiece, and one of the greatest pictures of the period. Milestone achieves a perfect marriage of film and theater. The picture has a vividness not matched in a newspaper subject until *Citizen Kane*. Pat O'Brien's Hildy Johnson, the tough reporter incarnate, has an excellent foil in Adolphe Menjou's jaded and suave editor, the pair of them wringing every last drop out of an escaped convict story. It has been claimed that the film's brutally truthful picture of newspaper life is due entirely to the stage play, but Milestone's use of Richard Day's brilliant newspaper office set is so fluent, its editing and camera movement so dazzling in their complexity, that the criticism makes no sense. Macabre and funny all at once, the picture is at its most typical in a scene in

which a crazy prisoner is being interviewed by an equally crazy psy-
chiatrist (Gustav von Seyffertitz) and, in demonstrating all too clearly
how a certain gun released his inhibitions, shoots his interrogator dead
and effects an escape. Few pictures until the heyday of Capra in the late
1930s had the electric vitality of this work.

*Rain* (1932) began with a demonstration of Milestone's almost
Curtiz-like sense of cinema, evoking the fans and ferns of a tropical
hotel in vain of heightened realism that whetted the appetite for more.
But the casting of Joan Crawford in the role that made Jeanne Eagels
famous was a mistake, and the sermons of Walter Huston (parodied by
himself in *Duel in the Sun*) were delivered much too theatrically.

*Hallelujah, I'm a Bum* (1933), with a late appearance by Harry
Langdon, and *The Captain Hates the Sea* (1934) were full of Milestone's shrewd observations. *Hallelujah, I'm a Bum,* written by S. N.
Behrman from by Ben Hecht, was in fact well in advance of its time, an
almost Brechtian verse play with an unconventional score by Lorenz
Hart. Bunger (Al Jolson) is a white-suited proletarian, living with his
close friend, an itinerant black, and other Depression deadbeats in
Central Park. His philosophy in Rodgers' words is "You've got the
grass/You've got the trees/What do you want with money?" The
rhymed dialogue, the daring transitional devices, a fine Eisensteinian
montage of mid-Depression faces crying for help, Al Jolson's sophisticated and intelligent performance, all combine with Milestone's highly
original direction to make for a unique entertainment. Harry Langdon,
puffy and ill-looking in his decline, is touching as the Communist gar-
bage collector. And there is one scene that sums up the essence of the
Thirties: Jolson and his girl friend (Madge Evans) dancing at a window
while the fox-trotting couples sway together in the windows of Funland
Dance Parlor across the street, illuminated by the flashing of a light sign
as Jolson softly sings a sad Depression tune.

*The General Died at Dawn* (1936) recalled Capra's *Bitter Tea of
General Yen* and von Sternberg's *Shanghai Express* replete with an
adventurer (Gary Cooper), caught up in revolution, pitted against a
stock company villain, the infamous General Yang (Akim Tamiroff).
Milestone ably decorates an adventure story. In a then revolutionary
technique, he divided the screen into panels, each panel separated by

Scene from ALL QUIET ON THE WESTERN FRONT

a ceremonial sword and showing a simultaneous but separate event. He also made extraordinary skillful use of dissolves, including one unique effect in which a close-up of a white billiard ball dissolves to a close-up of an identically-sized white doorknob. In many ways the film was as technically exciting as anything in the *oeuvre* of Orson Welles.

Milestone's humanity and strength of purpose did not desert him in the 1940s. His *Of Mice and Men* (1940), admirably adapted from John Steinbeck by Eugene Solow, showed his finest qualities—honesty, decency, strong command of narrative—at their best. Before the credits, two men, George (Burgess Meredith) and Lennie (Lon Chaney, Jr.), are seen fleeing a posse. They hide in a ditch, board a train, and the titles appear on a boxcar. The mood is set with dynamic swiftness, and the events that follow—the farm scenes, Lennie's strangling of the farm boss' wife, George's mercy killing of Lennie—are set against a movingly observed portrait of rural life, as fine as anything in Ford or Vidor and informed by an instinctive sympathy for the pathos, loneliness, and tawdry pleasures of the itinerant farmhands.

*The Red Pony* (1949) offers a similarly tender and affectionate portrait of country life harking back to the best qualities of silent films. Based by Steinbeck on his own story, *The Red Pony* told of the affection of a boy (Peter Miles, later the author of *That Cold Day in the Park*) and a pony, Galiban. The delicate color photography and the simple woodwind score of Aaron Copland were most felicitous, but it was from beginning to end a director's film. In between these personal works, Milestone spent the war years giving his special touch of distinction to such routine subjects as *Edge of Darkness* (1943) and *The Purple Heart* (1944), both of which were superior to Ford's or Hawks' war films. *The Strange Love of Martha Ivers* (1946) was a fine steamy melodrama, perhaps owing more to the producer, Hal Wallis, than to Milestone.

After the war Milestone directed little of interest, save for the first-rate action scenes of the underrated *Kangaroo* (1952), which may have suffered from the poor script by Harry Kleiner and Martin Berkeley and the studio's lack of interest in the project, but which offered a drought sequence and a cattle stampede that gave Harry Watt's *The Overlanders* quite a run for its money. Excitingly shot by Charles G. Clarke, using a mixed British, Irish, and Australian cast, *Kangaroo* once again demonstrated that as a master of natural environments, Milestone was second to none, capturing the sweat and dust and saddle leather of Australia's

*Myrna Loy, Louis Calhern, Robert Mitchum, Peter Miles, Shepperd Strudwick,* THE RED PONY

outback to perfection. Illness and the collapse of *Mutiny on the Bounty* (1962) at the box office finally wrecked Milestone's splendid, grossly undervalued career.

Other extrovert directors were legion in the 1930s. W. S. Van Dyke was a craftsman of great talent, who moved from beautiful works like *The Pagan* (1929)—an evocation of the life of the Society Islands— and its not so good but still wonderfully made predecessor *White Shadows of the South Seas* (1928) to the extraordinary, haunting *Trader Horn* (1931) with its twelve thousand-mile African safari and strange white goddess (Edwina Booth, today a Mormon missionary). Other Van Dyke films included *Tarzan, the Ape Man* (1932); *Eskimo* (1933), a poetic work about the frozen North; *The Thin Man* (1934); the best of the Jeanette MacDonald films, *Rose Marie* (1936) and *San Francisco* (1936) with its great earthquake scene based upon Russian principles of montage. His *Marie Antoinette* (1938), based in part on Stefan Zweig by Claudine West, Donald Ogden Stewart, and Ernest Vajda, was typical of the director in its warmth, spaciousness, and physical command; admirably played by Norma Shearer, Robert

Morley (the infantile Louis XVI), and Anita Louise, it also offered a brilliant performance by Joseph Schildkraut as the painted fop Philippe Egalité, and some of the most terrifying mob scenes on record. The logical progression of Marie Antoinette to the guillotine was masterfully realized, her journey by tumbril and execution almost unbearable in their realism. The film, underrated at the time, remains Van Dyke's masterpiece, a peerless evocation of the period.

Two hard-bitten directors who learned the cutting techniques but did not adopt the sentiment of Griffith were Henry Hathaway and Raoul Walsh. Both proved extraordinarily durable, their careers stretching into the contemporary period. They believed, like their master, in the rapid juxtaposition of shots, the dynamic use of screen narrative to convey fundamentally simple rural values. Hathaway made a number of Westerns with all the energy though little of the romantic feeling of Ford, emerging as a major director with *The Lives of a Bengal Lancer* (1935), a rousing account of life on the northwest frontier of India. Hathaway's *Trail of the Lonesome Pine* (1936) was the first three-color picture shot out of doors, alive with a genuine feeling for the American wilderness, harking back in its formal groupings, beams of light slanting through trees, and sweeping panoramas to the earliest Griffiths. In *Souls at Sea* (1937) Hathaway rose to the challenge of a story of a shipwreck, re-creating with a skill approaching Ince's the details of a mass drowning and rescue. *Spawn of the North* (1938) again showed Hathaway taking on a theme of the wilderness, evoking the atmosphere of Alaska with a semi-documentary accuracy. His *The Real Glory* (1939), made for Goldwyn, was set in yet another exotic location: the island of Luzon in the Philippines during the Spanish-American War. Its opening scene of an assassin, knife in teeth, slithering out of the water in the port of Manila to strike an official down is interesting. Unfortunately, however, the direction of the jungle battle scenes, full of ingenious traps and springs is very labored.

Despite poor scripts, Hathaway's distinguished career continued at a high level until the 1970s. *Brigham Young* (1940), a story of the first Mormons and their heroic trek to found their dynasty in Salt Lake City, was done on an epic scale, its best scene a locust attack, the women beating the crawling creatures back, the sky dark with wings as though with thunderclouds. No nonsense here, as in Metro's *The Good Earth,* about faking the locust plague. Hathaway typically had his cast go to a locust-infested area, shooting their agonized struggle with the creatures exactly as it happened, registering the stench of the dead insects on the players' faces. In the mid-1940s he turned to softer subjects. *Home in Indiana* (1944), about trotting races, was a typically attractive example. In the middle of the decade he went to the forefront of the new school of semi-documentary film-makers with *The House on 92nd Street* (1945), in which the activities of espionage agents were carefully documented. Other films in the genre were *13 Rue Madeleine* (1945), about American spies in Europe, and *Call Northside 777* (1948), dealing with the pursuit of the truth of a long-buried murder case by a dogged reporter (James Stewart). It was characteristic of Hathaway that he should bring his sense of realism to this essentially indoor subject: the film's best scene, in which Stewart confronts an aging woman in a sleazy walk-up, the elevated rushing by, was not faked in a studio, but was shot in an actual Chicago tenement.

Hathaway's *Fourteen Hours* (1951)—about the man-on-the-ledge case of the 1930s—was informed with all of his technical skill, ability to involve an audience, and command of suspense. Richard Basehart, on an actual ledge for portions of the film, played with fine suppressed feeling the role of an emasculated mother's boy who does not quite have the courage to jump, and, as his mother, Agnes Moorehead gave one of her most inspired performances. Her entrance is unforgettable: rushing along a corridor, scattering reporters, and thrusting aside police, she arrives at the window, almost causing her son to fall because of her sudden unbridled attack of hysteria. Hathaway achieved the scene in a sustained take, conveying to perfection the milieu: the crowded offices, the sensation seekers below, the whole jazzed-up frenzy of a public incident.

Hathaway's most accomplished film was *Niagara* (1953). Ostensibly a vehicle for Marilyn Monroe, it was in fact a masterly example of fluid screen narrative, as intricate and complex as anything in the sound cinema. The story, which concerns a honeymoon couple at Niagara Falls, an insane killer, and a pursuit by a detective, is not worth repetition. As so often is the case in the American cinema, it is the physical execution alone which counts, and here the execution dazzles. The great cameraman Joe MacDonald was an immeasurable help to the director, excitingly using the three-color palette. Several sequences deserve to be singled out, among them the marvelously worked-out episode in which the song-chiming carillon of the Falls is shown in a series of almost monochromatic dissolves, the intricate machinery of the bells charged with a subtle menace. Other scenes of equal power are the pursuit through the Falls, with yellow raincoated figures outlined against gray smoking arcs of water; Marilyn Monroe's visit to a funeral parlor, her lipstick the only spot of color against the deep blacks of her mourning outfit and the gleaming white of the shroud; and her death in the carillon tower, shot from above through a complex of metal stair rails. This extraordinary film, its craftsmanship ignored at the time, showed that as a maker of the dramatic film, Hathaway was second to none in his field.

CinemaScope seemed to damage Hathaway artistically, and it was three years before he made another interesting picture. *Twenty-Three Paces to Baker Street* (1956) was a first-rate suspense story, overlooked at the time, about a blind man (Van Johnson) haunted by a sinister voice, made at the end to walk along the boards of a crumbling building in pursuit of a diabolical killer. The raincoated female killer effectively resembled the mannish predator played by Signe Hasso in *The House on 92nd Street*. Hathaway expertly played on the audience's knowledge of blindness: the unnatural loudness of sounds, the constant nervous probing of a stick through the blackness of the world. Nigel Balchin's script from a Philip MacDonald novel was the best Hathaway had worked with to date, and he made the most of it. The energy of this interesting director has not failed him in the films made since: *North to Alaska* (1960), which took him back to the setting of *Spawn of the North*; the best passages in *How the West Was Won* (1963); the gentle, unsentimental *True Grit* (1969).

Like Hathaway, Raoul Walsh is an extrovert director with little sublety in scenes of intimacy but a fine command of action sequences. He had a long career in silent films, beginning in 1912 with a life of Pancho Villa. His most interesting silent was the Fairbanks *Thief of Bagdad* (1924), an omnibus of Arabian Nights fantasies some of which Alexander Korda actually adapted in a more sophisticated remake (1940). More typical of Walsh was *What Price Glory?* (1926), a boisterous comedy set during World War I. His *Sadie Thompson* (1928) offered Gloria Swanson in the part that Jeanne Eagels made famous on the stage. Despite Miss Swanson's practiced playing and the careful atmosphere of the South Seas, the film, like Milestone's sound version, lacked the weary sophistication of Maugham, substituting for it a mindless bounce.

More interesting, *The Red Dance* (1928), staged during the Russian

Revolution, evoked in authentic detail both a period and a series of dominant personalities, Rasputin figuring in the action. Walsh used the film's scenes of revolutionaries being driven down flights of stone steps once more in a mediocre sound picture, *The Yellow Ticket* (1931). The problem with Walsh's films of this period is that they had an unemotional coldness quite out of keeping with their highly charged subjects. Even *The Big Trail* (1930), a Western that would have been thought to have stirred Walsh's blood, was as lethargic as Cruze's *Covered Wagon,* which provided its inspiration.

During the Thirties Walsh made a string of inferior films set largely indoors, including a predictable Mae West vehicle, *Klondike Annie* (1936). During the Forties, he shot Errol Flynn adventure stories like *Northern Pursuit* (1943) and *Objective Burma* (1945), as well as the energetic Bogart vehicle *High Sierra* (1941). His best films of the period were *Pursued* (1947), a Western written by Niven Busch using the elements of Greek drama in Busch's characteristic style and staged in the oppressive heat of Arizona. James Wong Howe's low-key photography gave the film a constant visual distinction. Almost equally good was *White Heat* (1949), which achieved a Curtiz-like intensity in its

*Judith Anderson, Teresa Wright,* PURSUED

story of a crook (James Cagney) tied to his mother's apron strings who frequently goes berserk, tormented by agonizing head pains. One extraordinary scene, shot in a sustained take, the camera feverishly tracking, shows Cagney in the grip of a seizure, rushing headlong through a prison refectory, moaning with pain.

In the 1950s and 1960s Walsh's films were as before—ploddingly routine for the most part, the dull progression interrupted by occasional moments of excellence. *Captain Horatio Hornblower* (1951) and *The World in His Arms* (1952) were full of glowing seascapes reminiscent of Cruze's *Old Ironsides*. *Battle Cry* (1955) was a proficient account of American troops in New Zealand, made with unobtrusive skill and a fine narrative rhythm. Even his last film, *A Distant Trumpet* (1963), with a rousing score by Max Steiner, had all the polish and authority of his best work, and suggested a greater command of editing than he had hitherto shown.

Another extrovert director, with a taste for comedy, Tay Garnett has had an extraordinarily varied career, including that Cuban Frankie and Johnny *Her Man* (1930) and the sentimental but skillfully made story of doomed love *One-Way Passage* (1932), which remains a quintessential Thirties film in its cruise ship setting and its languid playing by Kay Francis and William Powell. *China Seas* (1935) was an amusing story of another ocean voyage, this time an account of the lives of passengers plying down the China coast. Jean Harlow was raucously on form as a kept woman, snarling at a Chinese lady in the saloon ("Hi there, jingle bells"), and there was some enjoyable repartee between her and Clark Gable; the film's best scene involved a steamroller which breaks loose on deck during a storm, crushing the coolies in its path.

Garnett's talent for the action film was shown in *Slave Ship* (1937), the Hollywood satire *Stand-In* (1937), and the noisy *Seven Sinners* (1940), in which the major attractions were Marlene Dietrich and the screen's longest and most savage barroom brawl. During the war years, Garnett at M-G-M turned to more stately subjects—*Mrs. Parkington* (1944), an account of the lives of a patrician family, and *The Valley of Decision* (1945), another Galsworthian chronicle based on a novel by Marcia Davenport. Better than these was Garnett's version (screenplay by Niven Busch and Harry Ruskin based on James M. Cain's novel) of *The Postman Always Rings Twice* (1946), which had already been filmed—as *Le Dernier Tournant* (Pierre Chenal, 1939) and *Ossessione*

*John Garfield, Lana Turner,* THE POSTMAN ALWAYS RINGS TWICE

(Visconti, 1942). Garnett's film captured the hardness of Cain's world even more skillfully than Curtiz' *Mildred Pierce*. The story of a murder, similar to the same author's *Double Indemnity*, of a roadside dinery manager by his wife (Lana Turner) and her lover (John Garfield), the film has a classic authority and concision. Garnett's hard-bitten style is just right for the subject, dodging the occasional hints of sentiment in the writing. Lana Turner, implacable, dressed ironically in white, gives her best screen performance, and John Garfield, vulnerable and uneasy under a veneer of sexual charm, makes a perfect foil. In an excellent touch the girl drops her lipstick case; it rolls along the floor to be picked up by Garfield, who sees her superb legs and is immediately and fatally attracted.

Victor Fleming was another extrovert director who achieved a large commercial reputation in this period. Fleming's two major films of the late 1930s were *The Wizard of Oz* and *Gone With the Wind*, both released at the end of the decade. *The Wizard of Oz*, adapted by Noel Langley and two other writers from L. Frank Baum's celebrated children's book, previously filmed by Larry Semon in the silent period, was a distinguished example not so much of Fleming's direction as of a combined effort of studio technicians. Each of these people deserves equal credit: the brilliant production design of Cedric Gibbons; the special effects work of Buddy Gillespie; the photography, fine-grained as the best of the silents, of Harold Rosson; and the inventive production skills of Mervyn LeRoy, recently arrived from Warners. The young Judy Garland's performance as Dorothy has a fragile, nervous beauty, justly legendary and conveying precisely the right quality of innocent wonder. The scenes in which the tornado carries Dorothy away, her smiling face greeting a cow as it whirls past the windows of her house, are brilliantly staged in sepia. The arrival in the land of Oz is magical in its charm, with the various figures of legend perfectly brought to life. A triumph of casting was Margaret Hamilton as the nasty schoolteacher Miss Gulch, who emerges as the Wicked Witch of the West. With her evil familiars darkening the sky, a sinister horde of flying monkeys, she is a wholly successful creation. The film's sense of transcendent release in the flying scenes together with the evocation of the Witch. owes an immeasurable amount to Disney.

David O. Selznick's *Gone With the Wind* has entered American legend as the most successful example of Thirties entertainment. It is essentially the success story of a hoyden in a society (the 1860s) in which women were largely repressed. It succeeded in fulfilling female dreams—of emerging victorious from the world of men, conquering all obstacles including war and famine, hooking an exceptionally handsome husband, and occupying a mansion beyond the dreams of avarice. Its only daring touch was to leave this determined woman stranded at the end, when the one man she appears to love walks out on her. Magnificently designed by William Cameron Menzies and Hobe Erwin, handsomely shot by Lee Garmes and Ernest Haller, the film still stands up as a solid piece of craftsmanship, even though the plot tends to run out of steam toward the finale. Fleming could bring just the right touch to the war itself and its aftermath, and to the increasing importance of the figure of Rhett Butler, played to perfection by Clark Gable. Vivien Leigh's celebrated performance of Scarlett O'Hara struck just the right note: initially, her skittish, ruthless charm was fascinating to watch. In the second part, when she had to carry the film into realms of domestic melodrama, the actress conveyed a startlingly vivid sense of desperation.

*Thomas Mitchell, Barbara O'Neil, Evelyn Keyes, Oscar Polk, Ann Rutherford, Hattie McDaniel, Vivien Leigh,* GONE WITH THE WIND

Unfortunately as the spectacle of southern collapse and reconstruction falls away, the script by Sidney Howard reveals a thinness stemming from the book itself, and Leslie Howard's poor playing of Ashley Wilkes was a handicap. Despite reservations, though, the film, with its massive sweep and authority, is a worthy culmination to the grand effort of so many Thirties film-makers. Substantial portions of it were directed by Sam Wood, William Cameron Menzies, and George Cukor.

The Warner Brothers team worked well under Darryl F. Zanuck or Hal Wallis during the 1930s. Zanuck moved to 20th Century-Fox in 1933, where he engaged Henry King and Frank Lloyd, reliable director of *Cavalcade*. The production heads of Warners demanded and obtained a particular kind of "headline" film-making when their primitive early sound musicals lost their initial popularity. Although the Warner approach was closer to that of muckraking yellow journalism, designed to sell pictures in difficult times, than to genuine social criticism, it resulted in many good pictures written by such scenarists as Casey Robinson and Julius J. and Philip G. Epstein, and directed by the Warner team, a rugged collection of craftsmen headed by Michael Curtiz, Mervyn LeRoy, Roy Del Ruth, Lloyd Bacon, Alfred E. Green, Ray Enright, William Keighley, and Archie Mayo. The working conditions were the toughest in Hollywood; many films were shot entirely in first takes. Jack Warner ran the studio like a tabloid newspaper, ordering that the pictures explode with violence and feature aggressive dialogue, slambang dramatic situations, and city room tactics.

Of the Warner directorial team, Michael Curtiz was the champion, his command of the medium sure and his pictorial sense extraordinary. A Hungarian, he had made his first films in Europe, and remained a very UFA-esque director. His career included every category—crime stories, soap operas, musicals, Westerns, costume dramas—all executed with a sophisticated edge. His weakness was that he was devoid of original ideas, and was thus utterly dependent on his writers. It would take a longer book than this adequately to evaluate the work of this prolific craftsman. Of his early sound films, the most impressive were *Strange Love of Molly Louvain* (1932), a portrait of low life in which Lee Tracy gave an unsparing portrait of a yellow journalist; *Cabin in the Cotton* (1932), with Bette Davis in a carefully worked-out portrait of a southern flirt; and *Twenty Thousand Years in Sing Sing* (1933), a prison melodrama in which Spencer Tracy and Miss Davis acted with great intensity. Two horror films, *Dr. X* (1932) and *The Mystery of the Wax Museum* (1933), are more personal than the aforementioned works, reminiscent of the best films made at UFA in the 1920s. Of the two pictures, the second is the more striking, and is of special interest as the last of the two-color Technicolor films. In order to obtain a high degree of stereoscopic separation, the photographer Ray Rennahan achieved an amount of light so intense that it caused cast and crew great suffering. The results are among the most extraordinary images ever put on a screen, startling and at times overpowering in their three-dimensional immediacy. Essentially a black comedy, the film moves un-erringly from newspaper farce to the most terrifying scenes of horror ever shown to an audience. The wax museum with its deranged pro-prietor (Lionel Atwill) may be a ridiculous concept, but the wax figures —almost alive, corpselike presences—and the art direction of the museum by Anton Grot are in the finest Gothic tradition. Curtiz' meld-ing of sound and image is superbly assured: the clock striking and the pallid green rain at the outset; the hullabaloo of New Year's Eve as a black-clad little knot of figures makes off with a dead man; the squeak of a shroud against wood as a body slides off a mortuary table, the snap and creak of the rope lowering it to its last journey; the pale pink flames and sputtering of wax as the figures are caught in a fire, the process of decay seemingly caught by the camera as the faces melt away. The film is a masterpiece of the macabre.

Later in the Thirties, Curtiz had little opportunity to display his in-tensely personal Gothic sense. He ranged from exotica like *Mandalay* (1934) with its glistening portrait of a tropical port, to *Black Fury* (1935); from *Kid Galahad* (1937) to *The Charge of the Light Brigade* (1936), in which Errol Flynn rode—not a moment too soon—into the Valley of Death. *The Adventures of Robin Hood* (1938) was a rousing epic about the Sherwood Forest bandit. *Four Daughters* (1938) and *Daughter Courageous* (1939) were sensitive and moving accounts of middle-class life.

Curtiz really came into his own in the 1940s with *The Sea Wolf* (1940), a version by Robert Rossen of Jack London's novel. The open-ing sequence, in which two ships collide in a harbor fog, is superbly managed, and so is the transition to the sinister ship captained by a psychotic sadist (played by Edward G. Robinson in the finest perform-ance of his career). On board the vessel, the characters emerge very fully: Alexander Knox, the soft and pampered intellectual who is unable to face up to the challenge of physical brutality and stupidity; John Garfield, vulnerable and tense, a passenger against his will; and Ida Lupino, puritanical but gradually discovering the reality of personal affection. Curtiz conveys with impeccable mastery the atmosphere of the ship: the low ceilings on which the reflection of the ocean glitters, the cramped corridors in which figures suddenly loom, the lamps that sway as the heavy swell arises, the constantly moving pools of light and darkness. It was a Germanic, powerful work almost devoid of compromise.

Almost as striking technically, *Casablanca* (1942) was a startling example of Curtiz' virtuosity. Set in the North African town during the first troubled months of World War II, it introduces a gallery of bizarre and fugitive characters: Rick (Humphrey Bogart), a jaded bar owner; Ilsa (Ingrid Bergman), a sad and adrift mistress of a resistance leader; a fat restaurant proprietor (Sydney Greenstreet); and a cynical and corrupt police chief (Claude Rains). Totally synthetic, the film worked on its own melodramatic terms, and many aspects of it have gone into legend, including the playing of "As Time Goes By" by Dooley Wilson and the Blue Parrot Cafe of Sydney Greenstreet. The film, written by Julius J. and Philip Epstein and Howard Koch from an obscure play, contrived to present war as a somewhat enjoyable if hazardous experience, exactly what audiences needed as escapist fare in those harrowing times.

The film established Curtiz once again as the major director at Warners. He increased his reputation still further with *Mildred Pierce* (1945), which gave Joan Crawford her opportunity for an Oscar-winning performance. It was the story, based faithfully in spirit on the novel by James M. Cain by Ranald MacDougall, of a hard-up suburban housewife who takes a job as a waitress to pay for her daughter's music lessons and by a rather startling series of maneuvers turns herself into a restaurant tycoon with a chain of medium-priced restaurants stretching down the Pacific coast from Malibu to beyond Santa Monica. This wish-fulfillment fantasy delighted millions of women, who, house-bound like the heroine and struggling with cramped wartime budgets, dreamed of escape to the sort of glamorous world that Mildred occupied. The film became an almost seminal work, expressing Forties romanticism at its height. Here were the glittering interiors, the sumptuous furs and silks, the handsome men, and pretty locations which women leafed through magazines to look for. Curtiz brought the whole thing to life with a

Germanic, low-key flourish, and the music by Max Steiner, thudding away constantly behind the action, added an even further charge of Middle European Gothic extravagance.

Even more Gothic were *The Unsuspected* (1947), a richly executed account of a murderous radio storyteller, played magnificently by Claude Rains, and *Flamingo Road* (1949), an excitingly developed story about an ambitious woman, played by Joan Crawford.

Curtiz' *annus mirabilis* was 1950: in that year he made three of his finest pictures, *Young Man with a Horn, The Breaking Point,* and *Bright Leaf. Young Man with a Horn* was based on the brilliant career of the trumpeter Bix Beiderbecke, with Kirk Douglas in the leading role. The opening scenes were marvelous, representing Curtiz at his most authoritative. In striking low-key images by Ted McCord, he evokes the world of jazz cellars, of streets wet with rain, of clanking streetcars, entirely in the studio. His fabulous command of technique has never been so clearly expressed as in these scenes of a young boy discovering the pleasures of music, and the treatment of his black mentor (Juano Hernandez) is deeply sympathetic and devoid of the condescension typical of the time. Though purists might complain that Harry James's dubbing of the track is a poor substitute for Beiderbecke's own playing, his strident performances are stunningly executed, with orchestrations by Ray Heindorf, and intoxicatingly recorded by the Warners' sound team. The final sequences of Beiderbecke's downfall are equally well done, particularly in a nightmarish journey through the Manhattan streets, the angles distorted and the natural street sounds surrealistically increased and distorted.

*The Breaking Point* was a remake of Hawks' *To Have and Have Not.* It succeeded in catching more of Hemingway's spirit than Hawks had done and was superior both in terms of visual narrative and of writing, which perfectly hit off the cool intelligence of the author's dialogue. John Garfield made an admirable central figure, playing with his customary intelligence the gunrunner forced into crime by financial problems. As his wife, Phyllis Thaxter was competent, but she was outclassed by the really first-rate playing of Patricia Neal as the society beauty improbably involved with the shipping of rifles. The relationship between Neal and Garfield is played and directed with a sharp edge of sophistication, and Curtiz' direction has never been more authoritative than in the final battle on the high seas, in which the multiplicity of camera setups is astounding.

*Bright Leaf* (1950) was a story of the tobacco wars and the personal tensions of a tobacco baron played admirably by Gary Cooper. Directed with all of Curtiz' skill and flair, the film was ravishingly photographed by Karl Freund, particularly in the sequence when the rival tycoon, so excellently played by Donald Crisp, dies in his carriage which rolls driverless up to an ornamental gate.

Curtiz' last film of importance, similar in mode to *Young Man with a Horn,* was *The Helen Morgan Story* (1957), which used with great assurance the medium of black-and-white CinemaScope. Despite the inadequacy of Ann Blyth in the leading role, this was an admirably mounted and physically impressive evocation of the Helen Morgan era. Curtiz was at his best in such sequences as the Morgan night-club tour, with a superb presentation of "Deep Night"; in the sequence in which the star is discovered in a seedy bar, beginning her descent into obscurity; and above all in the long track-in to the Chez Morgan Club, with the star on her white piano, the band behind a sequined curtain, and the Prohibition officials breaking in to smash her mirrors and bottles in a frenzy of rage. Curtiz had many gifted followers at Warners,

*Gary Cooper,* BRIGHT LEAF

*Ann Blyth,* THE HELEN MORGAN STORY

including Jean Negulesco (*Johnny Belinda, Humoresque*), Irving Rapper (*Now, Voyager, Deception*), and Vincent Sherman (*Nora Prentiss, The Damned Don't Cry*).

Of the other Warner alumni of the 1930s, Mervyn LeRoy was the most skilled after Curtiz. His films were marked by a Warner vigor and punch, and at his best he created memorable artifacts. In the last scene of the prison drama *I Am a Fugitive from a Chain Gang* (1932), a fugitive's face disappears into the blackness of the Depression with the words "I steal." *Two Seconds* (1932) is the story of all a man remembers as he is about to die in the electric chair. LeRoy's best film of the Thirties was the masterly *They Won't Forget* (1937). To an already fine script by Robert Rossen and Aben Kandel, based on the Leo Frank lynching case of 1913, LeRoy added a brooding intensity. This story of a small-town killing and the hounding of a supposed killer, a black, brought out LeRoy's finest qualities, humanism, decency, a stunning narrative drive. The casting and acting are inspired. Among many fine performances the film contains a definitive portrait of greed in Allyn Joslyn's excellently played reporter. Unfortunately, LeRoy's later career was a very ordinary one, ranging from Greer Garson vehicles at Metro

*Claude Rains, Otto Kruger, Elisha Cook, Jr.,* THEY WON'T FORGET

to *The Bad Seed,* which brought him back to Warners. But even in dealing with the most indifferent scripts, LeRoy's professional skill remained constant.

Most Warner directors were simply expert hacks, hired to slam across the studio's distinctive brand of muckraking. Archie Mayo in such films as *Svengali* (1931), with its Germanic sinister sets and fantastic camerawork, *The Petrified Forest* (1936), which made of Robert Sherwood's phony liberal tract a stylish melodrama, and the astonishing *Black Legion* (1937), a gripping story of xenophobia in American factories, offered more. And there were flashes of individual talent in Alfred E. Green; Roy Del Ruth, whose *Lady Killer* (1932) was a brilliant black comedy; and Lloyd Bacon, whose *42nd Street* (1932) was the best of the Depression musicals. Busby Berkeley was, of course, a special case, creator of the exotic musical routines of films of the period, object of camp cults in the 1960s and 1970s.

Howard Hawks emerged as a director with a Curtiz-like sense of stark realism, insisting on correct light sources and unvarnished sets in his films. He did not have Curtiz' virtuosity: his films were deliberately compressed and narrow in their visual and aural range. His austere masculine approach was not appreciated in his time; it has taken our own age, with its laconic casualness and mistrust of the baroque, to appreciate him. Long before it became fashionable, Hawks kept his cool. His films are technically uninteresting, as geared to the proscenium arch or the conventional landscape composition as any pre-1927 silent film.

Hawks' career began in the silent period, where his style was at odds with both the sentiment of a Griffith or the sophistication of a Lubitsch. The cool detachment of *A Girl in Every Port* (1928), in which Louise Brooks appeared, was quite atypical of its period. At the outset of sound, Hawks made *The Dawn Patrol* (1930) from a laconic script by the talented John Monk Saunders, an ex-airman who also wrote the bittersweet, Scott Fitzgerald-like *The Last Flight* (William Dieterle, 1931). The writing is the film's best feature; Hawks' direction is ploddingly naturalistic. Elmer Dyer's handling of the aerial sequences is distinguished. It was *Scarface* (1932), a crude and brutal, violently ugly film, that established Hawks as a figure to be reckoned with, though Ben Hecht's script in fact contained every image and Lee Garmes handled much of the technical execution. The picture was compromised by censorship: in the original ending the Al Capone figure, played by Paul Muni, was to fall on his face in a pile of horse manure. The opening sequence, shot in a sustained take, as the camera explores a deserted, streamer-hung party scene and shows a man being gunned down in an alleyway, was all most carefully detailed in Hecht's script. Hawks' handling of this scene was confident, and rather more than that in such scenes as a shooting in a nightclub and the final showdown in a tear gas-filled room, where the director was admirably served by Garmes and by Ann Dvorak's playing as Scarface's sister.

*Scarface* showed that, given a good scenario, Hawks could be a very capable director, though his insensitivity and stagy direction of actors were drawbacks. The untidy, overdone *Viva Villa* (1934) dealt with a character as archetypal as Al Capone—the Mexican patriot Pancho Villa—but Wallace Beery was laughably miscast in the role and much of the picture vitiated by the falsified script and by the commonplace direction of Jack Conway, who handled portions of it. *Twentieth Century* (1934) was based rather obediently on the play. Hawks' role here was merely to support the writing discreetly, to stand back and let the two leading players (John Barrymore and Carole Lombard, impersonating, respectively, a producer and a temperamental star) give a championship display of competitive histrionics. *Barbary Coast* (1935) was a feeble Goldwyn concoction, *The Road to Glory* (1936) a lachrymose war drama crudely played by Warner Baxter and marred by the self-conscious awkwardness of Fredric March. Only the scenes of the front, reminiscent of *All Quiet* but without the tenderness, have any degree of power, and the ending, with Fredric March addressing the troops, has all the sentimental heroic pretension of the worst Ford films.

Hawks' most interesting film of the 1930s was *Only Angels Have Wings* (1939) despite its boring theme of brotherly self-sacrifice complete with man-to-man death scene at the end. Jean Arthur arrives in Barranca, a South American port, on a freighter, where she meets airmen engaged in running a mail service. The excitements and tension move Hawks back to the adventure films of a decade earlier. The execution is strong and forthright, the jungle setting cleverly simulated, and Joseph Walker's photography (except for two obvious model shots) skillfully low-key. By contrast, the much admired *Bringing Up. Baby* (1938) seems to me a very arch comedy, with Katharine Hepburn indulging her worst mannerisms, and Cary Grant intoning nasally the predictable Philip Barry lines.

During the 1940s Hawks continued to produce cold, clean-cut pictures. *His Girl Friday* (1940) was a talkathon inferior to its original, *The Front Page*. *Sergeant York* (1941) was another Fordian hymn to the military. *Air Force* (1943) was a stagy affair with several stars trying to re-create a feeling of comradely intimacy in a studio bomber. *To Have and Have Not* (1944) was a conventional Warner melodrama, unlike Curtiz's version a travesty of Hemingway's novel.

*The Big Sleep* (1946) was better: Bogart was at his most intelligent as the Chandler detective Philip Marlowe, and there were some nicely observed characters including the nymphomaniac of Martha Vickers and the beady-eyed little guy classically impersonated by Elisha Cook, Jr. Hawks expertly caught the atmosphere of the Beverly Hills mansion with its aged owner living like a bottled spider preserved in the heat of a greenhouse, the bookshop with its sexy custodian and leather-bound first editions, the camera concealed in the antique figurine, the raffish

*Walter Sande, Humphrey Bogart, Lauren Bacall,* TO HAVE AND
HAVE NOT

night life and bourbon breakfasts in Southern California.

For the next twenty years, Hawks continued to seize on a great
variety of scripts, making it difficult to understand what consistent mode
could be discerned by critics in this scattered *oeuvre*. *Red River* (1948)
covered the first cattle drive over the Chisholm Trail, from Texas to
Kansas, in 1866, told with a stark simplicity that improved on Ford's
approach. Studio interiors were not well contrasted with exterior sequences, but the start of the trek, the camera swinging around the
figures on horseback, the stampede, and the arrival at Abilene were
quite vigorously done.

In recent years, taken up by *Cahiers du Cinéma, Sight and Sound,* and—finally—the American critics, Hawks has won praise for *Rio Bravo* (1959), *Hatari!* (1962), and *El Dorado* (1967) among other films, all of which I find stale, slow-moving, tedious, and childlike in their portrayal of human character. *El Dorado* and his last film at time of writing, *Rio Lobo,* were sadly lacking in Hawks' best qualities of firmness, tightness, and concision.

■ ■ ■ ■ ■ ■ ■ ■ ■ ■ ■ ■ ■ ■ ■ ■ ■ ■ ■ ■ ■ ■ ■ ■ ■ ■ ■

# 4. Pictorialists

■ ■ ■ ■ ■ ■ ■ ■ ■ ■ ■ ■ ■ ■ ■ ■ ■ ■ ■ ■ ■ ■ ■ ■ ■

A number of directors, coming to film from the stage, expressed an entirely different quality from the extrovert figures of Milestone, Ford, and Hawks. They were intensely sophisticated figures, greatly influenced by European models, and with an intense visual feeling somewhat interior and baroque in approach. These could be called the true pictorialists of the Thirties film, painters in celluloid, whose interest in the medium was chiefly in providing a glittering, sumptuous, and original series of images with which to delight audiences. Among the most brilliant of these was Rouben Mamoulian.

This gifted mannerist's inventiveness was first expressed in his stage career. His production of *Porgy* was described by reliable witnesses as a masterpiece. He adapted techniques used in it to evoke an awakening city in *Love Me Tonight* (1932). His first talkie was *Applause* (1929), in which he used two microphones and moving cameras in defiance of the restrictions of the time. The performance of Helen Morgan—a greater actress than she was a singer—as the raddled, aging burlesque queen partly surmounted the novelettish foolishness of Beth Brown's screenplay. Her suicide, presaging the actress' own tragic decline into alcoholism, with the sounds of the city surrealistically distorted, showed Mamoulian already sophisticated in the new medium.

*City Streets* (1931) was as artificial and unconvincing a crime story as von Sternberg's *Underworld,* full of obvious symbolism (cats represent jealousy; a flight of pigeons, freedom) and arty, often pointless camera

*Joan Peers, Helen Morgan,* APPLAUSE

effects, similar to those of von Sternberg at his worst. *Love Me Tonight* was an often captivating operetta, though, if truth be told, it owed as much to Clair and Lubitsch as *City Streets* owed to von Sternberg. *Dr. Jekyll and Mr. Hyde* (1932) remains of the greatest interest. The opening shot, in which we leave Jekyll's house, enter a carriage, and arrive at a medical lecture, is flawlessly executed in subjective camera, mirroring the best of Murnau's techniques. Unfortunately, Jekyll's transition into a monkeyish grotesque is comic rather than horrible and the evocation of Victorian London is very insecure.

Mamoulian's next three films—*Queen Christina* (1933), *Song of Songs* (1933), and *We Live Again* (1934)—were exercises in the baroque which added little to his reputation. Even the carefully timed scene in *Queen Christina* in which Garbo touched the objects in a bed-

(Left) *Holmes Herbert, Fredric March,* DR. JEKYLL AND MR. HYDE

*Miriam Hopkins,* **DR. JEKYLL AND MR. HYDE**

*Holmes Herbert, Fredric March,* **DR. JEKYLL AND MR. HYDE**

*Rouben Mamoulian*
directs *Fredric March,*
DR. JEKYLL AND
MR. HYDE

room, seeking to memorize a night of erotic fulfillment, was damaged by
John Gilbert's asking her at the end of her excursion. "What are you
doing?" Again and again Mamoulian's scripts undercut the effect of his
sumptuous visuals, seen at their richest in the beautifully made *Song of
Songs. Becky Sharp* (1935), one of the first three-color Technicolor
films, was superior to all of these works: directed in a series of period
tableaux, it was a graceful account of the rise of Thackeray's heroine,
cleverly telescoping *Vanity Fair*'s somewhat prolix narrative, and notable
for the carefully thought-out performance of Miriam Hopkins. Of Mamoulian's films of the late 1930s, the most successful was *High, Wide
and Handsome* (1937), an ingenious blend of the elements of melodrama, musical, and action film, staged with brilliant energy.

In the Forties, with the improvement in film lacquers and black and
white and color processes, Mamoulian improved strikingly. He had
better scripts, and by now his flamboyant talent had become fully
disciplined. *The Mark of Zorro* (1940), much superior to the Fairbanks
silent version, united him with an equally fine craftsman, the cameraman
Arthur Miller, and the results were spectacularly good. Mamoulian cap-

tured the hard shadows and glaring sunlight of Spanish California, the sombreroed heads propped against posts, dust under the carriage wheels, a sense of torpor interrupted by the sudden slash of a rapier on an ancient door. *Blood and Sand* (1941) was even more exciting, splashed with the luxurious palette of the three-color Technicolor system. Granted that its view of Spain was false and two of its leading characters, as played by Tyrone Power and Linda Darnell, were hopelessly American. Granted, too, that it had elements of kitsch, particularly in the scenes featuring the seductress Doña Sol, played by Rita Hayworth. But it was wonderful nonetheless: in its tensely erotic dance performed in a smoky *boîte,* in its ferociously accurate scenes of the *corrida,* above all in the sequence (not shot but planned by Mamoulian) of the training of the young bull, bathed in rich Goyaesque moonlight on location in Mexico.

Mamoulian made one more film of interest: *Summer Holiday* (1948), a version of *Ah, Wilderness!* as sensitive as Clarence Brown's version of the early Thirties, with the additional bonus of a lovely musical score.

*Jackie "Butch" Jenkins, Selena Royle, Mickey Rooney, Walter Huston, Agnes Moorehead, Frank Morgan, Shirley Johns,* SUMMER HOLIDAY

The family scenes, the dance of the young couple across a rolling lawn, the open-air Fourth of July picnic with jellies wobbling, ale tankards downed, a child stealing a slice of cake, the moonlight conversation of the parents—the whole was a brilliant reflection of Mamoulian's Theatre Guild experience, making one regret all the more that he did not direct the screen versions of *Oklahoma* and *Porgy and Bess*.

Another director with a strong theatrical background was the British James Whale, too often associated exclusively with the horror film. No addict of the macabre, he in fact spoofed UFA-esque conventions of horror. Whale came to America after a career that established him as the most promising young director in the West End. His films had a Shaftesbury Avenue polish and gentility, and he frequently used British players—the overwrought Colin Clive, the effete Ernest Thesiger, Boris Karloff, Valerie Hobson, and others—and his films were full of camp British private jokes. In *The Old Dark House* (1932) the withered ancient of 102 hidden in the attic is listed as being acted by a "John Dudgeon" in the credits, whereas in fact Whale had him played by a false-bearded old woman.

Whale was brought to America by Universal in 1930 to re-create his London stage success *Journey's End* by R. C. Sherriff. Set in the world War I trenches, the film seemed cinematic thanks to Whale's immediate grasp of editing principles and ability to keep his figures moving within a tiny central set of a dugout. The exteriors of trench warfare were brief but striking, shot silent to the accompaniment of gunfire, paralleling Milestone's famous tracking effects in *All Quiet on the Western Front*. *Waterloo Bridge* (1931), despite a sentimental story which even Griffith might have quailed at, was also very fine, lovingly re-creating a London boarding house down to the chamber pot under the bed and the mobcap worn by the skivvy, poetically evoking the damp and misty streets in a studio setting. It was for *Frankenstein* (1931) that Whale was better known. This updated and radically altered version of Mary Shelley's novel achieves a rare and effective balance between cinematic and theatrical techniques. The opening sequence is pure expressionist theater, like a scene composed by Piscator: Dr. Frankenstein (Colin Clive) and his hunchbacked assistant (Dwight Frye) rob a graveyard of a fresh corpse. Cleverly lit by Arthur Edeson against a backdrop, the scene with its quirkish charnel humor and bizarre angles involving vertical objects—spades and gibbets slanting against the artificial sky—is quintessential Whale. Also typical of his humor is a shot of Frye robbing a

*Courtesy of Universal Pictures.*

*David Manners, Mae Clarke, Edward Van Sloane, Colin Clive, Dwight Frye,*
FRANKENSTEIN

*Courtesy of Universal Pictures.*

*Boris Karloff, Dwight Frye,* FRANKENSTEIN

laboratory of a brain for the monster, dropping the healthy brain on the floor and making off with a diseased one instead. Boris Karloff is excellent as the monster, eyelids raised with painful slowness like windows pried open. Karloff more than compensates for the overplaying of Clive and Dwight Frye. The final sequence, in which the burghers storm the fortress and burn the old mill where the experiments take place, comes entirely from Ingram's *The Magician*. An original and quite inspired concept is Whale's idea of raising the inanimate patched-up figure of the monster on a platform to receive the lightning in the midst of a convenient thunderstorm, returning it to an electrical forest of gadgets where the final experiments begin.

Whale's *The Old Dark House* (1932) was an even more enjoyable piece of spoofery, by Benn W. Levy and R. C. Sherriff, based on *Benighted* by J. B. Priestley. A group of lost travelers in a storm— Melvyn Douglas, Charles Laughton, Gloria Stuart, and others—take refuge in a house of horrors presented by Whale with even more relish than Priestley himself: the dwarf whose gnarled hand slides round the bannister in an echo of the silent serials; the 102-year-old ancient behind the locked attic door; the monstrous drunken butler played by Boris Karloff who shatters a window in an outbreak of sexual rage; the hag woman with her carving knife; and a brother (Ernest Thesiger) who is a tippling pantywaist. *The Old Dark House* was in essence not a horror film at all, but an unbridled camp fantasy directed with great wit. The contribution to the film of Benn W. Levy, author of many successful West End farces, has been an underrated one.

*The Kiss Before the Mirror* (1933), a drama of marital infidelity, contained more authentic terrors, especially in a surrealist trial scene and in the extraordinary sequence when the wife (Nancy Carroll) is frightened by the multi-paneled images of her mirror. *By Candlelight* (1933) was a feeble Ruritanian romance, and *One More River* (1934) a clumsy version of Galsworthy. But *The Invisible Man* (1933) was a meticulously faithful page-by-page version of H. G. Wells' novel. The megalomaniac invisible man, exulting in his power, assumes in the R. C. Sherriff version the antic wickedness of a poltergeist, and Claude Rains' voice superbly conveys the agony and desperation of the character. Whale showed a strong sense of environment in such scenes as the snow being printed with mysterious footprints, the inn with a hysterical Una O'Connor, the darkness of the night that hampers the police but makes no difference to the man in his cloak of invisibility.

*Courtesy of Universal Pictures.*

*Eva Moore, Gloria Stuart,* THE OLD DARK HOUSE

*The Bride of Frankenstein* (1935) has an enormous cult following; suffice it to say that it surpasses *Frankenstein* in its Gothic satire, and presents two haunting creations: Ernest Thesiger's epicene Dr. Pretorius, brooding over miniature shrunken figures in glass bottles, and the bride, with her electric, white-streaked busby of hair and her hiss of doom like escaping gas when the switches are thrown to destroy her. Whale never equaled this powerful Swiftian work again.

*Show Boat* (1936) confounded those who believed Whale could only succeed in offbeat areas of melodrama. Universal's faith in entrusting him with this venture was more than justified by the results, and of the three versions of the musical, this one is the finest. No longer tied to his theatrical origins, Whale made this his most purely cinematic film, effectively using a back lot ambience to create an illusion of a Mississippi setting. He was also at his best in the handling of an exceptionally distinguished cast, including Irene Dunne, Allan Jones, Charles Winninger, and two geniuses of the musical theater, Helen Morgan and Paul Robeson.

The opening of the film is screen narrative at its best. The show boat arriving, crowds gathered along the wharf, the steam whistle triumphantly sounding, sirens blowing, skirts swirling in a wholehearted visual approximation of the flow of Jerome Kern's score. Later, the film achieves a warmth, intimacy, and charm equal to the best of Ford. As always, Whale's period sense is beyond praise. His evocation of the show boat's first night is magical, with Irene Dunne, more animated than usual, charmingly in blackface singing "Gallivantin' Around," and Charles Winninger executing a remarkably agile performance of several characters in a period barnstormer, the audience whipped into a fierce excitement. Helen Morgan's "Bill," tenderly delivered at an audition, and Paul Robeson's "Ol' Man River," thrillingly sung and still more

*Courtesy of Universal Pictures.*

*Colin Clive, Elsa Lanchester, Boris Karloff, Ernest Thesiger,* THE BRIDE OF FRANKENSTEIN

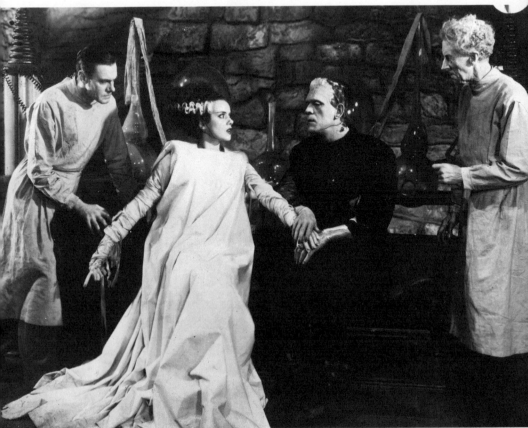

*Paul Robeson, Irene Dunne, Hattie McDaniel, Helen Morgan,* SHOW BOAT

*Paul Robeson,* SHOW BOAT

thrillingly shot in a 360-degree pan around his seated figure on a wharf, are not only fine examples of Whale's direction, but irreplaceable records of peaks in the popular musical repertoire.

Unfortunately, Whale's later career was somewhat disappointing. *The Road Back* (1937), from a Remarque novel, was an unsuccessful attempt to recapture the greatness of *Journey's End*. *The Great Garrick* (1937) was a lovingly authentic but somewhat loosely constructed biography of the actor, and *Wives Under Suspicion* (1938) was the first proof that a career was slipping: a remake of an earlier success (*The Kiss Before the Mirror*) in every way inferior to the original. *The Man in the Iron Mask* (1939), though a travesty of history surprising in the *oeuvre* of so meticulous a man, had some very interesting passages: the masked man in silent agony in a prison cell; the heir to the French throne gazing into an ornate mirror; and Fouquet (played with flawless accomplishment by Joseph Schildkraut) dying at swordpoint in a carriage. *Green Hell* (1940), a South American adventure story, was a waste of Whale's talents, and *They Dare Not Love* (1941) contained little of interest. Whale retired for several years, a rich man. He returned in 1949 to make for Huntington Hartford *Hello Out There,* based on the play by William Saroyan, a film designed to illuminate the minimal talents of Hartford's then wife, Marjorie Steele. Most of the action took place in an expressionist jail cell, in which a prisoner waits for a lynching. The bars of shadow, the intense whiteness of the lamps indicate that Whale's usual style remained more or less intact, and the set was admirably designed. Unfortunately, though, the acting of Miss Steele and the condemned man of Henry Morgan was scarcely distinguishable from the amateur. Only in the arrival of the lynch mob headed by a ferocious Lee Patrick was the film properly reminiscent of the best of Whale. Dissatisfied with the film, Hartford never released it. Whale died in 1957, by drowning accidentally in his swimming pool, forgotten by the industry.

Another director of extreme refinement and visual inventiveness, now entirely overlooked, Roland West was ruined by the suspected murder of his mistress Thelma Todd. Like Whale, he was concerned in a joking Swiftian spirit with the macabre, which he had effectively dealt with in the best of all Lon Chaney vehicles, *The Monster* (1926), a stunningly directed horror film about a lunatic who literally runs an asylum, luring travelers to destruction. It is a totally surrealist masterpiece, devoid of compromise. West also showed his sense of the macabre in his magnificent *The Unknown Purple* (1923), about a man who dissolves his victims inside a movable purple funnel of light controlled by his transcendent will. West wrote his own scripts, insisting on—and getting —absolute autonomy. He had a sense of cinema shared by few other directors, as daringly creative as any of UFA's leading spirits. *Alibi* (1929) was an unrelenting melodrama, overplayed by Chester Morris in the leading role, but notable for its staccato editing and bizarre camera angles far in advance of the period. *Corsair* (1931), about the bootlegging industry, was very fine, a work so totally German expressionist in mood it might have been made by Murnau or E. A. Dupont, though an improvement on both.

But it was *The Bat Whispers* (1931), a remake of his own admirable silent version of Mary Roberts Rinehart's *The Bat,* which revealed his pop art genius most completely. The story is an absurdity about a bat-cloaked man who climbs buildings and swoops on his victims like the gaunt famished Fantomas of the Feuillade serials. Chester Morris again overplays the central role with a hysteria that grates on the spectator's nerves. Yet the action scenes are an astonishing experience—and must have been still more so when, at moments of tension, the screen expanded to 65 mm., stereophonic sound was introduced, and the bat's eyes glowed with a supernatural intensity, filling the entire screen and terrifying the audience. The camera never stops moving, winding through labyrinthine miniatures of city and country mansion; focusing through a high window on a UFA-esque bank robbery; swinging as though on a pendulum through a midnight office as the bat flies in for the kill.

Tod Browning was another director of great imaginative flair, with a taste for the funny/macabre, who had made several excellent silent films (*The Legion of Death, The Unknown,* and *The Road to Mandalay,* with Lon Chaney). His *The Thirteenth Chair* (1929) was an admittedly strained effort about spiritualist séances, a subject enjoying a vogue at the time. But *Dracula* (1931) was an interesting film, with several passages that relieved the screenplay of Garrett Fort's too close reliance on a stage success. The opening in the crypt of the bat-Count was well done, with coffins creaking open and evil familiars scurrying about—an armadillo, a spider, a rat—and the superb use of sound (the groan of hinges, the stirring of an unidentified creature among the ribs of a skeleton's chest cage, the rolling over of leg bones) had a bravura flourish. A fine sequence offered the insane assistant Dwight Frye addressing his master (Bela Lugosi) on a ship in a heavy swell, the coffin moving with each roll and pitch of the vessel; there was a brilliant se-

*Courtesy of Universal Pictures.*

*Bela Lugosi,* DRACULA

quence, too, in which he was seen moaning in private agony at the barred window of an asylum. Browning re-created with the skill of a Leni the atmosphere of the asylum, where we experience the conical operating theater  designed and shot with Germanic brilliance, rows of white figures arranged in perspective as we peer through a glass observation screen, and the hysterical sobs and laughter of patients being wheeled around the grounds.

Browning's *Freaks* (1932) is also a remarkable work, set in a traveling circus in which the unfortunate creatures try to make a world of their own. The film is dominated by the performance of Harry Earles as the midget, a bald-faced, wizened, brilliantly evil gnome whose passion for a normal woman (Olga Baclanova) is thwarted by the strong man. In the original version the creatures crawl under a caravan in a rainstorm and cut off the strong man's testicles to prevent his enjoyment of his bride.

Browning's *Mark of the Vampire* (1935) is a pitiful travesty of the vampire legends, but *The Devil Doll* (1936) is a very interesting effort, about miniaturized people involved in a series of robberies. Browning's quirkish sick humor and fine visual sense were strongly in evidence as Whale's, though he lacked Whale's sophistication. It is unfortunate that Browning's career faded out as a result of several box office failures, including *Miracles for Sale* (1939).

Another director who declined sharply in the late 1930s was William K. Howard, who had a pronounced visual flair but a heavy-handed approach to actors. His works include the admirable *White Gold* (1927); that labored film *The Valiant* (1929); *Transatlantic* (1931) (poorly played but extremely well-lit by James Wong Howe and designed by Gordon Wiles to give an illusion of life on a liner); and *The Power and the Glory* (1933), scripted by Preston Sturges, which in its transitional narrative devices and use of flashbacks influenced Welles. Howard's best-made films were the expressionist *Mary Burns, Fugitive* (1935); and a handsomely mounted Elizabethan story, *Fire over England* (1937). He also made a soft and tender version of Hugh Walpole's novel *Vanessa* (1935). Heavy drinking wiped out his always shaky professional career.

A film-maker whose career was even more abortive than Howard's, Jean de Limur came to America from France. After making two vehicles for Jeanne Eagels, *The Letter* and *Jealousy* (both 1929), he returned, disappointed by conditions of work at Paramount Long Island, to his native country. His *Jealousy* was a feeble effort, but *The Letter* makes fascinating comparisons with the William Wyler remake of some eleven years later. Jeanne Eagels, ill, evidently stricken with the effects of drugs, is not quite the commanding genius of *Man, Woman and Sin* nor what was presumably her greatest achievement, the stage production of *Rain*. Her opening scene, as the camera in a sinister slow dolly, shot through leaves, arrives at a Singapore plantation house and she confronts her lover (Herbert Marshall) for the last time, is played as though she were utterly removed from life itself. It is an unsettling experience watching her poor acting here. But in the following scene, as she goes to trial for her lover's murder, lying and lying about the circumstances of his death, she is superb. Her half-smiling, half-anguished statement with the fluttering eyes and rapid speech of the

*Courtesy of Twentieth Century-Fox.*

*William K. Howard, James Wong Howe* shooting TRANSATLANTIC

practiced liar surpasses Bette Davis' performance of the same lines in the second version. And later, as she descends a long dark staircase to the infernal cellar where the Chinese woman waits to receive her blackmail money, as she puts her hand to her throat and drops her head forward when she is threatened with death by hanging, her actress' touches are sure marks of greatness. De Limur's primitive part-talkie direction is aided by George Folsey's beautiful lighting of various Singapores dives, but it is for Jeanne Eagels' nakedly emotional, nervous, and vulnerable performance that the film deserves to be remembered.

# 5. Blending Film and Theater

Mamoulian, Whale, West, Browning, William K. Howard, and Jean de Limur were originators in matters of technique and presentation, chiefly interested in visuals, in exploring the medium in new ways. Their command of dialogue, its pacing and emphasis, often left something to be desired. Another group of directors—William Wyler, George Cukor, and Frank Capra—showed a peerless command of screen conversation, evidenced from the very outset of sound, while adding little that was vividly inventive. Though the first two directors had little to say, contenting themselves with providing highly polished entertainment, a little startled to rear themselves described as artists, and though Capra's ideas were rudimentary, all three had superb skill with players, a sophisticated knowledge of sound techniques.

Wyler had come to Hollywood as a young man from Germany, worked his way up through cheap Westerns, and emerged at the outset of talkies with a reputation for making pictures quickly (which he rapidly lost). Shooting from dozens of angles, he would select the best one, often reducing actors to exasperation in the process. And often the results were too perfect, too slick, mechanical, and pat.

Wyler, though, did have a very definite personality as a craftsman; he was disciplined, rigid, Germanically precise. Unlike Roland West or Mamoulian, Wyler accepted the theatrical restrictions imposed by sound, skillfully using stage techniques in that excellent movie *Counsellor at Law* (1933).

*Counsellor at Law* was an ample demonstration of Wyler's most accomplished craftsmanship: his ability to give the audience a complete sense of the geography of a setting, and to build tiny details of characterization until a whole human being emerges in the final scenes. Brilliantly edited, each effect calculated to perfection, *Counsellor at Law* is a perfect realization of Elmer Rice's play about an attorney cracking up. John Barrymore in the central role gives one of his greatest performances, surpassed only by his professor in *Topaze*. His energy, jubilation, and gradual breakdown are relentlessly observed, particularly in the extraordinary scene at the switchboard in the last reel when he discovers his wife's infidelity. Wyler, characteristically, directs the entire sequence in three very long takes, implacably closing in on the ruined man. The use of the newly built Empire State Building as a setting, the flawless ensemble playing of the cast (headed also by Bebe Daniels, magnificent as Barrymore's loving secretary) are proof of Wyler's early maturity as a director.

*Dodsworth* (1936) was a faithful and moving version by Sidney Howard of Sinclair Lewis' novel, affirming the values of middle-class solidarity in a way that suggests a middle-brow reinforcement of Babbittry. It was carefully directed and effulgently played by Mary Astor as the Other Woman. *These Three* (1936) tactfully and delectably made, showed Wyler's command of sound. The voices of the three principals, embattled figures in a private school, are carefully counterpointed and contrasted, while the whispers of the evil child who accuses them and the hushed accusations of adultery behind locked doors show an extraordinary knowledge of the effect of off-screen sounds. The film was exquisitely played by Joel McCrea, Merle Oberon, and Miriam Hopkins.

*Dead End* (1937) was something of a letdown, an all too sophisticated version (by William Hellman) of the Sidney Kingsley play about life in a stagy New York slum. This film showed Wyler's chief limitation, his inability to break completely loose from the confines of the proscenium arch (he had learned much by the time of *Detective Story* [1951], which showed a far more authentic sense of the real New York).

Wyler's *Wuthering Heights* (1939), adapted from Emily Brontë's novel by Charles MacArthur and Ben Hecht, photographed by Gregg Toland, is a rather better film than critics have suggested. The reconstruction of a diffuse plot is firm, and the dialogue—brilliantly timed by Wyler—is a skillful telescoping and adapting of Miss Brontë's lines. In the opening scene, Lockwood, the new tenant at the Grange (Miles

Mander), arrives at Wuthering Heights on a windy night, to be greeted by loping mastiffs and a sullen proprietor whose housekeeper (Flora Robson) tells the tragic story of the house on the moors. The use of aural narration is extremely skillful and not common in the period, and the telling of Heathcliff's doomed romance with Cathy Earnshaw, the counterpointed story of the Lintons, is immaculately charted. Technically, the film is nearly perfect, except for one or two distracting backdrops, James Basevi's art direction and Toland's photography striking a clever balance between the drab shadows and rushlight of Wuthering Heights and the dazzle of gaslight illuminating the Linton house. The playing has generally been underrated. Merle Oberon makes convincing Cathy's fragility and gentility and her confused attitude to Heathcliff; Laurence Olivier is a passionate and virile hero; Geraldine Fitzgerald is a touching Isabella Linton; and Hugh Williams, Flora Robson, and Donald Crisp are flawlessly in period throughout. Perhaps the film's only major weakness is that it does not quite convey a raw sexual passion which could make of it more than a genteel, infinitely careful approximation of the novel. The cold hand of Goldwyn lies on every frame.

Two vehicles for Bette Davis, *Jezebel* (1938) and *The Letter* (1940),

*Bette Davis, George Brent, Henry Fonda, Margaret Lindsay, Fay Bainter,*
**JEZEBEL**

showed both director and actress at their best. *Jezebel* was a black and white, cut-rate *Gone With the Wind*, a companion piece to King Vidor's *So Red the Rose*. It is as false in its portrait of the South as these films or as *The Birth of a Nation*, the progenitor of them all. Yet Wyler, through selection and emphasis in the handling of dialogue, and Bette Davis, playing with a skilled and uncommon restraint, made far more of it than the Ferber-ish screenplay suggested. In scenes of dinner-party, the guests framed between the branches of silver candlesticks; of a sudden outbreak of yellow fever, with the dead carried off in cartloads; of a tense confrontation between Jezebel and her chief rival (Margaret Lindsay), Wyler showed himself to be at least the equal of a Victor Fleming as a master of period melodrama.

Wyler's career continued with great distinction in the 1940s and beyond. His first film of the new decade was *The Letter* (1940), based by Howard Koch on the play by Somerset Maugham which had provided vehicles for Katharine Cornell and Gladys Cooper on the Broadway and West End stage, and for Jeanne Eagels, as we have seen, in the cinema. The film, set in Malaya, concerns the murder of her lover by a planter's

*Bette Davis, James Stephenson,* **THE LETTER**

*Reginald Owen, Jeanne Eagels,* THE LETTER

wife who manages to convince almost everyone that she killed him in self-defense. In many ways it seems heavily dated, and Max Steiner's music is annoying at moments when we need to feel the silence of the plantation, the scrape of crickets and creak of bamboo which would play on the lonely wife's nerves, the constant irritation of tropical sounds. Yet by sheer force, Wyler pulverizes the audience into submission, piling on one visual effect after another: shadows of blinds that seem to resemble prison bars on the wife's face, the recurrent image of the moon, rubber dripping from a tree. The images, realized by Tony Gaudio, are heavily lacquered, exquisite as fine carvings in jade. Bette Davis as the murderous woman plays with striking repressed passion, erotic tension concealed behind the tight memsahib's face, hands forever stitching at a lace bedspread, each tiny oval worked with filigree care as a symbol of her will power, ability to build a pattern of deceit, and method of steadying her nerves. It remains her finest performance on the screen.

In *The Little Foxes* (1941) Wyler's technique worked less well. Bette Davis here seemed awkward and ill at ease in the role of Regina Giddens, evil scion of a southern clan, and the copperplate execution, aided by Gregg Toland's speckless fine-grained images, failed to make up for the coldness of the Lillian Hellman dialogue and the too obvious playing of the supporting cast. A version of Henry James by Ruth and Augustus Goetz, *The Heiress* (1949), worked much better. Wyler expertly created the ambience of 16 Washington Square: the proud mortally stricken Dr. Sloper (Ralph Richardson), ashamed of his unbeautiful daughter Catherine (Olivia de Haviland) and trying to protect her from fortune hunter Morris Townsend (Montgomery Clift): the cold rituals of dinner, brandy, and cigars which disguise a mortal suffering. Sliding doors emphasize the isolation of the characters; mirrors point up the father's awareness of mortality and the daughter's consciousness of her own unattractiveness. The house is used not merely as a stage setting, but as a living thing, at once reflecting the characters' moods and casting shadows on their lives. The timing is assured. A tap on a coffee cup announces the end of a sojourn in Paris, the snip of a pair of scissors on the last thread of an embroidered alphabet concludes Catherine Sloper's feelings for Morris Townsend. Wyler had not forgotten the dramatic power of sound.

In *Carrie* (1951), written expertly by the Goetzes, he again cleverly guided the performances and minutiae of detail which could reveal aspects

*Montgomery Clift, Olivia de Havilland,* THE HEIRESS

of character. Dreiser's novel is faithfully reworked in screen terms; the story of the headwaiter Hurstwood (Laurence Olivier) married to a rich woman (Miriam Hopkins) but ruined by involvement with a struggling actress (Jennifer Jones) is here given an agonizing reality, played to perfection by the principals. Wyler is at his best in such scenes as Hurstwood's discovery that he has accidentally burned his trousers; the sense of poverty, of money scrimped and saved, of the horror of unemployment is excellently conveyed. The scenes in the flophouse are overpowering: the camera craning along wire-meshed cubbyhole ceilings as drunks and deadbeats cough and Hurstwood, reduced to an unshaven, shivering wreck, breaks into helpless tears. At the conclusion, Wyler achieves a moment of greatness. As Hurstwood leaves Carrie for the last time in her theater dressing room, heading into the night to starvation and certain death, the hiss of the dressing room gas stove indicates the last gasp of their expiring relationship and the probable method he will, use to destroy himself. The finest version of Dreiser ever put on the screen, *Carrie* mirrors its author's heartbreaking logic, his knowledge —equal to Frank Norris'—of the terror of life without money and without hope.

Wyler's later films altogether lacked the intensity of his best work of the 1930s and 1940s. The box office failure of *Carrie* virtually destroyed him as a serious artist. Faced with the fact that uncompromising realism was not possible in the American cinema, a lesson also learned by von Stroheim, Wyler simply became a smoothly efficient maker of mass entertainment, though his efficiency deserted him in the unfortunate remake of Fred Niblo's *Ben-Hur* (1959). The enormous success of this film proved to him that what the public wanted at the time was grandiose vulgarity. Of Wyler's other films of the 1950s and 1960s there is little to be said. *The Desperate Hours* (1955) was a shallowly developed melodrama in which a family is menaced by a gang headed by an aging Humphery Bogart. *The Big Country* (1958) and *Friendly Persuasion* (1956) were, respectively, stories of a landowning clan and a Quaker settlement, which seemed to be efforts to emulate the open-air, free-sweeping approach of a Ford, King Vidor, or Henry King, made without the necessary lyricism or strong response to landscape. As always, Wyler was happiest in the interior sequences.

It was almost shocking to see him, in a new version of *These Three*, *The Children's Hour* (1961), providing a film that in every respect, except a courageous introduction of the lesbian theme to be found in Lillian Hellman's original play, was inferior to the original. What had been taut and crisp, if a trifle bloodless, became slack and badly organized. The performances without exception were inferior to those given by the earlier players. *The Collector* (1965), made partly in England, was a carefully crafted version of John Fowles' celebrated novel about an impotent young man (well played by Terence Stamp) who keeps butterflies in boxes and imprisons a young woman in the same fashion in a cellar of a country house. Gradually, it is disclosed that he is unable to consummate his banked-up feelings for her, and the scene in which he tries to make love to her recalls for a moment the better, more emotionally committed Wyler of *The Letter* and *Carrie*, dealing in states of psychological breakdown with a detached and kindhearted intelligence. But the synthetic elements in the novel eventually overwhelm even his skill, and the pressure behind the direction is never as strong as it should be. As a piece of craftsmanship, though, for all its faults, the film almost measures up to Wyler's Forties films.

Since then, Wyler's only film worth mentioning has been *Funny Girl* (1968), an inaccurate and indeed hokum-laden biography of Fanny Brice, based on the stage success which launched the career of Barbra

*Barbra Streisand,* FUNNY GIRL

Streisand. The opening of the film is very practiced. Aware that enormous public interest had built up in seeing Miss Streisand on the screen, Wyler began with a shot of her back as she disappeared down a brownstone alleyway in New York. Suddenly, she emerges in an empty theater, after stopping at a mirror, looking at her far from lovely reflection, and saying, "Hello, gorgeous!" with an ironical chuckle. This immediately puts the audience on her side, and the shot of her alone in the orchestra stalls makes her seem effectively lonely, isolated, and fragile. Despite the rather faded browns of Harry Stradling's overly dark camerawork, and the essentially theatrical personality of the star, Wyler manages to give the film a degree of interest through his usual timing and pacing of lines, especially in a comic scene of seduction and in his subdued and simple direction of the songs. His period feeling is strong, and though Walter Pidgeon scarcely makes a convincing Ziegfeld, substituting for the man's sardonic brooding drive a British headmaster's hauteur, the evocation of the Ziegfeld era of show business has an authentic tawdry bustle and excitement. The score is extremely well recorded, and in one scene music and image combine with great effectiveness: Fanny runs along a New York pier clutching a bedraggled bunch of roses and some heavy luggage, misses her lover as he leaves for Europe, boards a pilot boat, and sails out into New York harbor, singing triumphantly and holding her roses high in imitation of the Statue of Liberty and its torch. Observed in a remarkable helicopter shot, the image of the lonely figure seen for below against the gray water of the harbor is, despite indifferent color, a beautiful one. Wyler has since that time rested on his laurels.

George Cukor is superior to Wyler as a director of the minutiae of gesture. His concentration on details of expression is more subtle, more complex even than Lubitsch's. His films are constructed around an actor's style, each shot designed to illuminate a player's most expressive characteristics. The rhythmical structure of a sequence is designed to expose details of a performance that would escape a stage audience's eye. Though he is not the "theatrical" director many have claimed, for Cukor the actor is the expressive center of a film. He is impatient with virtuoso techniques; like Lubitsch, with whom he worked on *One Hour with You,* he shoots a great deal in medium shot, and he has preferred to use the studio. The emphasis on sound stage shooting, on the discipline of interiors, is one of his distinguishing marks as a craftsman.

Beginning, unlike Wyler, in the sound period, Cukor was promoted from dialogue director to co-director after working with Milestone on *All Quiet on the Western Front*. Of his earliest films, *Girls About Town* (1931) and *The Royal Family of Broadway* (1930) were the best. *Girls About Town*, the story of two gold diggers played by Lilyan Tashman and Kay Francis, opens brilliantly: society women dancing through models of skyscrapers behind the credits, then the camera dollying forward through swinging doors into a salon crowded with bored and exhausted blondes, while at home the gold diggers' black maid, disguised as Whistler's mother, keeps guard against wolves at the window. Later scenes, such as a madcap party on a yacht with pajamaed women guests jumping into the sea, have an almost home-movie quality in their calculated casualness, but Zoe Akins' vulgar script finally ruins the mood of careless sophistication achieved by the direction.

*The Royal Family of Broadway* survives better. This is a neat jest at the expense of the Barrymore family, written by Edna Ferber and George S. Kaufman and impeccably played by Fredric March and Ina Claire. The film is slightly handicapped by a subplot involving the heroine's affair with a business tycoon who returns from South America to sweep her off her feet. But when the temperamental star returns from his first brush with Hollywood, storming upstairs, stripping off his clothes, and denouncing his director to his astonished family from the shower, Cukor's flair brilliantly shows through.

In this period came, notably, *Tarnished Lady* (1930), a soggy Tallulah Bankhead vehicle. *A Bill of Divorcement* (1932), greatly admired for the playing of John Barrymore and Katharine Hepburn, but dated today; *What Price Hollywood?* (1932), an expert portrait of life in the world of movie-makers; and *Our Betters* (1933), a smooth version of Maugham's comedy.

None of these films quite equaled the style and sharpness of *Dinner at Eight* (1933), Cukor's first major film. The film's wit discloses itself at the outset, in the credits, when the faces of the cast—guests of a lavish, mid-Depression dinner given by a society hostess—appear grinning foolishly on dinner plates. The Ferber-Kaufman play was a microcosm of the American upper-crust scene in the early Thirties. The aging Manhattan "aristocrats" of an older generation, including Lionel Barrymore's ailing speculator, Marie Dressler's ravaged actress, and John Barrymore's falling star, clash with and are pushed out by the materialist New Rich, led by Jean Harlow's gold digger and Wallace Beery, her illiterate tycoon bedmate. In the midst of it all the hostess flutters, unaware of the downfall of her world. Obvious and rather crude social comment by today's standards, perhaps, but the writing still has a savage bite. The script strips away the pretensions of the upper set, showing, for example, the hostess' absurd attempt to lure an English nobleman and his wife to the dinner party, and the washed-up actor's determination to stay on in the most expensive hotel room in New York. In scene after scene the director displays a full command of his veteran cast: in the bitter, wounding attack of the agent (brilliantly played by Lee Tracy) on the nervously trembling Barrymore; in Barrymore's suicide, doors locked, curtains drawn, a lamp arranged to illuminate the famous profile as he lies down and sets the gas hissing like a snake; above all, in the final scene, Barrymore's death announced, Marie Dressler staring with coalpit eyes as she says, "Death is so terribly final," as the guests troop into dinner, joking emptily, the actor's disappearance from the scene already forgotten, doors closing on a perfectly self-contained world.

*Little Women* (1933), which Cukor himself admired for its carefully authentic re-creation of period houses and costumes, seems faded

*Jean Hersholt, John Barrymore, Lee Tracy,* DINNER AT EIGHT

by contrast, but with *David Copperfield* (1934) he returned to form. Hugh Walpole's intelligent adaptation of the novel (with Howard Estabrook) preserves most of its two-dimensional characters and much of its good-natured humor. Cukor, taking a more literal, more detached approach to Dickens than David Lean was to do in his 1940s version of *Oliver Twist,* is content to step back and let the story take its course. The casting is the film's chief triumph: in particular Edna May Oliver's Aunt Betsey, Roland Young's Uriah Heep, and Lennox Pawle's Mr. Dick are all quite exemplary.

It would be kindest to draw a veil over *Sylvia Scarlett* (1935), an ill-advised attempt at a British comedy of manners; *Romeo and Juliet* (1936), a wholly disastrous version of Shakespeare, anemically played by Norma Shearer and Leslie Howard; and the inane romantic trifle *Zaza* (1939). Cukor, it seemed, after the major triumphs of the mid-Thirties, was marking time. Of his films of this period, the only one to emerge in strong colors today is *Camille* (1936), an elegantly mounted version of Dumas *fils'* Parisian romance which framed one of Garbo's most celebrated performances and contained at least two impressively directed sequences: the laughing scene between Marguerite Gauthier and the Baron de Varville at the piano, and the dinner scene in the Gauthier house when the procuress Prudence (played with cigar-puffing bravura by Laura Hope Crews) passes a lewd joke around the table.

In 1939 Cukor made *The Women,* in 1940 he made *Susan and God* and *The Philadelphia Story,* comedies in which the brittle, clever dialogue shot barbed insults into the hide of the American rich; in which women clashed with men in an effort to assert their own identities; and in which the timing, the use of silence and of bursts of razzle-dazzle repartee excited critics of the period and reinforced Cukor's already substantial reputation as a master of dialogue delivery. The films remain more notable for their playing—Joan Crawford and Rosalind Russell, Katharine Hepburn and James Stewart—than for their cinematic structure. It was not until *A Woman's Face* (1941) that Cukor could again show what he was capable of in developing film narrative, in showing off the cinema's resources. Paradoxically, this melodrama, about a scarred nursemaid who revenges herself on the world, was the worst-written of all Cukor's films (it had an odd pedigree, from a Paris play via a Swedish film version with Ingrid Bergman and the efforts of a dozen scriptwriters, including Isherwood and Elliot Paul). But as though this release from the overpowering personalities of the playwrights he had

been adapting gave him a new injection of vitality. Cukor rose above the dialogue's idiocies to show an unprecedented skill as a technician.

The opening is immediately riveting. A woman prisoner hurried down a stone corridor by wardresses, an iron door clanging shut behind her as she is pushed into the glare of a courtroom's lights. Her statement to the judge, and the statements, too, of several witnesses, carry the spectator into the past of the accused murderess Anna Holm (Joan Crawford). The film moves with a beautifully muscular fluency and grace, from Anna's first meeting with the corrupt aristocrat Torsten Barring (Conrad Veidt) through the scene of the attempt to murder their infant charge while crossing a waterfall on a scenic railway, to the final sleigh ride through the snow when Anna and her evil genius meet for the last time.

There are memorable episodes throughout: a surgeon's removal of the dressing from Anna's face after an operation, the silence punctuated by the metallic click of surgical instruments in a bowl, the final snap of the scissors timed with the precision of an orchestra conductor; Anna's search for a job, her black-hatted face framed in mirrors along the pavements; a half-sinister, half-jocular little party, candles flickering on a cake, the guests jigging to an eerie Norwegian spinning tune; the journey on the scenic railway, with the movements of the child, the slow slide of the nursemaid's hand toward the safety catch of the gate, the rushing waters of the falls, and the woman's brow knitted in an agony of conscience, all intercut with unerring skill. Best of all is the final chase: a torch flung out into the night; sleighs whirling with bright bells through dunes of snow; faces tormented with anger or grief; furs sparkling with frost; the pursuing sleigh glimpsed through the undercarriage of its forerunner; and finally a shot fired by the desperate Anna Holm, the dying aristocrat falling into the pines of the canyon below. The playing of Conrad Veidt and Joan Crawford, Bronislau Kaper's music, and Robert Planck's gloomy, UFA-esque camerawork still carry a powerful charge.

*Keeper of the Flame* (1943) harks back to the somber mood of *A Woman's Face,* though its story, from a novel by I. A. R. Wylie about a fascist mistaken for a hero by the nation's boys' clubs, works on a rather high level of intelligence. The opening reels carefully build up an atmosphere of tension and menace: a car racing through storm-swept

*Conrad Veidt, Joan Crawford,* A WOMAN'S FACE

trees at night, crashing down a canyon; the dead occupant, like Charles Foster Kane, mourned by millions while only his intimates know his true character; weeping crowds under umbrellas while the predatory reporters gather in the nearby hotel, trying to gain access to the lonely mansion on the hill where the dead man's widow (Katharine Hepburn) and his secretary (Richard Whorf) try to hide their secrets from the mob.

The parallels with *Citizen Kane* are interesting: the secretary's press conference stems directly from the *March of Time* sequences in Welles' film; the iron gates and forbidding stone walls, even the mansion itself, bring back shades of Kane's Xanadu. But from the moment when the characters of returned war correspondent (Spencer Tracy) and widow trying to keep him at bay take over, the film steadily declines and Katharine Hepburn's intolerably high-falutin' performance does nothing to save it.

With his perennial ability to surprise, Cukor returned to form the following year with *Gaslight* (1944), perhaps his most aesthetically pleasing and technically consummate film. The plot is pure ham, a creaking Patrick Hamilton melodrama previously (and flatly) filmed by Thorold Dickinson. And again Cukor was able to raise the level, re-creating the play in purely cinematic terms, guiding camerawork and editing with impeccable skill. *Gaslight* is mostly set in London. A famous soprano is murdered by her greedy jewel-addicted lover, who seduces her niece into marriage and tries to drive the girl mad in order to obtain possession of the dead woman's gems. The credits immediately establish the film's authority; a gas-jet shining on a Victorian wall while an off-screen soprano voice—the murder victim's—sadly and wordlessly sings a phrase from "The Last Rose of Summer." With a brilliant stroke of imagination, Cukor shot the opening sequence, which takes place several years before the main action of the film, in soft focus, suggesting the sinister gloom of a forgotten murder story: the bereaved niece hurrying out of the house, assisted by servants, climbing into a carriage and staring helplessly ahead of her as the vehicle moves slowly into the night.

The honeymoon with the seducer in Italy has a nice irony: a romantic abstraction of Victorian literary dreams, the villa by the water, vines trailing from a trellis and the bride rising happy from her bed while ahead lie madness, attempted murder, and the prison cell. And when the couple enter the house with its eternally sliding claustrophobic doors and stifling bric-a-brac, when the patient cruel husband torments his wife by day and desperately searches the dead singer's belongings in the attic at night, the tension unbearably grows. The surface gentility, emotions held firmly in check, is beautifully suggested, so that the outbreaks of emotion—a sudden scream down a stairwell, a breakdown at an impeccably correct musical soiree—are all the more disturbing and effective. Sound and image are orchestrated with triumphant skill: the guide in the Tower of London describing the thumbscrew while the wife looks desperately for a lost cameo brooch her husband has in fact stolen; her voice off-screen describing the singer's death while the camera probes over a chair into the black fireplace where the corpse once lay; the tune of a gavotte as a guest reads an invitation to a musical evening, the slapping of his gloves on the program timed exactly to the fading of the last note; the sinister flickering of Bronislau Kaper's woodwind and strings as gas lamps flicker and feet scrape across the bedroom ceiling. Charles Boyer and Ingrid Bergman, cast cleverly against type as sadist and victim, are minutely guided by the director, whose skill extends to the minor players: Angela Lansbury's vicious maid knowingly lighting her master's Russian cigarettes, Barbara Everest's deaf housekeeper oblivious to her mistress' agony.

Two years and two indifferent films later, Cukor began in 1946 one of the most successful phases of his career, working with the scriptwriters Ruth Gordon (whose performance in *Two-Faced Woman* had been memorable) and her husband, Garson Kanin, on a melodrama, *A Double Life* (1947); four comedies, *Adam's Rib* (1949), *The Marrying Kind* (1952), *It Should Happen to You* (1953), and *Pat and Mike* (1952); and Ruth Gordon's nostalgic family album, *The Actress* (1953). All these films were beautifully made, expertly written and played, and with the exception of *A Double Life* (the story of a famous Othello who identifies murderously with his stage role) directed deliberately in a minor key. *Adam's Rib* pitched the Hepburn-Tracy team into a battle of wits between warring lawyers. *The Marrying Kind* explored the problems of a young couple, struggling to make ends meet, losing their baby (in a half-humorous, half-sad manner reminiscent at times of Vidor's *The Crowd*). *Pat and Mike* again featured Hepburn and Tracy in a story about the temperament of sporting idols. Intensely American, polished, urban in feeling and location, these films form a still rewarding group; but there was nothing in them to suggest the wholehearted cinematic flair and drive of *A Star Is Born,* the major triumph which followed *It Should Happen to You* in 1954.

Together with *Dinner at Eight* and *Gaslight, A Star Is Born* remains the greatest of Cukor's films. And this despite serious flaws, including insensitive cutting by the studio to make room for an ugly musical number ("Born in a Trunk") not directed by Cukor, some unattractive costume design (by Irene Sharaff and others), and an uneven script (Moss Hart) that loses a good deal of the wit of the original 1937 version written by Dorothy Parker and Alan Campbell. Several scenes building up the difficult love affair of the new star, Vicki Lester (Judy Garland), and her husband, the fallen, drunken screen idol of the past, Norman Maine (James Mason), were cut, including one of which Cukor has said he was particularly fond, when the couple act a love scene on the sound stage and their words are cut by a live microphone and played back to them. Nevertheless, the film retains a clean, strong narrative flow and drive. Every detail is designed to expose the reality of Hollywood, the hissing spotlights and crisp white furs of Oscar night contrasting with the spiteful comments of bystanders, the falling matinee idol lurching drunkenly onto the stage; the awkward, desperate love affair of old and new star conflicting with the smoothness of their screen image; a predatory headwaiter offering Maine starlets in a Hollywood restaurant; the agent (Jack Carson), a reincarnation of Lee Tracy in *Dinner at Eight,* savaging the big-timer when he is down. Visually, the film is continually alive and striking, from the first moment when the camera shoots directly into a spitting arc to the climax when Norman Maine swims—this was based on a real-life incident—into the sea to his death. In this sequence, as technically sophisticated as any in *Gaslight*—the drifting curtains of the beach house, the surf reflected in the tall aluminum-framed windows, the husband twisting in agony on his bed, and the wife frantically looking for him as he steps down the sand —camera and sound electrifyingly combine. And in the slow track-in to the lonely girl singing her heart out at a late night band session; in the visit to the stricken husband in the alcoholic's home; in the dressing room scene when the girl bursts into tears through her clown's makeup; here again and again the direction has a bitter truth. Much has been written about Judy Garland's full-scale star performance, but James Mason's seems to me no less moving and accomplished, encompassing an early hysteric gaiety as well as the sudden depression following the alcoholic jag, the mouth opening with pain in the dark when the stricken man knows that all he can do is die.

Two years later, *Bhowani Junction* (1956), the story of a native revolt, powerfully staged in India, struck a more conventional note of location adventure, but in several scenes, including a mass show of passive resistance with the rebels stretched on railway tracks, a Sikh wedding, and the heroine's nightmarish train journey, a montage of railway tracks diagonally slashing the CinemaScope frame to express her pain, Cukor was at his best. All the more pity then that immediately after this excellent (and neglected) film he should strike a patch of indifferent scripts. From the late Fifties one prefers not to remember a feeble musical, *Les Girls*; a cumbersome Anna Magnani vehicle, *Wild Is the Wind*; the hideously garish *Heller in Pink Tights* and *Let's Make Love*; the disastrous Wagner biography, *Song Without End* . . . This was the worst period in Cukor's career, in which his skill was relentlessly squandered on mediocre material and he apparently felt disinclined even to preserve his normal standards of good taste.

*The Chapman Report* (1962), oddly enough (though critically disliked), was in fact Cukor's best film in several years, full of sharp observation, wit, and adroit performances. Based on Irving Wallace's ludicrous novel about a Kinsey-like research team and its effects on women's lives, the script plays up the potential comedy in the book and cleverly underplays the crudity and violence (Richard Zanuck later recut the film to restore some of the vulgar emphases Cukor had avoided). The design is pleasing throughout, and the playing—especially of Jane Fonda and Claire Bloom—as delicate and subtle as any in the Cukor repertoire. There is at least one waspishly funny episode which bears the director's unmistakable stamp: that involving the frustrated Teresa Harnish (Glynis Johns), who recites Dowson on the beach, eyes the local muscle men, and lures one of them to a seduction, only to find that his love-making technique leaves her as frustrated as before.

With *My Fair Lady* (1964), Cukor's career comes full circle: from *The Royal Family of Broadway* to the mannered musical comedy of Lerner and Loewe it forms a very satisfactory graph. In this latest film, after a long hiatus, Cukor's personality is very much in evidence, dominating even that of Cecil Beaton, whose costumes and designs express a no less striking intelligence and flair. In the relaxed, elliptical playing of Rex Harrison and Audrey Hepburn, in the subtly unobtrusive flow of editing and camerawork, in the marshaling of the supporting cast into agreeable patterns within the frame, Cukor's skill shows an undimmed luster.

Whereas the films of George Cukor are measured, civilized, and prim, Frank Capra's are fast-moving, energetic, brashly direct. Never a sophisticated director, he was the least constipated of craftsmen, able to achieve a pace and freedom in the sound film which recalled the best of the silent comedies (including his own). As thinkers, he and his writer, Robert Riskin, cannot always be taken seriously. Their view of politics and of the common man was sometimes caricatured, and they saw morality in simple blacks and whites. Their stories of hick town Galahads pitted against the bigwigs of commerce seem dated and unconvincing today, but the unequaled brilliance of the execution, immeasurably aided by Capra's superb cameraman Joseph Walker, is such that while the films are being watched, they must sweep away all but the most cautious judgment.

Capra's *Ladies of Leisure* (1930) announces his irreverent, racy style in a story (excellently played by Barbara Stanwyck) of call girls, remarkably frank in its sexual explicitness and disillusioned portrait of life in a big city. *Dirigible* (1931) was a hymn to Air Force heroes in the worst Hawks or Ford mold. More interesting was *The Miracle Woman* (1931), in which Barbara Stanwyck plays with intensity a tormented, hick-exploiting evangelist, a role based on Aimee Semple McPherson. Unfortunately for veracity, she is swayed at the end by true love, but up to that feeble-minded sop to the public, the picture has a grainy toughness equivalent to the best Warner films. The climax, in which the tabernacle catches fire, is spectacularly well handled.

In 1931 Capra also made the energetic, raucous Jean Harlow vehicle *Platinum Blonde*; and in 1932 that important study of mass psychology *American Madness*. *American Madness* is the story of a banker (Walter Huston) whose most trusted employee (Gavin Gordon) aids a bank robbery and simultaneously attempts to seduce the banker's wife (Kay Johnson). After the robbery, performed by a master criminal, there is a run on the bank, its ruin narrowly avoided by the actions of the chief cashier (Pat O'Brien). Capra achieves with an extraordinary degree of realism the atmosphere of the bank, from the first shot of a complicated, cylindrical steel safe being laboriously opened to the long tracking shots through the tellers and the scenes of mass panic as hysterical crowds demand their money back. Important as an almost Warner-ish reflection of Depression attitudes, Riskin's script conveys with tough assurance the psychology of the executive class as exemplified by the board of directors, blocking every adventurous move, refusing to help when the chips are down. Despite the conventional elements in the portraits of the characters, and the rudimentary nature of the playing (except for Huston), the film is persuasively and powerfully made.

*The Bitter Tea of General Yen* (1932) showed Capra entirely off his proper territory, directing in a rather awkward style a story of a Chinese provincial governor Yen (Nils Asther) and a missionary girl (Barbara Stanwyck) emotionally drawn together in a palace that looks like Grauman's Chinese Theatre. Nils Asther, resembling an animated tea cosy and delivering lines in a Swedish accent, and Barbara Stanwyck, talking at remarkable speeds in a display of missionary emotion, are weirdly miscast, and there is one very funny moment when his Chinese mistress approaches the warlord and addresses him in their native tongue. "Stop that and speak English!" he snaps, thus making it possible to communicate to the audience. The film showed most Chinese as unreliable, vicious turncoats. This was scarcely a help in a time when there were major political problems in Shanghai, and the film was banned in many countries. Only the final scene, when Yen takes poison after a

*Nils Asther, Barbara Stanwyck, Toshia Mori,* THE BITTER TEA OF GENERAL YEN

© *Columbia Pictures Industries, Inc.*

brief unsatisfactory embrace with the captive girl, offers any indication of Capra's directorial talent.

*Lady for a Day* (1933) and the famous *It Happened One Night* (1934) further developed Capra's reputation. These were essentially light entertainments, without serious intent. *Mr. Deeds Goes to Town* (1936) established Capra as a major director dealing in important themes, with an unusually fluent narrative style and an unabashed sentimental patriotism which even allowed his central figure to deliver a bashful flag-waving speech in front of Grant's Tomb. *Mr. Deeds Goes to Town,* based on a Clarence Budington Kelland story, was a completely successful escapist entertainment for the Depression masses which succeeded in hoodwinking some sophisticated critics as well. Gary Cooper played with considerable skill the role of Longfellow Deeds, the Vermont greeting card poet whose wise saws and tuba-playing antics astonish everyone when he inherits a fortune from an uncle dead in a car crash. A corrupt firm of lawyers tries to cheat him, a typical Thirties girl reporter, "Babe" Bennett (the excellent Jean Arthur), takes him for a ride. At the end he becomes a champion for the downtrodden, arranging mass ventures in collective farming and throwing a courtroom into an uproar by defending the charge of insanity leveled against him. In the world presented by the film, established poets are drunken and ruthless, ready to make fun of a hick; exploitative editors and reporters have hearts of gold; opera is a waste of time; a judge turns out to be a kindly old curmudgeon; and an accused man can strike to the ground a prominent attorney in mid-trial without the slightest repercussion of the law. The Philistine absurdity of the proceedings unredeemed by a single moment of reality was compensated for by Capra's and Riskin's mastery with punch lines, amusing repartee, and inspired use of the American language ("doodling" and "pixilated" entered the popular vocabulary as a result of the film).

*You Can't Take It with You* (1937) was a satisfactory transcription by Riskin of the successful play, without much in the way of additional material. The casting, though, was inspired. A crazy New York family, holding out against the incursions of a syndicate that wants to buy their home and throw them into the streets, is brilliantly played on a note of exaggerated cornball caricature. Spring Byington's novel-typing Mom, in print dresses, using a cat for a paperweight; Lionel Barrymore's crusty, income tax-defying paterfamilias; Mischa Auer's ungainly ballet dancer; Donald Meek's toy-manufacturing clerk: these and the other characters are brought to life with an irresistible charm. Wholesome as apple pie, the film manages yet another Capra/Riskin onslaught on capitalism, in the portrait of Edward Arnold, black-coated and beetle-browed, as an evil industrialist. Needless to say, the left-wing argument is sold out at the climax, with Arnold and Lionel Barrymore, joined in loving camaraderie, playing harmonicas. If only the capitalist lion would lie down with the proletarian lamb (the dramatists and their Hollywood adapters are jointly saying) all would be well in this wicked old world. It was a message that Thirties audiences (and even critics) had little trouble in swallowing.

*Lost Horizon* (1937) was Capra's most ambitious film of the 1930s, a masterpiece of technique. Based by Riskin on James Hilton's novel, photographed exquisitely by Joseph Walker, it opens in Baskul, China, on March 1, 1935. The British diplomat Robert Conway (Ronald Colman) is evacuating groups of refugees from a war-torn province, eventually flying out with a handful of British and American subjects— a paleontologist, a swindling business chief, a tubercular girl, and Conway's brother. The opening sequences are extraordinary. We see the evocation of a swarming mob, flare path lights illuminating contorted faces, hysterical Europeans gathered in an airport building, plane after plane roaring out into the night. Once in the air, Capra flawlessly inter-cuts studio and Elmer Dyer flying footage, staging excitingly the plane's refueling on the borders of Tibet. Shangri-La, the glistening world which the travelers find as they follow their discoverer Chang (H. B. Warner) to a secret valley, is magnificently achieved by the art director Stephen Goosson, its faintly Chinese character suggested with subtlety, doves flying past a white palace, arbors, glades, waterfalls, and ornamental glades assuming the look of Paradise. In a room with a single candle, the French priest who arrived in Shangri-La in 1713 lingers on 222 years later as the High Lama (Sam Jaffe) until his life is snuffed out. As he dies, a breeze blows out the candle beside him, an obvious metaphoric device which works beautifully in the context.

The scenes in which Conway, his brother, and his brother's girl friend make their way back to China across the snowy wastes are the finest in the picture, the evocation of icy wastes astonishing in its power. The film's playing is almost uniformly admirable, each actor's limited skills seen at their best because they are cast to perfection within those limitations: Ronald Colman's puzzled charm is perfect for Conway; H. B. Warner makes an ideally spiritual, refined Chang; Sam

*Ronald Colman, Isabel Jewell, Edward Everett Horton, Thomas Mitchell,*
**LOST HORIZON**

Jaffe in a triumph of makeup is convincingly venerable as the High
Lama. Only John Howard as Conway's brother seems unable to handle
an awkwardly written role. Fundamentally absurd though its entire concept is, the film still has the power to move an audience.

*Mr. Smith Goes to Washington* (1939) reworked the theme of *Mr.
Deeds,* with James Stewart as the idealist boys' club cheerleader put
into office as a senator by a corrupt combine which hopes to make use
of him. Aided by Jean Arthur, once again a chirrupy girl reporter, he
turns the tables on the enemies of democracy, foiling a plot to feather
the nests of the local governor and his fascist manipulator, Boss Taylor

(Edward Arnold). For the first two thirds of the film, the writing (by Sidney Buchman, approximating quite neatly the Robert Riskin tone) and direction are little more than competent, the scenes composed in a monotony of medium shots, devoid of pictorial variety. Jefferson Smith's visit to various Washington monuments is as embarrassingly patriotic as Mr. Deeds' before him. But the last third of the film is superlatively good cinema, as Smith filibusters in Stephen Goosson's extraordinary ceilinged set of the Senate chamber. It is a sequence in which for all the absurdity of the situation—a hick confounding the caricatured representatives of the forty-eight states—the effect is deeply moving. Stewart's impassioned delivery of the lines, sinking to a whisper as he is gradually reduced to exhaustion, and the ferocious retorts from "the Silver Knight," Senator Claude Rains, can still bring tears to the most jaundiced eye. Rains is nothing short of magnificent, flawlessly creating the tension of an elder statesman torn between duty and chicanery, delivering his harangues with an eloquence, a fervor that places his in the short list of the screen's greatest performances. It is to Capra, though, and Capra alone, that the overwhelming power and electric vitality of the film's last third are due.

*Meet John Doe* is of special interest for its portrait of the Nazi-like political boss again played superbly by Edward Arnold, an elaboration of the similar figure played by Arnold in *Mr. Smith Goes to Washington.* Just before America entered World War II, Capra alerted the country to the dangers of Fascism: the fatly pitiless and complacent figure in his pince-nez surveying his black-clad storm troopers in their motorcycle maneuverings or ordering the arousal of mass hysteria from his mansion near New York is one of Capra's and Riskin's most brilliantly menacing embodiments of power. The portrait of the mob is more complex here than in other Capra films: the crowds are swung with alarming ease from one political pole to another, manipulated without any trouble by the crime boss, their inanity observed with extraordinary ambivalence, the attitude toward them at once contemptuous and sentimental. Although the idealist tramp-turned-public idol, the girl reporter, and her editor are impossible figures even as played by Gary Cooper, Stanwyck, and James Gleason, Arnold is more convincingly real. Like Disney, Capra and Riskin are fascinated by evil and portray it far more successfully than goodness, while providing moralistic messages of which Griffith would have approved. More urgently than any other film-maker, Capra asserts the superiority of the common man, for all his short-

comings, to intellectuals, do-gooders, and politicians of most colors, the film's rampant Philistinism right in the Hollywood mainstream.

With the Forties, Capra achieved an even greater confidence. *Meet John Doe* (1941) and *It's a Wonderful Life* (1946) remain his best-made films. *It's a Wonderful Life* is justly regarded as Capra's best-made picture, a masterpiece of moralistic fantasy, executed with a skill that surpasses Welles at his best. It may not be too much of an exaggeration to say that it is the most brilliantly made motion picture of the 1940s, so assured, so dazzling is its use of screen narrative to tell a fundamentally silly and banal story about the character of a small town.

As the camera tracks along the sin-ridden streets to show the "horrors" of dives, pintable parlors, and sordid movies, the camerawork of Joseph Walker is amazing in its virtuosity. Capra has done nothing of interest since. It is a misfortune that he could not match to his command of the technique of film-making—a command second to none—something of the sophistication and detachment of the Cukor films.

In the fields of comedy and social satire or melodrama in which Cukor, Capra, and the other great directors here discussed had distinguished themselves, many minor figures too large to enumerate gave color and vibrancy to Hollywood's escapist or realist fare of the 1930s. Mention should be made of such skillful movie-makers as Gregory La Cava, whose *My Man Godfrey* (1936) was a witty object lesson in the perils of Thirties "slumming," and John Cromwell, who brought a civilized intelligence to bear on many movies, similar in some ways to the equally intelligent and subdued George Stevens discussed in Part III. John M. Stahl in such pictures as *Back Street* (1932) and the excellent *Leave Her to Heaven* (1945) had a practiced ease with the camera, and a knowledge of directing actors almost as complete as Cukor's. Alexander Hall, Lowell Sherman, Leo McCarey (extravagantly over-rated by the French in recent years), Mitchell Leisen—that capable follower in the Lubitsch tradition—all were worthy commercial craftsmen, heirs to the mantle of Mal St. Clair and Harry D'Arrast.

*Barbara Stanwyck, Gary Cooper, MEET JOHN DOE*

# PART THREE
## The Forties and After

*Humphrey Bogart, Sydney Greenstreet, Peter Lorre, Mary Astor,*
THE MALTESE FALCON

■ ■ ■ ■ ■ ■ ■ ■ ■ ■ ■ ■ ■ ■ ■ ■ ■ ■ ■ ■ ■ ■ ■ ■ ■

# 1. War and Post-War

■ ■ ■ ■ ■ ■ ■ ■ ■ ■ ■ ■ ■ ■ ■ ■ ■ ■ ■ ■ ■ ■ ■ ■

The basic structure of the studios changed little in the late 1930s. Paramount underwent a number of executive upheavals. Its chiefs Jesse L. Lasky and Budd Schulberg were ousted from office by internal maneuverings, but its Lubitschian policy—the director even ran the studio for a period—continued basically unchanged. Irving Thalberg's death did little to alter M-G-M's combination of lavish presentation and rearguard thinking. Warners continued to be run by Albert, Harry, and Jack, Sam having died on the eve of the premiere of *The Jazz Singer.* Universal underwent a number of shifts of power after its chief Carl Laemmle retired and his son took over, leaning more toward light-hearted musicals (Deanna Durbin's films particularly) and comedies as the Germanic influences waned. RKO was in constant difficulties and in the late 1930s it was virtually run by Floyd Odlum, head of the multi-million-dollar Atlas Corporation, from offices in New York.

New York, in fact, held the purse strings. After 1934, banks virtually kept the studios afloat, with the exceptions of the affluent Loew's/M-G-M. The banks backed up the Breen code (which Nicholas Schenck of Metro had helped to enforce) by insisting on well-laundered plots which their directors and directors' wives would approve. Needless to say, Schenck always made sure Mayer kept to the straight and narrow path, but Warners with its usual likable brashness often risked and even incurred the code's and the banks' displeasure. It was typical of the atrocious situation that existed by 1938 that the title of a film called

*Joy of Loving* had to be changed to *Joy of Living* because it was thought improper to suggest that sexual desire might be pleasurable.

By 1940 the term "pre-code" referred to a long-lost Golden Age of sophistication. Throughout the 1940s the sentimental values of the silent period returned in full force, and the mood of a country at war brought about a degree of flag-waving and jingoism harking back to the time of the first world conflict and the popular epics of the late 1920s. By 1940 the industry was virtually emasculated. Mae West, the Marx Brothers, and W. C. Fields had run out of steam. The New York wits who had given a freshness to the writing of early Thirties movies had either become alcoholics, died, or gone home to the sting of good conversation and the high challenge of the stage.

Perhaps the most serious development in the 1940s was the reduction in the power of the director. In the silent period the director had, as I have demonstrated, a great deal of power. In the early 1930s if he had had experience on the stage or could match the imported figures from the theater in handling stars and stories, he had an almost equal degree of influence, though producers obtained more and more control toward the end of that decade. It became the principle of most major studios to "cast" directors along with players. In the 1940–50 period many directors were subservient to producers.

Let us take as an example the major film-producing company, M-G-M. The system there was usually mandatory. The director came on the picture two weeks before it was begun, and left the picture four days after the shooting was finished. Louis B. Mayer became disenchanted with directors due to what he called their extravagance, and in order to limit their influence he made it the duty of his production staff to select the story, collaborate on the screenplay with the writers, choose the casts, have the entire production fully ready, and edit the film when shooting was completed. The director could be, and frequently was, taken off a picture if his deadlines or budgets were not met. Directors were on weekly salaries (averaging $750 a week) and if they displeased, they could easily be replaced by other contractees. Warners, Paramount, and all the other studios followed M-G-M's lead in this matter. We can talk confidently of "Forties movies" because they were committee efforts for the most part, made to the precise dictates of fashion. To cite one example, *Mrs. Miniver* was far more the creation of its producer Sidney Franklin than of William Wyler, its ostensible director.

Of the independent producers of the 1940s, the two most influential

were Samuel Goldwyn and David O. Selznick. Both exercised considerable personal control over their productions, both signed directors,
players, and writers to long-term contracts and made a policy of loan-
ing them out. Both followed the Thalberg policy of lavish, tasteful films,
flawlessly made and somewhat bloodless. Of the two, Selznick had the
better record: *Gone With the Wind* was incomparable in terms of production values, whatever its shortcomings of substance, and most of his
Jennifer Jones films were capably made, especially *Portrait of Jennie,*
exquisitely shot by Joseph August. On Selznick's credit record can be
listed, retrospectively, Victor Schertzinger's *Forgotten Faces,* a tearjerker made tolerable by Olga Baclanova's penetrating portrait of a
greedy woman; *Topaze,* an agreeably acid account of a schoolmaster's
career; *The Four Feathers* of Cooper and Schoedsack; the Cukor films
*What Price Hollywood? David Copperfield,* and *Dinner at Eight*; Norman Taurog's beautiful early color film *The Adventures of Tom Sawyer*;
Hitchcock's *Rebecca*; and John Cromwell's *Since You Went Away,* the
best of the World War II home front pictures. Among much kitsch
masquerading as art, Goldwyn made a few quite good films, including
Frank Lloyd's *Madame X*; Wyler's *Wuthering Heights*; Irving Reis'
fluently told story of several generations in a London house, *Enchantment;* Archie Mayo's *They Shall Have Music*; and Wyler's *Dodsworth.*

There were a small number of fortunate directors who were able to
develop their own shrewd and penetrating scripts in the period, most
notably John Huston and Billy Wilder (I have already remarked on
Wyler's excellent work with Ruth and Augustus Goetz). Warners
achieved the only consistent standards in writing, giving their scenarists
an unusual degree of freedom. Warners was known as a "writers' studio,"
and Warner contractee authors like Casey Robinson, Julius J. and
Philip G. Epstein, Robert Rossen, Stephen Morehouse Avery, and
Howard Koch were widely envied in the business.

Technically the films of the Forties gained in sophistication and from
the perfection achieved through committee rule. In all of the modes—
the knockabout comedy, the women's picture, the war film, the musical,
the gangster melodrama, and so on—the skill became more and more
noticeable thanks to the knowledge of producers like Hal Wallis, Henry
Blanke, Victor Saville, Arthur Freed, and Pandro S. Berman.

The few films of major artistic merit in the period were frequently
Germanic in mode. We have already noted how King Vidor, Henry
King, and their confreres of the Griffith school pursued their rural con-

cerns into this new period. Lubitsch went on working with Preston Sturges and several Paramount directors, led by Mitchell Leisen, as camp followers. However, the most important new figures of the period —Welles, Huston, Wilder, Lang, Litvak, Preminger among them— revived the UFA tradition of Murnau, Leni, Dupont, and Robison.

The reason for the revival of the Germanic modes is not far to seek. Just as the native American comedy and drama started to decline due to code interference in 1934, the first wave of refugees from Hitler began to arrive in Hollywood. The makers of that noted German film *People on Sunday,* Robert Siodmak, Edgar G. Ulmer, Billy Wilder, and Fred Zinnemann, all made their way to America. Fritz Lang, after rejecting Hitler's offer to become head of the German film industry, also arrived. Along with them came a flock of writers, including, of course, several who did not work in the industry: Thomas Mann, Lion Feuchtwanger, Leonhard Frank, and others.

Lang's important first sound films made in America, *Fury* (1936) and *You Only Live Once* (1937), restored the UFA style, which had only been fitfully sustained since the deaths of Murnau (1931) and Leni (1929) and the advent of sound, which banished the majority of the other European figures. It had earlier been seen in Robert Florey's *Murders in the Rue Morgue* (1932), Curtiz' *The Mad Genius* (1931) and *Mystery of the Wax Museum* (1932), Archie Mayo's *Svengali* (1931), and Karl Freund's *The Mummy* (1932) and *Mad Love* (1935). Familiar images in these films were the sinister figures in the near-darkness, the menacing eyes peering through thick spectacles, the fans of light splitting around a raincoated presence at a street corner, the sense of a haunting, all-pervading evil fate. Lang, and Ford as well, developed these images, and art directors like William Cameron Menzies, cameramen like Bert Glennon, Joseph August, and Gregg Toland perfected the mode. Karl Freund was responsible for Gregg Toland's increased interest in the style; they worked together briefly in *Mad Love,* chiefly shot by the Germanic Chester Lyons. But in fact Toland employed it as far back as 1930, in *Bulldog Drummond,* designed by Menzies with low-ceilinged sets and deep focus. Gradually, it became obligatory in the late 1930s for directors making "serious" subjects to use UFA-esque low key. In the 1940s it became predominant at Warners, Universal, and—for nocturnal melodramas—M-G-M. The range of influences was actually extremely complex. And Welles' "influence" was not as great as it may seem. Forties melodramas looked not "Wellesian"

*Courtesy of Universal Pictures.*

*Boris Karloff,* THE MUMMY

but Germanic because of the great pressure exerted by the increasing influx of German and Austrian figures. Welles was simply the first of many directors in this decade to employ Germanic methods. Ceilinged sets and deep focus were also used effectively in *The Long Voyage Home* (1940), which Toland shot just before making *Kane*.

Due to a prevailing fashion, the problem film loomed large in the decade. In addition to those pictures dealt with in detail in later sections of this book, mention should be made of Edward Dmytryk's *Crossfire* (1947), a superficial but well-made film about racial prejudice; and the carefully manufactured *Gentleman's Agreement* (1947), which also concerned anti-Semitism. Better were the straightforward journalistic accounts of crime in the big city, such films as Hathaway's *Kiss of Death* (1947) and *Call Northside 777* (1948), distinguished by a semi-documentary realism recalling the same producer Darryl F. Zanuck's "headline" work at Warners fifteen years earlier. Anatole Litvak's *The Snake Pit* (1946) dealt with madness; Wyler's *The Best Years of Our Lives* (1947) with the problem of war veterans; Michael Gordon's *The Lady*

*Gambles* (1948) and *An Act of Murder* (1948) with, respectively, gambling mania and euthanasia. All were made without real profundity or understanding, and exploited rather than explored their subjects. As for war films, it would be kindest to ignore the majority of these, since they reflected the propagandist romanticism of the time, serving effectively as morale boosters without aspiring to the level of art. Decent and rare exceptions to the rule of mediocrity were Frank Capra's *Why We Fight* documentaries; William Wyler's beautiful *The Memphis Belle* (1945); and John Farrow's authentic account of the rise of Nazism, *The Hitler Gang* (1944).

Literary adaptions reflected the spread of mass education. Among the best of these were Robert Stevenson's *Jane Eyre* (1944) and his remake of Fannie Hurst's *Back Street* (1941); Robert Z. Leonard's *Pride and Prejudice* (1940); and, above all, Max Ophuls' and John Houseman's *Letter from an Unknown Woman* (1948), a brilliant version of Stefan Zweig. The action film was exemplified by the handsomely made Errol Flynn movies and Henry King's *The Black Swan* (1942) and *Captain from Castile* (1947). Westerns included fine new works by Ford and those rousing accounts of frontier life, Tay Garnett's *Seven Sinners* (1940) and Ray Enright's *The Spoilers* (1942).

Comedy retained a vestige of its screwball origins of the 1930s, both in the films of Preston Sturges and another follower of Lubitsch, Mitchell Leisen, and in such minor pleasures as William Keighley's *The Man Who Came to Dinner* (1941). Chaplin's *The Great Dictator* (1940) and *Monsieur Verdoux* (1947) were silent-style in technique but were written and played with a fine sense of irony. The comedies of Abbott and Costello and the Three Stooges were popular with the public, as was the *Road* series of Bing Crosby, Bob Hope, and Dorothy Lamour.

The musical reached its peak as an art form in the 1940s. The elegant, white-tie-and-tails approach of a Fred Astaire was gradually replaced by the more down-to-earth dancing of a Gene Kelly. Kelly tried to express the feelings, not of the rich and sophisticated, but of the soldier, the sailor, and the common man, in free, exhilarating dance routines. Betty Grable, a far better dancer than she was credited for, also provided an essentially earthy expression of balletic forms, particularly in her incarnations of waitresses or other simple members of society. Beginning with her *Moon over Miami* (1940), musicals began to move freely over locations, breaking with the theatrical conventions of the Ziegfeld era. The one director who fought these new developments was Vincente Minnelli, whose theatrical training influenced his famous series of films for M-G-M, including *Meet Me in St. Louis* (1944) and *The Pirate* (1947). The secret of the success of his musicals was their total artificiality, their stagy charm. Other directors understood the need for free, open direction and an extensive use of the American scene. In *Anchors Aweigh* (1945), a handsomely photographed musical about three sailors on furlough, George Sidney shot an entire sequence brilliantly in the Hollywood Bowl. Later, Stanley Donen and Gene Kelly staged their marvelous *On the Town* in part in New York, capturing the effervescence, the excitement of a great city in some of the most intoxicating sequences ever filmed. The last great musical of the period was *Singin' in the Rain* (1952), also duo-directed by Donen and Kelly, which used the whole ambience of its own studio, M-G-M, to re-create in comedy and music the devastatingly funny realities of the changeover period from silents to sound.

The visual richness and variety of Forties films was extraordinary, their lack of intellectual content compensated for by their polished execution, the great personalities of the performers of the time—Bogart, Bacall, Davis, Sheridan, Garland among them—and the sheer sense of exuberance that marked the era. These works were the last reflections of Hollywood as a place where people enjoyed making pictures. The blacklists of the late 1940s and the increasing desperation of the postwar years killed all that ebullience for good.

Film music grew more sophisticated during the decade. Each studio had by now firmly established a fixed style, but the expression of it by the individual composers was not wholly derivative and crass.

Each studio had a different approach to film music in the 1940s. Warners specialized in the lush, overripe scores of Max Steiner, Erich Wolfgang Korngold, Adolph Deutsch, David Buttolph, and Franz Waxman, the latter its most gifted composer. Waxman's score for *Dark Passage* (1947), subtly integrating the foghorns of a San Francisco setting, was particularly memorable. Steiner specialized in sweeping romantic scores, filled with a rich fund of melody; he set the tone for the Warner studio as a whole. M-G-M featured the rather sickly Palm Court music of Herbert Stothart. Paramount had some interesting scores by Frederick Hollander and Miklos Rozsa, who later moved to Universal. His angular, harsh music was effective in such films as *Double Indemnity* (1944) and *The Lost Weekend* (1945), though at times he fell into a monotonous reworking of the same themes. At 20th Century-Fox, Alfred

Newman and Hugo Friedhofer were constantly heard from, Newman improving on his usual mediocrity in a fine score for *Leave Her to Heaven* (1945). Columbia and Universal (before Rozsa) added little of interest. Other composers of the period were Hanns Eisler, Ernst Toch, Sol Kaplan, Gail Kubik, and Victor Young. Although certain films, such as *Kings Row* (1942), scored by Korngold, benefited enormously from the accompanying scores, a vast number seemed overloaded with music, which frequently fought with dialogue, trains, cars, and even with storms and hurricanes, making otherwise good films seem seriously dated today. Movie scores like Aaron Copland's for *The Red Pony* and *The Heiress* were rare in their acid freshness, and that fine but neglected composer David Raksin (*Laura, The Big Combo*) was all too rarely heard from. Hollywood's attempts at the biographies of serious composers can safely be passed over in silence.

# 2. The Advent of Orson Welles

The style of most major Hollywood directors developed rather than changed in the new decade. Few showed more than a passing interest in the one really great figure to make his mark in the period: Orson Welles. His genius was entirely different from any that had emerged in film before. He combined all the techniques and many of the ideas of film into his one masterpiece, *Citizen Kane* (1941), but he acted in defiance of the traditions which had given it birth. Whereas the other great filmmakers, even Capra, had worked firmly in a tradition of American humanism, accepting American virtues without question, Welles became the American cinema's first major radical, its first serious critic of society. He was given aid in this critique by the writer Herman J. Mankiewicz, a lightweight intellectual who had provided much of the brittle empty wit of 1930s comedies. But Welles, by the force of his direction, gave far more weight to Mankiewicz's satire than the essentially burlesque talents of Mae West and the Marx Brothers had done. *Citizen Kane* was an anti-American classic, the exact antithesis of the work of Ford or Wyler or Cukor in the period.

A sign hung over a wire-mesh gate at night, "No Trespassing"; at the top of a hill a Gothic castle, a light shining from a single window; a clutter of gondolas, caged monkeys, shapeless junk; Disneyish lit panes; a face in stony profile as rubbery lips breathe "Rosebud" and a glass paperweight spins out of a dying hand; the image of a nurse slanting through the paperweight glass as she comes through the door. The opening of *Citizen Kane,* accompanied by the grim rumble of Bernard Herrmann's score, is today very often mentioned. Yet each time one sees it, it reasserts its power, and so does the newsreel which follows, sputtering into life on the private screen with jungle music and the waving palms of Kane's palace, the opening lines of "Kubla Khan"; the glimpses of Kane's career as lion rampant, errant, and finally couchant; the intricate beauty of the sequence when, from an apple tree's bare branches, a hand-held camera peers coldly at the aged magnate pushed in his wheelchair through the orchard, a shapeless mummy wrapped in a winding cloth of time.

Orson Welles' tragedy was that he needed the resources of technique and money which, in the film industry only Hollywood can provide. Welles' genius fed on Hollywood's marvelous machinery. In Europe, his dependence on American skill cruelly shows through. All his American films show a profound understanding of the American character, of its ambition, its deceits, its absurdities, and its beautiful humor and resilience. *Kane, The Magnificent Ambersons* (1942), *The Lady from Shanghai* (1947), and *Touch of Evil* (1957)—his four masterpieces— explore facets of the native mind and emotions with a greater complexity than all save a handful of American novelists. His greatness has chiefly been thought to lie in his technical innovations or renovations, his experiments with lighting, cutting, and sound. But his true art was in breaking through the Hollywood conventions which shut out the truth about Americans or turned the authentic dramas of everyday life into comic strips of violence informed by cheap sociology. His genius was in breaking those barriers, and in showing how the cinema could explore life as ruthlessly as the novel or the theater. If Welles' desire for truthfulness destroyed him, he left the truth as his monument. And his films are not merely truthful. Rossellini's, for example, are truthful, too, and time has dealt badly with them. Welles' are beautiful, delectable constructs. Their richness of texture remains unequaled in the American cinema.

When, in *Kane,* Welles is showing the vulgarity and emptiness of the lives of the American rich, he is unable to resist a gourmand's gobbling of detail.

In *The Magnificent Ambersons,* Booth Tarkington's world is not only re-created but observed with piercing clarity below the surface, and the surface is marvelous. Welles broods with intense enjoyment over the Amberson house, its pretentious staircase leading nowhere, like Amer-

ican hopes; the children's velveteen suits, the cracking whips and mus-
cled horses of a morning ride; the winter outing, with its laughing
crowd perched high, bells tinkling brightly, whirling snow, and hiss of
parted ice.

Even *The Stranger* (1946), a film far better than Welles himself
thinks it is, contains a refined poetry of surfaces, of the beauties of
Americana. The Connecticut store, with its proprietor forever listening
to the radio, the square outside, dominated by a Strasbourg clock, the
complex woods, the boys weaving through glades in a child's game
while a murder is carried out only a few yards away. A microcosm of
American life is disclosed in the setting of a provincial town, violence
and beauty juxtaposed, suburban pleasantries barely hiding a deadly
cruelty.

*The Lady from Shanghai* displays a still more powerful imaginative
force. For the first time, Welles moves from North America, taking in
Acapulco, the coast of South America, and the Caribbean. Of all his
films, I find this one the most ravishing. It is a masterpiece of evocative
imagery, conjuring up as no other film has done the feeling of the tropics,
of the lazy movement of a yacht at sea, of the beauty of marshes and
palms, and of the misty calm of remote ports of call. For its somber, inci-
dental sniping at the rich, the film is essentially a romantic work. In its
most beautiful sequence—when the wife lies on her back on deck, singing, and the two businessmen exchange brutal wisecracks about money
("That's good, Arthur!" "That's good, George!")—Welles' love of
luxury, of relaxation and pleasure, flashes through the bitter social
comment and shows him essentially to be a poet of the flesh.

*Citizen Kane* has often been referred to as the story of a self-made
man. But it is, in fact, the story of a man who has inherited money and
power, whose fortune has come to him as the result of the discovery of
a mine on his parents' poverty-stricken farm. He is haunted by the
memory of the purity of the life of poverty, by the image of the sled
that symbolized that purity, the sled he once symbolically pushed into
the banker, Mr. Thatcher, who told his parents of his inheritance. The
use of this image indicates Welles' fundamental romanticism. He cannot
shake off the myth of the innocence of youth.

Charles Foster Kane is shown as childish, unable to come to terms
with reality. We see the failure of his friendships and his inability to enter
into another psyche or understand the needs of others. Welles and Mankiewicz expose the stupidity of Kane's various colleagues as they severally

*Joseph Cotten, Orson Welles, Everett Sloane,* CITIZEN KANE

describe him as Communist, fascist, and patriot. The fact is that Charles Foster Kane is an opportunist, as selfish as a baby.

The cynism of the film lies in its technique of showing different aspects of Kane's character as related by the various figures in his life. It quickly becomes apparent that most of these people are naïve, rather confused semi-intellectuals whom Kane has used for their negative qualities. Emily Monroe Norton, Kane's first wife, is a pompous bore; his second wife, that "cross section of the American public," is a ninny who ends up a slattern in a nightclub, blaming Kane for launching her on a failed career as an opera star. Jedediah Leland, Kane's dramatic critic, and his editor, Mr. Bernstein, are shown respectively as fuddy-duddy and sycophantic. It would be impossible to name one character in the film whose intelligence and sharpness are outstanding; most are quite inept. The fall of Joseph Cotten's Leland, pathetically trying to cadge a smoke in a hospital, to forget the past ("One of the greatest curses of the

*Orson Welles, Everett Sloane, Joseph Cotten,* CITIZEN KANE

*Orson Welles, Ruth Warwick,* CITIZEN KANE

human race, memory"), is typical. Leland becomes a gentle, unexceptionable but futile victim of Kane's will.

The film's best passages are those in which Welles' and Mankiewicz' own youthful, sardonic personae are exactly matched with that of Kane himself. On Kane's return from his honeymoon with Emily Monroe Norton, a party is thrown for him by the staff of *The Inquirer*. The various editors, subeditors, reporters, and friends are packed solid down the festive table. The air is heavy with lewd jokes and the acrid smoke of cigars. To a brass band overture, a chorus line of girls dances into the room kicking legs high and singing a sycophantic song in Kane's honor. The song has a military (or military college) air, emphasizing the regimented, forced camaraderie of the Kane empire.

No sooner has Welles shown us Kane reveling in his power as husband and newspaper magnate, than we see his marriage to the President's niece beginning to tame and emasculate him. Something vital and youthful is destroyed in him forever. Jedediah Leland's voice on the hospital balcony remembers crustily, "It was a marriage just like any other marriage." [77] There is a brief, tripping Bernard Herrmann gavotte on the soundtrack as we see three subsequent stages of a declining marriage. In the British-style antique dining room of Kane's house, the couple talk animatedly, squabble, and sink into absolute silence, cut off from each other by the unfolded pages of *The Inquirer*.

Inevitably, Kane seeks solace. On his way to the Western Manhattan Warehouse to look at the sled ("I am in search of my youth") and the other symbols of his innocence, he meets a sheet-music salesgirl, Susan (Dorothy Comingore). Susan has been stricken with toothache, and to cheer her up, Kane wiggles his ears, a trick taught him, he says, by "the present President of Venezuela" at the world's best boys' school. Kane exerts a simple charm: "I run a couple of newspapers. What do you do?"

The mounting acceleration of their relationship is expertly charted, from the girl's first nervous comprehension of her compromised position, to the marriage, to Susan's rise and fall as a singer.

While most of the film's first half is dashingly energetic and vital, the second half is—in keeping with Kane's advancing years—slower and more somber. The images are unforgettable: the giant jigsaw puzzle over which Susan meditates, the fireplace, her cluttered room, the mirrored corridor down which Kane's lonely figure walks, repeated to infin-

*Dorothy Comingore, Orson Welles,* CITIZEN KANE

ity. And the stifling garden, hinted at in the picnic scene, a black singer significantly moaning "There Is No Love," ferns clustering, and a quarrel between husband and wife breaking into a storm in the oriental marquee.

If the film's basic mood is anti-American it is also an American masterpiece, in its energy, its opulence, its ambition and drive. It takes in a whole range of types, from the crabbed, loyal Mr. Bernstein to the fat and hysterical Italian singing teacher Matisti; from the El Rancho nightclub in Atlantic City where Susan Alexander has sunk to a drunken entertainer, from the echoing offices of *The Inquirer* where Jedediah Leland makes his career to the silent hospital where he ends his days. Like Balzac, Welles and Mankiewicz take in the world of life, of a society, and only their discipline saves the structure from being blasted apart. Throughout, the electric energy is contained and the genius of these two extraordinary men successfully channeled.

*The Magnificent Ambersons* is on another American theme, the rise of the machine age. Booth Tarkington's novel, originally published in 1918 as part of a trilogy of Middle Western life (and a recipient of the Pulitzer Prize), is a small classic of Americana too seldom read. It gives a fine portrait of the greedy Indianapolis of the past, with its spanking horses, pretty women, and haughty landowners being replaced by the brash and thrusting new machine age. Tarkington, as chronicler of this changing world, observed with ironic affection the complacency of the old order while at the same time neatly demolishing its affectations. As the center of his drama, Tarkington created George Minafer, a young pup whose arrogance and viciousness infuriate everyone until finally, like the quasi-aristocratic age he represents, he gets his "come-uppance," receives injuries in (significantly) an automobile accident, and as a result is "tamed." The horseless carriage has broken the young stallion. George's love affair with Lucy Morgan is neatly counterpointed with her father Eugene's love affair with George's mother. And George's jealousy of Eugene, subtly suggesting the Oedipal relationship between him and his mother, gives further point to the drama.

The last passages in the novel show the Ambersons broken by the machine age. At first driven abroad by the fury of George, his mother and Eugene return and Indianapolis roars to the sound of the Morgan automobile. Along the line, George Minafer's Aunt Fanny provides marginal comments on the impossibility of the horseless carriage taking over the world.

*Dolores Costello, Agnes Moorehead, Anne Baxter, Joseph Cotten, Tim Holt,*
*Ray Collins,* THE MAGNIFICENT AMBERSONS

Few critics have observed how completely Welles preserved the novel
in his film version. The Amberson house and the ball are re-created
down to the last detail, even to the "flowers and plants and roped vines
brought from afar" that filled the big house to suffocation for the occasion.

As Welles' voice reads an adaptation of Tarkington's opening para-
graphs, sketching in the childhood of George Minafer riding around on
his carriage, wielding a whip and frowning under a mop of black curls,
it is clear that this is going to be a "version" rather than, as *Kane* was,
an original work of art. Most of the ideas the film contains, expertly
pointed up in the action as they are, belong by rights to Tarkington.
Brilliant as *The Magnificent Ambersons* is, it remains willed, a construct
rather than a created work.

As the narrator, taking Booth Tarkington's part, talks on with an
amused, lightly cynical detachment, it becomes clear that the irony of
the novel is being replaced by a sentimental romanticism. The novel has
George Amberson Minafer as its central figure, and everything anach-

ronistic and smug about Indianapolis is summed up in him. At first, it looks as though Welles is going to follow the same line, and as George, Tim Holt is fine. He has the ramrod back, the head held haughtily high, the aggressive masculinity barely concealing a vulnerable feminine streak, and the strutting gestures which betray his cruelty and vanity: this is a portrait which precisely embodies Tarkington's character. But unfortunately the emphasis shifts away from George, and the film loses its center. The characters are sketched in with an openhanded affection that works against the book's tone. Joseph Cotten's Eugene, genial and gentlemanly, seems to belong more to the old generation than the one which belongs in the horseless carriage. As a manufacturer of robust tastes with a revolutionary lack of the graces of the past, he is misconceived. Dolores Costello as the mother is too faded, too genteel; she lacks the beauty and force which, in Tarkington's writing, explain her power to attract her son and her automobile manufacturer lover. And old Major Amberson, who founded the great and short-lived Indianapolis fortune of the family, is sentimentalized as richly as a Ford character.

Another mistake, I think, was in throwing the emphasis of the film's main drama onto the rather marginal character of Aunt Fanny. In the novel she is ably used as a symbol of complacency and of resistance to the new order. But Welles builds her up for her own sake, allowing her, through the medium of Agnes Moorehead's accomplished but monotonous performance, to run through a whole gamut of emotions for no reason other than that he finds her hysterical frustrations interesting. The long arguments up and down stairs between Fanny and George and the famous kitchen scene when she sits with her back to the boiler and expresses her virgin's agony are mere cadenzas appended to the action rather than pointing up some essential aspect of it.

*The Magnificent Ambersons* concludes much as the novel did, with George injured in an automobile crash and Eugene Morgan ready to forgive and to accept the rebel into the glorious new age. Peter Cowie in his *The Cinema of Orson Welles* (Zwemmer, London, 1965) complains of the illogicality of George's softening at the end, but Welles has simply allowed Tarkington to dictate the terms of the climax. Where the softening does irritate is in the "family album" treatment of the visual details, as sumptuously nostalgic as in a Minnelli picture. Mr. Cowie describes with admiration the evocation of "quaint customs and habits" in the first reel: the streetcar, the high-top boots, the serenade, and the use of soft focus edging the frame to give the impression of oval photographs faded with time. I would say instead that this display of pictorial sentimentality is exactly what reduces the effect of the scenes in which the past is seen being taken over. Furthermore, the episode in which Welles tries to sum up the end of the carriage age—the ride in the snow which echoes the opening of the childhood scenes in *Kane*—is too warmly observed, too much like an animated series of Christmas cards, to convey the underlying irony, the implicit tragedy of the original.

After a disastrous adventure in Brazil, *It's All True,* Welles in 1946 filmed a screenplay by John Huston and Anthony Veiller, *The Stranger.* It is the story of a war criminal, Franz Kindler—played by Welles himself—who takes refuge in a small Connecticut town. Disguised as a schoolteacher—exactly what he produced in terms of degrees and references is far from clear—he marries the daughter of the local judge and appears to become a pillar of the local society. But a Hound of Heaven pursues him: a government repersentative, played by Edward G. Robinson, who tracks him down and finally brings about his death in a plunge from a clock tower.

*Konstantin Shayne, Edward G. Robinson, Billy House,* THE STRANGER

The film, made to very precise specifications for the producer, S. P. Eagle (later known as Sam Spiegel), is the most disciplined of Welles' works. Its cool, matter-of-fact intelligence probably owes as much to Huston as it does to the director. The measured pace is particularly impressive in scenes where a degree of suspense is called for, the contrast between the comfortable bourgeois complacency of the small-town people and the terrified demon in their midst admirably sustained. The best scene in the picture concerns Welles' sudden outburst of fascist demagogy at a dinner table. Beautifully written and played, it illustrates the character of a fascist with precision, and here Welles' acting is at its most assured.

Whereas *The Stranger* was a disciplined, tightly-knit work, *The Lady from Shanghai* is the result of comparative freedom. It is an abandoned, extravagant creation which shows the director's skill at full length. If *The Stranger* and *Ambersons* gently or genteely show up bourgeois affectations, *The Lady from Shanghai* is a scathing indictment of the whole of American corruption, of middle-class decadence. The character of Elsa Bannister, who contains within her beautifully lacquered shell a heartless cruelty that sums up everything Welles hates in the American female, is played by Rita Hayworth, the sex symbol of the middle-class filmgoer.

All the major and minor characters are in different ways illustrations of aspects of the American character; in fact, the film is Shakespearean in the complexity of its response to society. Elsa, as I have said, is the heartlessly corrupt (and fake) sex symbol that beams down from the billboards along the endless American highways and that glittered from the Hollywood press advertisements of the Forties. Her husband, Arthur Bannister, "the most famous criminal lawyer in America," is the American male destroyed by his mate. Professionally successful and unscrupulous, rich, widely known, on nodding terms with the greatest, but physically and spiritually a ruin, dragging himself along on two knotted canes which seem extensions of his ravaged body and soul. Only money has saved him from a lifetime flat on his back in a hospital; only money has won and kept Elsa, who now wants to destroy him for his money. The fact that he is impotent is piercingly suggested in the film's famous trial scene. Here the prosecuting attorney says to Elsa, "You have no children," and a shamed, bitter glance passes from Arthur to her and back again. In the film's conclusion, Bannister, who has escaped his wife's attempt to murder him, dies together with her in a hail of bullets.

Bannister's partner, Grisby, is the American hick incarnate. Vicious but naïve, sweating constantly, giggling and inept, he is the fall guy whom Elsa uses to assist in murdering her husband, then plans to dispose of. His involved and absurd scheme for organizing his disappearance with Elsa inevitably results in his death (from another hand, as it happens). Michael O'Hara, the Irish sailor who stumbles into this nest of vipers, is another variety of American hick, sympathetically observed this time. Tough and cynical on the surface, "a notorious waterfront agitator," he is fundamentally innocent, and is used with ease by Grisby and Elsa as the fall guy in their murder plan. But at the end he walks out of the place where Elsa and Arthur Bannister have died, and he experiences the taste of a San Francisco morning. For the simple and decent ones of the world, Welles is telling us, there is always a chance of renewal, of a rediscovery of childhood happiness.

Welles' attitude to the minor characters is affectionately cruel. The judge who presides at the trial is a feeble-minded, fussy old man who plays chess with himself, hums when alone, and is completely unable to control what is going on in his own courtroom. The officers of the law are handsome, well-built boobies. The jury is made up of scuffling, sneezing, giggling petty businessmen and housewives. The crew on the Bannisters' yacht and the sailors glimpsed in the New York hiring hall are cheerful clowns, randy and self-conscious. The range of faces in the film is astonishing, and no other film of Welles' has explored his own country with such precision—and with such ruthlessness. The final image of Michael walking free across a wharf wet with rain is a superb evocation of the release, the joy of the innocent American whose life is lived physically. Against the brilliantly malign performances of Everett Sloane as Bannister and Glenn Anders as Grisby, Welles himself plays Michael with a deeply moving humor and simplicity.

The opening scene of the film is staged in Central Park, where Elsa Bannister is riding alone in an open-air, horse-drawn carriage. A gang of toughs grabs her and pulls her into the neighboring bushes in an attempt to rape her, but O'Hara rescues her, and they continue on the nocturnal journey. She, with hair and face steely, settles back against the intense blackness of the carriage hood, talking of her past in China (she was born in Chifu), her eyes suggesting a lifetime of high-class prostitution and compromise. O'Hara is more whimsical, talking about his own journeys ("The nicest jails are in Australia"). Beautifully unacademic cutting and the elliptical nature of the conversation convey the couple's growing mutual attraction. Later Elsa asks her husband to have Michael engaged as a hired hand for a New York to San Francisco yacht cruise.

The husband's entrance into the sailors' hiring hall to sign up Michael is cruelly observed. A shot slightly above eye level shows him crawling like a broken spider, eyes tormented under their freckled hoods, cheeks freckled and spotted with perspiration like the skin of a fungus. His misery is contrasted with the jaunty, empty-headed sailors and the cheerful American symbol of the jukebox. The brilliantly used set conveys heat, boredom, an underlying animal vitality as the seamen gather round and watch the warped phenomenon in their midst.

Arriving at the yacht, Elsa's pet dachshund yapping and circling, O'Hara gradually learns that he is being drawn into a maelstrom of evil. Elsa uses rather obvious sexual innuendoes to show Michael her true feelings: "I've learned to smoke now. Ever since that night in the park, I've been getting the habit." Cleverly she appeals to his masculinity by making him feel that she is sexually neglected (whereas in fact she is as sexually lifeless as her husband), and her feelings as conveyed to him are ironically contrasted with a radio hair-oil commercial and its flavor of knowing lewdness, their conversation deliberately pointless and cryptic following it:

O'HARA:     Love. Do you believe in love at all, Mrs. Bannister?
ELSA:        I was taught to think about love in Chinese. It is difficult for love to last long. Therefore, one who loves passionately is cured of love, in the end.

Here Welles is having a joke at the expense of the audience: the few who would at once listen to the dialogue and seek out literary references would probably take it that Elsa's proverb came from Confucius, that she had intellectual or semi-intellectual interests, whereas in fact the quotation comes from that very American best seller, *The Wisdom of China,* by Lin Yutang!

The picnic party that follows is a brilliantly achieved set piece. The occasion is introduced by a laconic soundtrack comment by O'Hara: "It was no more a picnic than Bannister was a man." Down the river the little party punts, sweating and strained, as alligators slither into the water and flamingos flash through the liana roots. As torches spread out across an inlet, men wade through black water, and "Baia" echoes from far away. Bannister, Grisby, and Elsa swing in hammocks, exchanging sharp remarks. There is a hint in the story that Elsa somehow blackmailed Bannister into marrying her. Michael wanders along the beach and sees the unhappy rich in their Scott Fitzgerald traps. Sadistically (and rather stuffily) he tells them the story of the fight of a pack of sharks off the coast of Brazil: one had torn itself from a fisherman's hook, and the smell of blood attracted the others ("until all about the water was made of sharks . . . and more sharks . . . and the water torn"). At the end, he says, "I never saw anything worse, until this little party tonight . . ." And as Michael walks off with a moral tag on his lips, Arthur Bannister says, "George, that's the first time anyone thought enough of you to call you a shark."

From the unnamed picnic site, the scene changes to Acapulco, a location which gives Michael/Welles a chance to comment on Mexican and Western society: "There's a fair face to the land, but you can't hide the hunger and the guilt." A moment later a gigolo off-screen says to his female companion, "Darling, *of course* you pay me!" Along the precipitous cliffs above the bay, Michael and Grisby walk together, Grisby sweating and pouting and giggling, his body looming over the brilliant harbor below as he makes Michael a proposition. He asks him

*Orson Welles, Rita Hayworth,* THE LADY FROM SHANGHAI

to fake a murder: for $5,000 Michael is to pretend to murder him. Grisby will, he says, escape to an island beyond the reach of atom bombs, and since there is no body, Michael will not pay the death penalty.

Michael accepts the offer, confirming this on arrival in Sausalito. Elsa's Chinese servant tells Michael she will meet him in the local aquarium. Against the monstrous gaping of a groper fish, Elsa reads the fake confession. As her soft voice runs through it, the huge shadowy shapes beyond the glass are contrasted with her beautiful face, but they symbolize her true nature. A crowd of school children stumble on the lovers, and a schoolteacher tries to get a spinster's quick look at passion before she is dragged away, protesting, by her companion.

The faked murder is no less strikingly staged. We see blood smeared on the car windshield, hear a shot fired, and watch Grisby disappearing below a pier in a speedboat, as a crowd of people, led by a fat cafe proprietor, rush out of their shops to have a look.

The trial of Michael for murder is brilliantly staged. The scene opens with Michael's sailor friend helping Elsa Bannister to a seat. The old spinster in the aquarium is back, jumping up to stare at Elsa. Arthur Bannister is drawing laughs with a typical crack: "I object! The question calls for the operation of the officer's mind!" A moment later he discredits the prosecution's witness, Officer Peters, by proving that the prosecuting attorney's concern is faked, since Officer Peters has no wife and family.

It soon becomes clear that Bannister is deliberately going to lose the case for Michael, his client. Bannister cross-examines himself, damaging his own case by simply reasserting Michael's virtues. No single charge against the prisoner is avowed; inevitably, the case collapses. Elsa suggests to Michael that he should take an overdose of her husband's pain-killing pills, after Bannister says, "This is one case I've enjoyed losing . . . I'm going to come and see you in the death house, Michael. I'm going to ask for a stay of execution. I hope it will be granted. I want you to live as long as possible before you die."

Michael pretends to swallow the pills, setting off a riot during which he escapes from the courtroom just before the verdict is announced. Michael finds Elsa in a downtown Chinese theater, the actors' eyes darting in ratlike fear through their heavy makeup, the soundtrack ticking and scraping with the musical accompaniment.

The final scenes show Michael waking up in a fun fair crazy house after he has been kidnapped by Elsa's servants. Whirling down slides and through gaping papier-mâché mouths, Michael winds up in a hall of mirrors. There he meets Elsa; Bannister arrives, hobbling through the layers and layers of deceiving glass panes. Elsa shoots him down, and he kills her. Michael adds a brief homily before leaving her to utter a final, sentimental farewell ("Give my love to the sunrise!"). The harsh rattle of the exit gate terminates the relationship. As the camera swings up to take in Michael's last walk across the pier, he says, "Everybody is somebody's fool. The only way to stay out of trouble is to grow old. So I guess I'll concentrate on that. Maybe I'll live so long that I'll forget her. Maybe I'll die, trying."

This surrealist work has many baroque pleasures, and survives untouched by time.

*Macbeth* (1947) had some striking set pieces—the appearance of the white-haired, whirling witches emerging from the icy mists; Banquo's apparition, a blood-dappled corpse animated by an infernal passion for revenge; the advance of the human forest, which brings an authentic chill of terror. Welles' idea of stripping away the usual classy trappings from the play, of showing it as a story of murder and usurpation in a

*Alan Napier, Orson Welles,* MACBETH

barbaric and unlettered world, was a clever one: but Shakespeare's rhet-
oric defeats him, at all times bringing the tone back to the aristocratic
when Welles is striving for a flavor of plebeian viciousness.

Like *The Lady from Shanghai, Touch of Evil* is drawn from a routine
thriller and translated into a powerful moral drama. It, too, is an exploration of a world ruled by corruption and fear. This time the moral
protagonist, representing Welles' attitude, is not portrayed as a simple
and direct representative of the laboring classes, but as a forceful investigator, representing the Pan American Narcotics Commission, Vargas
(Charlton Heston). Vargas and his wife (Janet Leigh) arrive at a
small town, Los Robles, on the border of Mexico and the United
States. Immediately, they are plunged into an orgy of violence.

With a threatening chord on the brass, a couple—local tycoon Rudi
Linnekar and his blond floozie—swing laughing down a colonnade and
get into a car and drive off. Suddenly the Linnekar car explodes. The
whole sequence is shot in less than three minutes of screen time, in a
single take from a crane: the dirty town, the black night, the sense of
heat and tension and crowds swarming, all brought to life in complex
detail. There follows a typically black exchange: "An hour ago, Rudi
Linnekar had this town in his pocket. Now you could strain him through
a sieve." The DA hurries out of a euphemistically named "Tootsie's
Steakhouse" to the murder scene; Vargas coldly remarks of his presence
there: "I'm merely what the United Nations would call an observer."
It turns out that the murder has been committed by a disgruntled shoe
clerk who has murdered Linnekar because the tycoon has tried to prevent his marriage to Linnekar's daughter. The local police chief, Hank
Quinlan (Welles) sets out to track the clerk down. A second chase
parallels the first. Joe Grandi, local nightclub owner and dope peddler,
seeks to destroy Vargas, who has caught his brother on a narcotics
charge. The climax is reached when both hunters and their quests end
in death.

Immediately after Linnekar's murder, the film explodes into kaleido-
scopic images of walls covered in tattered posters, streets full of whirling
newspapers, a brothel full of swaying bead curtains and the relentless
grinding of a pianola. Mrs. Vargas, pursued by Grandi's sons and their
lesbian leader (Mercedes McCambridge), makes her way to a motel
in a dusty plain presided over by a neurotic manager afraid to pronounce
the word "bed." Exhausted and irritable, Mrs. Vargas tries to settle
down in one of the motel *cabañas,* but she is tormented by the sound

of a rock 'n' roll radio band from the adjoining *cabaña*. Finally, the Grandi boys break in, rape her, and pump her full of drugs in an attempt to blacken the drug investigator's reputation.

Meanwhile, in Los Robles, Quinlan conducts an interrogation of the murderer, Sanchez, breaking off the grilling to complain about not getting "doughnuts, sweet rolls." Quinlan makes a savagely graphic comment on the killing: "Last night an old lady on Main Street picked up a shoe. The shoe had a foot in it." He thinks that the only way he can trap the quarry is to frame him, so he plants sticks of dynamite in the boy's bathroom. Later, we find that Quinlan's relentless pursuit of Sanchez (who is part Indian) stems from an experience before World War I: his wife was killed by a half-breed, whom he never caught up with and who died in the trenches in Belgium ("The good Lord did the job for me"). At the end of the film, Quinlan murders Grandi, who he fears will implicate him in various scandals, and Vargas at once overhears and records Quinlan's final confession of guilt on a transistor radio/tape machine.

Despite its many brilliant passages—more technically assured, more aesthetically achieved than any since *Kane—Touch of Evil* suffers from an ambivalent attitude to the material. The central flaw lies in the character of Hank Quinlan. He is clearly intended to be a living illustration of a moral point: that the end does not justify the means, that the fact that he successfully performs his duty as a law enforcer, trapping the killer of Linnekar, does not excuse his deliberate planting of the dynamite in the murderer's bathroom. Nor does the fact that he is haunted by the murder of his half-breed wife, that he is still bent on vengeance against the unlawful, mitigate his behavior. His badge is, in fact, a badge of evil; he is as guilty as his quarry, and at the end, when he sinks into the oil sump under brooding towers against the night sky, he is as much a crushed monster as Arthur Bannister.

Quinlan is evil destroying evil and being destroyed himself: but here an ambivalence in the writing and playing dangerously weakens his forcefulness as a central presence. For one thing, Welles has miscast himself in the role. His neutral warmth, humanity, and irresistible personal charm break through the thick makeup, the padded grossness of the body, the obscene and ugly gestures. And in the writing, Welles has not been able to resist (as he so brilliantly did in *The Lady from Shanghai*) the temptation to make Quinlan "human"—or, to be more exact, sentimental. His floozie, the fortuneteller-cum-brothel keeper played by Marlene Dietrich, evidently loves him for his kindness of heart; at the end, when he dies, she provides a final comment which could, if one took it at face value, destroy Welles' whole central argument at a blow: "He was some kind of a man" (i.e. he may have been monstrously cruel, but he was involved in humanity, he *was* humanity, and that makes him lovable at the last). Perhaps we should give Welles the benefit of the doubt and call this her sentimentality, not his.

In one scene, when Quinlan is displaying his soul at its most vicious, he notices a nest of pigeon eggs on a window sill and gently fondles them. The comment implicit in this again betrays a definite sentimentality, even if the Dietrich observation only possibly does. It is as though, while swaying in his picnic hammock, Arthur Bannister were to have broken off some heartless observation to pat a peon's child on the head.

Another weakness of the film is that it contains too many "turns" or caricatures, which, instead of occurring as satirical illustrations of various aspects of American society, are introduced for their own sake. Too often the action degenerates into a macabre fancy dress party for Hollywood notables, and this has the effect of lowering the film's whole tone and seriousness. The business of spotting celebrities—including such unlikely occupants of a Mexican border town as Zsa Zsa Gabor, Joseph Cotten, and Miss Dietrich—may provide a "fun" game for the film buffs in the audience, but it almost fatally distracts one's attention from the film's main purport.

Since *Touch of Evil*, Welles has made two new American films, *The Other Side of the Wind* (1972), a sophisticated story about a director of the Hathaway breed who returns to Hollywood after a long sojourn abroad and discovers the changes there, and *Hoax* (1972), a study of Clifford Irving. Those who have seen them hold high hopes for their success. He has also worked extensively in Europe, making such films as *M. Arkadin* (1955), *The Trial* (1962), *Chimes at Midnight* (1965), and *The Immortal Story* (1968).

■ ■ ■ ■ ■ ■ ■ ■ ■ ■ ■ ■ ■ ■ ■ ■ ■ ■ ■ ■ ■ ■ ■ ■ ■ ■

# 3. Hitchcock's World

■ ■ ■ ■ ■ ■ ■ ■ ■ ■ ■ ■ ■ ■ ■ ■ ■ ■ ■ ■ ■ ■ ■ ■ ■

Aside from Orson Welles, Hitchcock was the most important director
to rise to prominence in the American cinema in the 1940s. Though
not quite the genius that Welles was, he had a brilliant command of
technique and an unerring sense of box office which put him ahead öf
the field. Unlike Welles, he was never a private artist; in fact he delighted in exploiting his own personality in public, made personal appearances in his films, and later introduced his own TV series with
macabre/funny remarks.

"Le cinéma, ce n'est pas une tranche de vie, mais une tranche de
gâteau . . ." ("Cinema is not a slice of life, but a slice of cake . . .")
This comment of Hitchcock's, from a conversation with Jean Domarchi
and Jean Douchet (*Cahiers du Cinéma,* December 1959), crystallizes
the director's attitude to the medium in which he has worked for almost
forty years. At heart, he has remained a practical joker, a witty and
sophisticated cynic amused at the French critical vogue for his work,
contemptuous of the audience, which he treats as the collective victim
of a Pavlovian experiment, perennially fascinated by his own ability to
exploit the cinema's resources.

The mechanics of creating terror and amusement in an audience are
what Hitchcock properly understands. The portrayal of physical or intellectual passion is beyond him, and he has never directed a sexual
encounter with the slightest apparent interest. He either exploits his
performers or mocks them, or both—certain mannerisms are seized on

and used merely to create a reliable response in the spectator. Occasional efforts to extend his range, to probe below the surface of a theme, have failed.

Hitchcock's much discussed and brilliant ability to use the revelatory personal gestures of a character is most strikingly displayed when he has a destructive comment to make. For example, in *Rebecca* (1940), the predatory American tourist squashes her cigarette in a jar of cold cream; in *To Catch a Thief* (1955) a similar lady thrusts her stub into the gleaming yellow eye of a fried egg; in *The Paradine Case* (1947) the English judge Lord Horfield's lecherous gaze pounces on a seated woman's shoulder. Conversely, when the script is saying something quasi-serious, the director withdraws with a yawn: Walter Slezak in *Lifeboat* (1943), James Stewart in *Rope* (1948), Joel McCrea in *Foreign Correspondent* (1940) can, respectively, utter their fascist, anti-Nietzsche, or patriotic speeches if they like, but Hitchcock is waiting to juggle the next lens.

Some critics have denounced Hitchcock as a sadist doing moral damage to his audience. His defenders feel that such criticism is merely puritanical and purse-lipped, that his films are simply there to be enjoyed, guiltily or not according to the state of one's psyche. Supremely detached, Hitchcock, of course, remains genially amused by this controversy and above it.

He remains at heart a cheerful London showman, with a tough contempt for the world he has made his oyster. Discussion of metaphysics in his work seems to me misguided, especially so in the various articles published in *Cahiers du Cinéma*. His own answers to the questions put to him in the *entretiens* which have appeared in that magazine should clarify for the doubtful his amusement at the earnest French inquirers. He has simply taken the most dynamic popular art form of the twentieth century, toyed with it superbly, and dared to explode some of the central myths it has established.

Where he has been most skillful of all is in his grasp of what can move the masses without fail. His mockery of human susceptibility springs from a belief in the essential absurdity of those susceptibilities. It is not a gentle mockery. We know, for instance, the response that the sight of a child or dog in danger can evoke even in the most brutally sophisticated people. No one save Hitchcock would dare to turn this natural responsiveness to his own advantage. In *Sabotage* (1936) the boy Steve Verloc carries a can of film, neatly wrapped by his sister

Sylvia, from the flat above the cinema where he lives into a bus headed for Piccadilly Circus. The tension is achieved, predictably, by keeping the audience guessing about the exact moment a bomb contained in the can will go off. Any competent director could have managed this. But Hitchcock was afraid that the boy's danger alone might not be enough to disturb the audience. So he gave the old lady sitting next to him a puppy to play with, concentrating on its gambolings until the exact moment of the explosion. The introduction of the puppy constitutes the Hitchcock touch.

In *Secret Agent* (1935) Hitchcock shows a dog frantically barking in a closed room as its master goes to his death on a mountainside miles away. Here again, the effect is exactly calculated, the audience's reflexes understood. In recent years, now that audiences have grown more cynical themselves, he has been able to exploit more cruel impulses. In *Psycho* (1960) the plunging of a knife blade into a woman's nude body in a shower is deliberately made to represent the thrustings of the sexual act, so as to unleash the repressed libidinous sadism of large numbers of spectators. Hitchcock's mastery of the medium is never more sharply expressed than in those sequences where he wants to make us release our repressions vicariously—as he has released his cinematically.

The skill with which he has engineered the mechanism of his films has varied sharply from work to work, but in those films dominated by morbidity, physical disgust, and terror his gifts have usually been in striking display. *Foreign Correspondent* (1940), *Rope* (1948), *Strangers on a Train* (1951), and *Vertigo* (1958) remain, in my view, his finest achievements in the medium. They succeed brilliantly as cinema, and they show that they are conceived, executed, and embellished by a dazzlingly clever mind.

Over the years, Hitchcock has gradually developed his technique of designing the production in advance, blueprinting each scene so that it is, in effect, edited before it is shot. Three of his productions were worked on in great detail by the designer Saul Bass, whose mocking brilliance seems exactly to fit with Hitchcock's own. This method of pre-planning the entire production means that the actors simply serve as pawns in a game played with—or against—the audience. This is very well when they have to be nothing more than acceptable props, but when they are called upon to express passion or terror the effect is mechanical. The love scenes Hitchcock so elaborately shoots, usually set in "high life" for the hicks to goggle at, are invariably sexless, antiseptic, and cold. For example, the often-mentioned earlobe feast in *Notorious* (1946) with Cary Grant and Ingrid Bergman necking against a cynically clumsy backdrop of Rio de Janeiro; in *Vertigo,* the flaccid grapplings of James Stewart and Kim Novak, mounted, we are told, on a revolving platform; the dull affair of Wilding and Bergman in *Under Capricorn* (1949)—all show an interest merely in camera manipulation. He is more at home with people who show no visible evidence of sexuality at all, notably an array of dead, middle-aged Englishmen and Americans who come on and off the chalk line in successive films to commit murders or shudder obediently in moments of disaster. And the perverted also fascinate him. One recalls the lesbian housekeeper Mrs. Danvers in *Rebecca,* caressing the transparent night-dresses of her dead mistress, and a succession of homosexuals, ranging from Peter Lorre's tittering assassin in *The Man Who Knew Too Much* (1934) to Leonard, the obedient and clinging secretary of *North by Northwest*'s (1959) smooth mastermind.

The numb hero and heroine, the sexless but useful character players, and the parade of sexually twisted oddballs in Hitchcock's films are, more often than not, engaged in a chase, and it is in the chase that he has found his central dynamic. To ensure universality, he has seized on monuments everyone can recognize and set his characters in motion across them—the British Museum, the Statue of Liberty, Gutzon Borglum's sculptured heads of the presidents on Mount Rushmore. The combination of *National Geographic Magazine* and *True Detective* audience appeal is beautifully managed.

Sometimes, of course, the chase runs below the surface of the work, rather than physically disclosing itself in the action. In *Vertigo,* for instance, and in *The Paradine Case,* it is the search for the true identity of a mysterious woman. Sometimes the chase is the director's own, such as an attempt to discover the way people die, or the way they react to danger. The observation, the degree of understanding, is adolescent, but the chasing after facts about modes of behavior is adult, similar to a novelist's insatiable curiosity.

What makes Hitchcock especially fascinating is that, by dealing with the studio bosses on the terms they understand, making money for them, he has now reached a point of freedom usually possessed only by those working outside the commercial cinema. *Psycho,* for instance, is a very free film indeed, not merely a commercial exploitation of a theme, but a personal work of genuine if unpleasant self-expression.

The obvious analogy is with the films of Kenneth Anger, which express without restraint the homosexual vision of life and death. In Hollywood this degree of freedom has been accorded to few, and usually only to those whose rather sickly brand of humanism has corresponded with that assumed cynically by the director's employers.

In the British films Hitchcock made during the silent period, there is an obvious impatience with the tired Shaftesbury Avenue conventions of the time. "Love" scenes are done with bored contempt; matinee idols and limp British leading ladies, cast in the film because of studio requirements, are barely directed at all. The scripts (mostly written by Eliot Stannard or Hitchcock himself) seem merely to provide opportunities for camera display. Hitchcock established a style by adapting the German technique of releasing the camera in the action, using heavily shadowed photography for melodramatic scenes, heightening the key for love scenes or comedy. Although his films of the British period have been praised for realism, they are in fact highly stylized, almost abstract in design, while the playing throughout is deliberately theatrical. Hitchcock takes his camera into seedy rooms, alleys, grubby theaters, but never attempts to make these places look like the real thing. Rather, he makes over a highly artificial and impressionist version of London or the English countryside into his own dream image, as, during the sound period, he was to do with many countries from Switzerland to Australia.

Hitchcock's American debut was remarkably confident. For David O. Selznick, he made *Rebecca* (1940), based by Robert Sherwood and others on the best-selling novel by Daphne du Maurier. Characteristically, in his first treatment for the film written with Joan Harrison, Hitchcock added touches of comedy at the expense of the characters: the hero is a victim of seasickness, the heroine has a comic game of golf. Wisely, Selznick had him return to the brilliantly worked-out structure of the novel, a marvelous example of popular fiction at its best. The result is not so much a Hitchcock work as a Selznick-du Maurier one, but the director has never made a more polished film.

The story, of course, is pure hokum: the lonely anonymous girl played by Joan Fontaine, trapped in companionship with a vulgar American tourist (Florence Bates), meets an ineffably romantic landowner named Maximilian de Winter, marries him, and, at his ancestral estate, experiences the constant unseen presence of Maximilian's dead wife Rebecca. It is a ghost story without a ghost; and Hitchcock's direction has an appropriate subtle eeriness, a sense of everything being slightly off-balance, which works to perfection. The camerawork of George Barnes has an intricate beauty, particularly in the very few sepiatone prints which were made. The playing is beyond praise: Laurence Olivier's odd, tight-lipped, haunted Max; Joan Fontaine's shy, inexpert wife; Judith Anderson's icy housekeeper Mrs. Danvers; George Sanders' odious Jack Favell; the small-part acting of Nigel Bruce, Gladys Cooper, and Leo G. Carroll are all perfectly woven into an immaculate if artificial whole.

For the producer Walter Wanger, Hitchcock later made *Foreign Correspondent* (1940), a picaresque romantic thriller set in Britain and Holland and on a clipper crossing the Atlantic. Humphrey Haverstock (Joel McCrea) is a hard-bitten reporter who discovers that his girl friend's father, a smooth and gracious English diplomat played by Herbert Marshall, is in fact the head of a subversive Nazi spy ring in London. With weary charm, the diplomat arranges for the kidnapping of a prominent political figure, uses a windmill as a guide for enemy planes, and prepares the destruction of McCrea at the hands of successive professional killers. Brilliantly designed by William Cameron Menzies, the film manages to create a totally convincing European ambience, though it was made entirely in Hollywood. A somewhat rambling narrative is interrupted by effective set pieces, showing the director at his best. These include the shooting of a diplomat's double in the Amsterdam rain, the gun concealed in a camera, the victim's face splashed with blood, umbrellas bobbing across a square; the sequence in the windmill, brilliantly utilizing the creaking of the sails, the spies talking in German, the machinery groaning on rusty hinges; and above all the clipper crash in the last reel, shot from inside the plane, a masterpiece of screen editing, sound recording, and physical reconstruction.

Again in *Suspicion* (1941) and *Saboteur* (1942) Hitchcock seized on features of setting which audiences could instantly grasp: the fox hunting and china teacups of England, the Statue of Liberty to which a man clings before plunging to his death. *Shadow of a Doubt* (1943) more subtly concerned a typical American symbol: the sunny little town which conceals deadly ambitions. Charlie Oakley (Joseph Cotten) is an aging gigolo who murderes rich widows, his psychosis hidden behind a blandly avuncular front. His family, naïve and concerned with everyday trivia, is oblivious of the evil in its midst. Hitchcock, like Welles in *The Stranger,* makes clear that most people live in cheerful ignorance, unaware of the sinister until it thrusts itself in their faces.

*Alfred Hitchcock*
directing a scene from
SHADOW OF A DOUBT

*Courtesy
of Universal
Pictures.*

*Courtesy of Universal Pictures.*

*Joseph Cotten, Patricia Collinge, Teresa Wright,* SHADOW OF A DOUBT

*Spellbound* (1945) dealt with the problems of psychosis in a superficial fashion, though the recurrent imagery of a man's psychosis—dark lines on a white tablecloth matched to the memory of ski marks in snow; the swirled soap-laden hairs of a shaving brush—makes a strong effect. The film is worth remembering also for Salvador Dali's brilliantly designed dream sequence, in which hangings filled with eyes, a conical roof where a faceless man waits, and a menacing card game achieve a surrealist purpose far beyond the film's general range. *Notorious* (1946) is a commonplace story of spies in Rio. It is raised above the average only by the performances of two important stage actors, Claude Rains and the great star of Reinhardt's *Sumurun,* Leopoldine Konstantin. *The Paradine Case* (1947) is more complex and intriguing. Taken from Robert Hichens' novel by its producer David O. Selznick, it is the story of Maddalena Paradine, who has killed her wealthy husband with the aid of his devoted valet and stands trial at the Old Bailey. Lee Garmes' camera movements are among the most fluent ever seen: for example, the sinuous spiral around Mrs. Paradine as she prepares for the police is a lesson in the functional use of imagery. This recurrent circling movement accompanies Mrs. Paradine everywhere, emphasizing the reptilian character behind the flawless Madonna mask. There are imaginative effects throughout: a snatch of the ballad "Annie Laurie" sung by a woman prisoner echoing through the jail when the visitors for Mrs. Paradine arrive; the jagged camera movements accompanying a confrontation in an inn; the enormous slow dolly shot around the dock as the valet leaves the court, Mrs. Paradine's face seemingly stretched in longing, her ears straining for the last of his footfalls. Hitchcock has seldom equaled this dramatic use of cinematography to convey the depth of an emotion.

*Rope* (1948) is for some reason critically *un film maudit,* perhaps because of its abandoning of editing in the use of reel-long takes. Yet the sharply directed playing of the cast, the impeccably disciplined camerawork on one set, and the sustained mood of tension and terror underlying the conventions of a New York bachelor's late afternoon party all show the director at his best. The story, based on the Leopold-Loeb case, has two homosexuals, Brandon (John Dall) and Philip (Farley Granger), murdering a friend, David Kentley (Dick Hogan), and hiding him in the living room chest from which they serve dinner to his sometime girl friend (Joan Chandler) and parents. There is a slight loosening-up of the film's taut structure toward the end, when the publisher Rupert Cadell, overplayed by James Stewart, decides to expose the killers after discovering what they have done, but until the final reel the film has admirable sharpness, precision, and delicacy. The situation evidently appealed strongly to Hitchcock, with his passion for irony, and assisted by Arthur Laurents' sophisticated script, he extracts the utmost from it. The color photography (Joseph Valentine and William Skall) and the use of a process screen which charts the changing light from late afternoon to darkness are admirable, and the players, especially Sir Cedric Hardwicke and Constance Collier as the dead boy's father and aunt, act with intelligence and style.

By 1948 it was clear that Hitchcock had matured enormously as a craftsman, and that he had far more interest in details of performances than in the Thirties, where his actors (with odd exceptions like Peter Lorre and Mary Clare) were indifferent. His pace and handling of editing had changed, and his films had grown more deliberate, more subtle. In England and America his critical reputation had reached a low point. Most reviewers were nostalgic for *The Lady Vanishes* (1938) and *The Thirty-Nine Steps* (1935), which were actually much inferior to *The Paradine Case* and *Rope* (though it is still sacrilege to say so), and did not like the "new" Hitchcock with his elaborate technical effects and eschewing of rapid editing. I think, looking back on the reviews of that period, that they were wrong, but unfortunately Hitchcock added fuel to their fire with almost all the films of the next few years, which suffered from slowness and deadness to a remarkable degree.

Few films of a major director can have been worse than *Under Capricorn* (1949), or *Stage Fright* (1950), or *I Confess* (1953). Of his films of the 1950s, one passes over the long list of indifferent works —*To Catch a Thief* (1955), *The Trouble with Harry* (1955), *The Wrong Man* (1957), the remake of *The Man Who Knew Too Much* (1956)—all of which showed Hitchcock's worst faults, archness, facetiousness, hollowness of content, at their most galling. *Dial M for Murder* (1954) was conventional, and so was *Rear Window* (1954), despite an undercurrent of voyeurism. The remaining films of the period, *Strangers on a Train, Vertigo,* and *North by Northwest,* deserve more serious and detailed analysis.

*Strangers on a Train* (1951) seems in retrospect like an oasis in the desert of Hitchcock's worst period in the sound era, closer in its sophistication and ingenuity and (except intermittently) rather slow pace to the films of the very late 1950s than to those of 1950 and 1952. Like

*Rope,* it deals with homosexuality, but in a far more flippant way. Bruno (Robert Walker), the simpering, girlish villain of the piece, is second cousin to the characters played by Peter Lorre in the films of the 1930s. The film opens with a famous sequence shot from ankle level of two pairs of feet carrying their owners through a railroad station, onto a train, and into a saloon car, when they meet for the first time. The different walks—one brisk and athletic, the other loose and effeminate —are beautifully distinguished. Bruno makes a big play for Guy Haines, a tennis champion (Farley Granger), on the train journey between Washington and New York. Flattering, cajoling, and batting his eyes, he suggests with a giggle that they exchange murders: Bruno is to kill Guy's rejected and spiteful wife in return for Guy's murdering Bruno's father. Since neither will have a motive for the executions they perform, neither will be apprehended by the police.

The rest of the film shows Bruno's murdering Mrs. Haines after Guy scornfully rejects the arrangement, Bruno's desperate journey to the fairground island where he has killed her to plant Guy's cigarette lighter at the scene of the crime, and a final showdown on a carousel that has gone wildly out of control. Aside from some feeble sequences involving Guy and his girl friend (Ruth Roman, whose performance is a decided liability) the film is one of the most sophisticated Hitchcock has made: a dazzle of cynical observation, ruthlessly cruel exposition of character, and glittering visual glamour.

The textbook sequences—the tennis match intercut with Bruno's journey to the murder scene; the murder itself, reflected in the dying girl's glasses—are deservedly renowned, but perhaps rather conventional. Where the film succeeds most strikingly is in the treatment of silly, predatory, middle-aged women, who seem to hold a special fascination for Hitchcock. Marion Lorne's performance as Bruno's mother—painting an inane daub, giggling and obsessive—is matched by that of Norma Varden as a monstrously infatuated partygoer, almost strangled by Bruno in a moment of accidentally induced rage (a bespectacled girl, played by Patricia Hitchcock, reminds him of his former victim). Robert Walker daringly plays Bruno, and there is an unforgettable display of nerves, nastiness, and edgy sensuality by Laura Elliott as the ill-fated Mrs. Haines.

*Vertigo* (1958) has been unmercifully treated in the English-speaking world, its peculiar dreamlike pace and deliberate air of surreality completely wasted on the majority of critics. Carefully examined, it shows a complete and exciting departure for the director, and the complex visual texture, owing much to Saul Bass (more than 780 separate shots were drawn up in advance), deserves full-scale examination on its own. The story of *Vertigo* involves a detective, Scottie Ferguson (James Stewart), in a search for the vanished wife of a friend, Gavin Elster (Tom Helmore). He finds her, only to see her plunge to her death from the bell tower of an old Spanish mission. Soon after, Ferguson meets another girl with an odd resemblance to the dead Madeleine, and the script springs its surprises from that moment on.

What Hitchcock manages is a total suspension of disbelief in the impossible goings-on before one's eyes. If one surrenders to the film, it invades one's consciousness with rules of its own. This is one of those films (Charles Vidor's *Gilda* is another) that completely create a decadent, artificial world unrelated in any way to the real one. It has taken the French, not bound by the American requirement of verisimilitude, to see that the unreality of *Vertigo,* its free play with time and space, makes it a genuinely experimental film. It opens with a dream in which Scottie is clinging in terror to a gutter. His fear of heights, and the subsequent vertigo from which the film's drama springs, is conveyed with dazzling skill. The whole of the pursuit of the apparently resuscitated girl, across a graveyard, into an art museum, through a redwood forest, is shot with a marvelous and deliberately sustained air of fantasy.

*North by Northwest* (1959) is by comparison a lightweight, but (though not nearly as well made as *Vertigo*) at times it is brilliantly directed. The set pieces—Cary Grant being machine-gunned by a crop-dusting plane, the last frantic scramble over the Mount Rushmore stone heads—are enjoyable, but the film's greatest success is with the playing of the cast. James Mason's master criminal, Eva Marie Saint's ambiguous heroine desperately switching sides, and Cary Grant's smooth advertising man may be conceived on a comic-strip level, but they are played with splendid sophistication and brio. The mocking, cynical script of Ernest Lehman, Robert Burks' photography, and above all the pounding score of Bernard Herrmann admirably serve Hitchcock's requirements.

In recent years, Hitchcock's films have shown an increasing boredom with the laborious process of film-making, while he himself has grown more mellow, more genial. The shocker *Psycho* (1960), made in harsh blacks and whites, was a study of impotence and murder executed with extraordinary skill, especially in the shower scene in which the thrusting of a knife into a girl's body symbolizes the thrusting which the nervous motel keeper cannot achieve sexually. *The Birds* (1963) was considered by some a gimmicky version of a Daphne du Maurier story about the onslaught of birds on a small town. Inexpressive leading players (Rod Taylor, Tippi Hedren) were compensated for by some beautifully executed passages: a line of crows forming sullenly on wires behind an unsuspecting character's head; a bird's-eye view of the town, perhaps Hitchcock's most extraordinary effect; the whole of the sequence involving a tweedy ornithologist (cleverly played by Ethel Griffies) before an attack on a gas station and the death of a man in blazing oil.

Since that time, Hitchcock did little of interest for nine years. There is little point in discussing critically such failures as *Marnie* (1964), *Torn Curtain* (1966), or *Topaz* (1969). Dead films, they simply offer the surface tricks, the polish, without the heartfelt passion for film-making which distinguished the best of Hitchcock's work. *Frenzy* (1972) falls outside the scope of this survey, which concludes with 1971.

*'Tippi' Hedren,* THE BIRDS

# 4. Wilder and Other Immigrants

We have seen how the first wave of Europeans who arrived after Lubitsch fled, with the onset of sound. The second wave—caused by the advent of Hitler—was headed by Billy Wilder, who was encouraged by the still-resident Lubitsch in the mid-1930s, at the still-"European" Paramount studios.

Together with Hitchcock, Wilder remains the English-speaking cinema's most persistently cynical director. His laughter at humanity, smartly bantering in his scripts written with Charles Brackett and others during the Thirties, savage and wounding in the series of major works culminating in *Ace in the Hole* (1951), has sounded increasingly hollow in recent years.

Wilder has been one of a handful of Hollywood directors whose films express an individual philosophy, and between 1934 and 1951 the development of a personal outlook could be charted. Before the war, he was working in the tradition of the Viennese operetta he knew as a boy, a tradition in which life was a frivolous amusement, the class barriers were broken down, and the wishes of the underprivileged were glamorously fulfilled. Taxi drivers and chorus girls hobnobbed almost effortlessly with the rich, who unbent over glasses of champagne to the tune of a Strauss waltz. Not a hint of reality intruded into his dream world, the rules and artifices of which Wilder recaptured in *Music in the Air* (1934), *Champagne Waltz* (1937), *Bluebeard's Eighth Wife* (1938), and the elegantly droll *Midnight* (1939).

This mode ceased to amuse in 1939, and Wilder and Brackett charted its disappearance in *Arise My Love* (1940), set against a collapsing Europe, and *Hold Back the Dawn* (1941), in which a gigolo (Charles Boyer) who could well have figured in any of the comedies of the Thirties is discovered trying to get into the United States via Mexico by cynically marrying an innocent American schoolteacher. *Hold Back the Dawn* is full of speeches in praise of the Land of the Free. The immigrant European's enchantment with the New World is further shown by *The Major and the Minor* (1942), which is set in a plush New York hotel, a fine express train, and an Iowa town where houses are Home Beautiful and the local military academy is lavishly upholstered by Hans Dreier.

Disillusion sets in with *Double Indemnity* (1943), set in a shabby and dusty Los Angeles villa, a cheap apartment, and a hideous insurance office; while *The Lost Weekend*'s (1945) vision of New York remains among the most unsparing ever recorded on film. Here is a nightmare of litter-strewn streets, a cluttered apartment looking onto a desolate stone wilderness, the elevated clanging up Third Avenue in the dirty light of a summer morning. *Sunset Boulevard* (1950), again set in

*Fred MacMurray, Barbara Stanwyck,* **DOUBLE INDEMNITY**

Los Angeles, evokes an old Hollywood with cockroaches in the interstices, a new one stupefyingly vulgar and brash. *Ace in the Hole,* framed desolately in and around Albuquerque, seems to be taking place at the end of the world.

In the major works made in the eight years between 1943 and 1951 —the works on which Wilder's critical reputation chiefly rests—his vision grows increasingly more distinct. The world is ugly and vicious, selfishness and cruelty are dominant in men's lives. Greed is the central impetus of the main characters; and even the walk-ons—the waiter who serves the alcoholic writer Don Birnam a martini in *The Lost Weekend,* or the tailor's assistant in *Sunset Boulevard*—are cruel. Bim Nolan, the male nurse in *The Lost Weekend,* is impersonal, tough, and efficient, but a simpering homosexual sadist. Leaving Birnam in the alcoholic ward in the early hours of a Sunday morning, he says, "It's like the doctor was just telling me, delirium is a disease of the night—good night!" Another example of Wilder's attitude to people occurs in the same film, when Birnam staggers along Third Avenue to try to pawn his typewriter. In Charles Jackson's novel, two men see Birnam trying desperately to gain admittance to a locked-up shop, and one of them snarls, "What's the matter with you, it's Yom Kippur!" Wilder, with Brackett's assistance, adds a characteristic joke. Don says, "What are you talking about, how about Kelly's? How about Gallagher's?" The man replies, "They're closed too. We've got an agreement. They keep closed on Yom Kippur and we don't open on St. Patrick's Day!"

In this forbidding world populated by malevolent strangers, parasites, or useless do-gooders, Birnam, Chuck Tatum in *Ace in the Hole,* Walter Neff in *Double Indemnity,* and Norma Desmond in *Sunset Boulevard* become increasingly isolated from reality, driven by obsessive lusts—for alcohol, for money, for a comeback to the big time. All are weak. Birnam is a failed writer, Tatum a failed journalist, Neff a failed insurance man who cheats his boss, and Desmond a failed actress who also has failed as a writer with a botched scenario of *Salome.* Except for Birnam, who is given a fresh chance, these people destroy themselves, die, or go mad, and whether it's Edward G. Robinson's insurance boss in *Double Indemnity* or Hedda Hopper's ferocious impersonation of herself in *Sunset Boulevard,* there is always someone around at the end to provide a pitiless final comment.

Even a love relationship—that release which Hollywood has usually granted even its most jaded creatures—is denied Wilder's people, and

the sexual relationships in his films have a predatory quality that suggests the matings of praying mantises. The parallel is exact in *Double
Indemnity,* in which the heartless ex-oilman's wife destroys the insurance
salesman through his sexual appetite for her. In *Sunset Boulevard* the
relationship between the star and the young writer shows barely a hint
of anything that is not ravening and predatory. The sexual encounters
between Tatum and his girl in *Ace in the Hole* are observed with austere
disgust, and are concluded when the girl plunges a pair of scissors into
Tatum's back. The vision of human love is as desolate as the vision of
business and of the masses at play.

Wilder's early career as a sports and crime reporter in Viennese and
Berlin newspapers during the Twenties and his work as a Berlin cabaret
entertainer fashioned the outlook which in the last twenty years has
turned sour. In many ways, in fact, the most characteristic Wilder films
have sprung from a crime reporter's view of life. His first script was for
*People on Sunday* (1928), a half-comic, half-melancholy little fable
about four young middle-class people spending a day at the Wannsee
in Berlin. Robert Siodmak directed, and Fred Zinnemann, Edgar G.
Ulmer, and Eugene Schufftan also worked on the production. Some
script work on *Emil and the Detectives* (1930) followed, along with
about fifty vanished scenarios for obscure UFA films of the period. Then,
in Paris, Wilder directed *Mauvaise Graine* (1933) with Danielle Dar-
rieux; this film, too, seems to have disappeared. Arriving in Hollywood
an unknown, Wilder hawked story ideas for two years and worked as a
gag man for Lubitsch before selling two synopses in a washroom to a
Paramount producer. By 1934 he was on the payroll, producing scripts
to suit the studio's policy of escapist entertainment set in European
high life.

Many of Wilder's scripts from this period still remain fresh, and of
his work between 1934 and 1937, *Music in the Air,* directed by Joe
May, and *Champagne Waltz,* directed by A. Edward Sutherland, released at the beginning and end of the period respectively, are probably
the most rewarding. *Music in the Air* has as its central figure a fascinating
embryo Norma Desmond, played with immense virtuosity by Gloria
Swanson, a prima donna who reduces everyone around her to nail-
chewing desperation with her tantrums and frenzied self-admiration.
Wilder's script (with Howard Young) is already crammed with characteristic touches. The plot line is a safe hack job: two simple Bavarian
villagers (June Lang and Douglass Montgomery) arrive in Munich and

pair off with John Boles, Swanson's leading man, and Swanson herself, thereby breaking up the most celebrated love affair on the European opera stage. The exchange of partners predictably makes each of the quartet see where his or her real affections lie. This sliver-thin story serves as an excuse for some brilliantly written set pieces: the irruption of the prima donna into a music publisher's office with her mate and co-star, the pair ripping off a complete rehearsal of their new opera with deafening brio; or a speech on amateurism in the theater delivered by a temperamental conductor (Joseph Cawthorn). The devastating mockery of opera's more fatuous conventions remained practically unique in a Nelson Eddy-Jeanette MacDonald age until *Citizen Kane.*

*Champagne Waltz* shows Wilder's unashamed Philistinism, this time in a spoofing of ragtime and the Viennese waltz tradition, both of which were enjoying a vogue when the film was made. Buzzy Bellew (Fred MacMurray), conductor of the Tiger Jazz Band, arrives in Vienna on tour, thereby threatening the business of a *Walzpalast* where Franz and Elsa Strauss, scions of the celebrated family, have previously been earning their living. The story develops out of the conflict between jazz and operetta (Elsa, like her predecessor in *Music in the Air,* is a temperamental prima donna) and the situations come at breakneck pace, working toward a reconciliation in New York, where, in a very Wilderian scene, Buzzy is found conducting a wretched supper band and Elsa in her *Walzpalast* is the toast of the town. A dream sequence, in which Johann Strauss plays the "Blue Danube" (for Franz Joseph), and a ruthless shot of the Tiger Jazz Band members twitching like spastics in the middle of a ghastly trained seal act bear the unmistakable Wilder stamp.

*Bluebeard's Eighth Wife* (1938, directed by Lubitsch) united Wilder for the first time with a man of comparable talent: Charles Brackett, a forty-six-year-old former theater critic of *The New Yorker* and a novelist (*That Last Infirmity, American Colony*). Though Brackett undoubtedly contributed sparkle and brio (and a partial counterbalance, probably, to Wilder's jaded vision), the dominant personality in the partnership was always Wilder's, and on the evidence of their films made solo, the philosophy was Wilder's and Wilder's alone. Writing for Lubitsch or Leisen, the pair achieved some of the most delectable comedies of the Thirties—artificial, witty, and ranging from a world which, if it ever existed, has vanished forever.

Until an ugly last reel set in a mental institution, *Bluebeard's Eighth Wife* has an agreeably feline asperity. The opening sequence is directed by Lubitsch with great zest, cynicism, and assurance. Brandon (Gary Cooper) is a millionaire who believes that the male pajama business is based deliberately on a false hypothesis: in his view, men only wear the top halves. Convinced the public is being taken for a ride, he expounds his theory to a bewildered Riviera shop assistant. The assistant goes to the first floor to talk to his department manager, the two men's expostulations and grimaces observed through the glass doors. In dumb show, they go up to see the vice-president, and he in turn telephones the president, who is dressed only in a pajama jacket. Embarrassment is averted at the last minute by the arrival of an impoverished French saleswoman (Claudette Colbert) who buys the trousers only for her father because he cannot afford the jacket.

The subsequent marriage of the millionaire and the impoverished lady is dealt with quietly and elegantly by Lubitsch, who rather softens the script's edge. But Wilder's personality shows through in the character drawing, particularly that of the prize fighter, played by Warren Hymer, who is hired by the wife to beat up her husband. In one scene, Hymer expostulates on the pleasures of being K.O.'ed: "You dream of Japan, pink cherry blossoms. Constantinople . . . I tell you, Mrs. Brandon, you get to see all those places you could never otherwise afford to visit." The last scenes in a sanitarium are evidently the result of Wilder's participation in the script, and show him at his most misanthropic: the inmates are cruelly observed, and there is a cruel final shot in which the hero wriggles out of a strait jacket to take the heroine into a typically jaded last-minute clinch. A modern variant on *The Taming of the Shrew, Bluebeard's Eighth Wife* remains an essentially bitter comedy.

In 1939 *Ninotchka* and *Midnight* were released. Both set in Paris, they showed Wilder and Brackett at the top of their form. *Midnight* has been almost totally forgotten perhaps because its director, Mitchell Leisen, has never been a critic's pet. The film's origins in Viennese operetta, its whipped-cream-and-Apfelstrudel view of life, put it in a class with *Music in the Air* and *Champagne Waltz*. Splendidly upholstered in the best Paramount-Hans Dreier tradition, it gives a stylized but penetrating exposition of an upper class that vanished almost immediately after the film was completed, with the outbreak of World War II. The parallel with Renoir's *La Règle du Jeu,* made in the same year and on much the same territory, hardly needs stressing.

The story is a perfect example of quasi-Viennese nonsense. A fugitive American chorus girl on the make in Europe (Claudette Colbert) arrives broke in Paris from Monte Carlo, after somehow smuggling herself onto the train in full evening dress. Meeting taxi driver Don Ameche (as unlikely a hackie as Paul Lukas in *Decision Before Dawn*), she persuades him to drive her around the Paris night spots while she auditions in each as a singer. Mercifully, we are spared examples of her efforts (except for a brief dying chord heard off-screen) and, still unemployed, she escapes from Ameche's by this time amorous clutches to wander into a superbly funny piano recital in a smart hotel. She sits next to a lecherous John Barrymore. He sizes her up expertly as, thinking herself unobserved, she blissfully removes her shoes. He pockets one. "I had an idea you had an idea," she tells him later.

After the recital, Colbert joins Barrymore, his wife (played with glittering malice by Mary Astor), and his wife's lover (Francis Lederer) at a classic card game during which she announces herself as Baroness Czerny. Lederer insists on escorting her to her hotel and, in a wonderfully played and written scene, leaves her safe at the bedroom door. Next morning, after she has spent a chaste but luxurious night in her suite, Barrymore arrives. He tells her that he knows she is a fake, but offers to pay good money if she will continue the deception, thereby provoking his wife's jealousy in an effort to win her back from her lover.

Colbert obligingly goes for a weekened to his country mansion (the parallel with *La Règle du Jeu* is once more remarkable), while Don Ameche and the entire Paris taxi force look for her. When she is located, Ameche arrives disguised as Baron Czerny, at the height of a party (during which Hedda Hopper leads the conga line with irresistible *élan*). Next morning there is a breakfast table sequence during which Ameche goes incredulously to the telephone to answer a long-distance call from his "daughter," supposedly measles-stricken in Hungary. There's a "little girl" voice on the line which actually belongs to John Barrymore, hilariously impersonating the non-existent infant on the telephone. Brittle, heartless, and stylish, this film remains one of the peaks of Wilder's career.

Some less impressive films followed, suggesting that Wilder and Brackett were marking time. *What a Life* (1939) is the least characteristic. Based on a Henry Aldrich Broadway farce, it is set in a college where the tougher sophomores bully the naïve hero, who of course gets the girl. Toward the beginning the bullying and crude college japes have a characteristic cruelty. After that the film, fluently and persuasively directed by Jay Theodore Reed and wittily acted by Betty Field as the hero's girl friend, becomes very good entertainment. *Ball of Fire* (1940), directed by Howard Hawks, rewrites the old nightclub-girl-meets-professor story in sometimes witty terms. *Arise My Love* (1940) and *Hold Back the Dawn* (1941), both by Mitchell Leisen, begin promisingly with racy and amusing situations, then suddenly deteriorate. The first starts with a girl reporter (Colbert) rescuing a flier (Ray Milland) from a firing squad in Spain. After some sharp observation of Europe in decline (the film was criticized at the time for bad taste), things become increasingly dull and repetitious. *Hold Back the Dawn* also starts well. In Mexico, two stranded immigrants, a wildly improbable Australian (Paulette Goddard) and a Romanian gigolo (Charles Boyer), are reunited; at Goddard's suggestion, Boyer sets out to find a simple American girl to marry so that he can cross the border. He settles on a schoolteacher (Olivia de Havilland), ruthlessly seduces her, and embarks on a union as thorny as the Cooper-Colbert marriage in *Blue-Beard's Eighth Wife*. The familiar Wilderian situation of the decadent European being snared by the apparently innocent American is amusingly exploited in the early scenes, but after that the writers seem to tire of the whole thing and only Leisen's unfailingly skillful direction keeps it going to the fade-out.

*The Major and the Minor* (1942) was Wilder's first job as a director in America, and the first sequences clearly show his hand. The film opens with a scalp-treatment demonstrator (Ginger Rogers) arriving at a New York hotel to massage a businessman's head, only to find herself being predatorily chased around the settee. Leaving the building in high dudgeon, she quells an elevator boy's eye-rollings by cracking an egg on his head. Disillusioned and beat, Ginger disguises herself as a twelve-year-old brat, complete with pigtails, apple, and balloon adventurously snatched from a child bystander, in order to pay the half-ticket rate, and hies home to her Iowa mother (unforgettably played by Mrs. Rogers). Adopted by an army major (Ray Milland) on the train, she is taken to his home and quickly summed up by his kid sister, wittily played by Diana Lynn. Although it flags slightly in the second half, this is a rather Sturges-like comedy with an agreeable edge.

A potboiler, *Five Graves to Cairo* (1943), was followed by *Double Indemnity* (1944), scripted with Raymond Chandler's assistance from James M. Cain's novel. Perhaps the purest, the least compromised and sensationalized of all Wilder's films, *Double Indemnity* retains an undiminished power. Its story of an insurance salesman driven to murder by an attractive woman is written and directed with relentless assurance from the credits, with a shadowy figure (the murder victim) limping cameraward, to the final sequence, in which the salesman returns, bleeding to death, to his office to dictate the story into a machine. Aided by John F. Seitz' harsh photography, Wilder liverishly explores a world shorn of beauty and decency. The tension, the sense of futility as the lovers realize they have committed murder for nothing are pitilessly developed.

Several sequences stand out: the desolate Chinese checkers game played by the wife (Barbara Stanwyck) and her stepdaughter; the wife's appearance at the insurance office after the killing, lying desperately, exchanging almost imperceptible glances with her lover; the killers' meeting in the supermarket, she implacable in white sweater and dark glasses, he nervous and irritable, arguing in whispers across the bean cans; the desperate attempt to start the car when it stalls after a murder which has been entirely conveyed through the expression on the wife's face; the lovers' final showdown in a shuttered room. The whole film is pitched deliberately in a minor key, understressed, to convey the pettiness of the crime, the sadness that seems to hang around enterprises of this kind. The use of a beautifully detailed soundtrack, especially in interiors, as well as the concentrated playing of Fred MacMurray and Barbara Stanwyck, ensure one's sense of involvement. The wife's cheap anklet, fluffy slippers, and her habit of drinking iced tea in tall glasses; the shoddy Spanish-style villa she inhabits; the dusty streets of Los Angeles with their scrubby palms—all become real and alive in a way that immediately establishes Wilder's command of physical detail.

This mastery was to be as strikingly displayed in his next film, *The Lost Weekend* (1945), set in an equally brutal and heartless urban world. Don Birnam is a once promising writer whose inner conflicts (in Charles Jackson's novel, he is a homosexual) drive him to the bottle. Apart from a clumsily produced flashback showing how he met his girl friend (Jane Wyman) the script concentrates on Birnam during four days of agony, following him to a hospital, his favorite bar, dirty streets, and rooms dominated by huge foreground objects—in one memorable shot, a fallen standard lamp. There are some irritating concessions to the box office (notably a floozie, played by Doris Dowling, who flirts with Birnam) and some unnecessarily sensationalized episodes underlined by Miklos Rozsa's raucous score. But the long episodes in which Birnam is alone obviously fascinate Wilder the most, and these are observed with

*Ray Milland,* THE LOST WEEKEND

*Ray Milland,* THE LOST WEEKEND

*Ray Milland,* THE LOST WEEKEND

cold detachment. The famous sequence of Birnam's D.T.'s, in which he sees a bat pounce on a mouse, the blood trickling down the wall (this was deleted in England), is ferociously directed. A hangover is masterfully conveyed in a single giant close-up of one of his eyes. The camera noses about everywhere: into a whisky glass as Birnam expatiates on the splendors evoked by alcohol in a speech which develops the earlier lines of Warren Hymer in *Bluebeard's Eighth Wife*; along the bar with its glittering liquor rings; through the refuse of Third Avenue, the elevated clanging and swaying overhead. In one virtuoso sequence, which takes place in Harry and Joe's Bar, Birnam steals a purse. As the waiter throws Birnam out, a sad little pianist leads the crowd in "Somebody Stole My Purse!" The Wilderian version of people's reaction to a man desperately sick and in need of help is as cruel as ever: the odiously jocular male nurse ("Good morning, Mary Sunshine!"), the people in Harry and Joe's, the bystanders on Third Avenue. All these people are brilliantly sketched in, scrupulously directed and played, whereas the limp, indifferent figures of Birnam's girl and his brother—the "good" characters—obviously bore the director.

The whole film stands or falls on the portrait of Birnam himself, and here the writing is consistently good, until the last-minute concession which gives him a new chance. Birnam's weakness, his dwelling on small-time past successes, his cravings for oblivion, and his overdone literary speeches to the barman are excellently conveyed, with Ray Milland's performance suggesting the charm, the softness, to perfection.

Two indifferent films followed. *The Emperor Waltz* (1947) was a feeble attempt to recapture the brio of *Champagne Waltz,* and *A Foreign Affair* (1948) was a repulsive onslaught on American and German post-war attitudes. Then, with *Sunset Boulevard* (1950), the film which marked the end of the Wilder-Brackett partnership, and *Ace in the Hole* (1951), Wilder returned as a major director. Both films are dominated by egomaniacs: Norma Desmond, the savage, self-obsessed Twenties star, and Chuck Tatum, the vicious reporter down on his luck, longing as desperately as Norma for a comeback. Such small sympathy as Wilder can manage is reserved for these monsters; the others, the representatives of the world outside, are almost uniformly vile, and when someone decent is attempted (Nancy Olson's Hollywood intellectual, Jan Sterling's bitter waitress) the characterization slips back into the conventional.

*Sunset Boulevard* was a partly compromised portrait of Hollywood which was nevertheless daring for its time. In the opening scene, the

*William Holden* and *Gloria Swanson,* SUNSET BOULEVARD

camera prowls along a sidewalk, while the dawn of Los Angeles breaks and a patrol car screams up to a shuttered villa in the Los Feliz district. A body, shot to pieces, floats above us as we gaze through the sterile glitter of a swimming pool. The victim is a gigolo-writer (William Holden) and the killer a rotting star (Gloria Swanson). We follow their doomed relationship from the moment when he arrives at his house dodging creditors in his car to their final confrontation when she destroys him. Wilder weakened the film by showing the "fresh young Hollywood" of the studio reader (Nancy Olson) to which the writer could have escaped; a braver film would have shown that no escape was in fact possible. But Wilder has never been better than in the scenes in the villa with its rat-infested pool, a butler with white gloves (Erich von Stroheim) playing an organ, a monkey ritually interred, the old star watching her movies on a silent projector late at night. Gloria Swanson's courageous playing as the star reflected Wilder's ability to wring the best from a player.

*Ace in the Hole* purports to attack sensationalism, in the brutal way in which press and carnival promoters exploit the sudden burial of a shopkeeper in a New Mexico cave. Actually, the film itself exploits the situation no less heartlessly. Tatum (Kirk Douglas) has fallen from the big time because of a sudden blackballing. Winding up on an Albuquerque tabloid, he sees the chance of a return to the top in the interment story (the parallel with the Floyd Collins case of the Twenties is deliberately stressed). Tatum keeps the excitement whipped up for a week, while deliberately delaying the rescue so as to keep the story alive. The buried man dies, and Tatum is stabbed to death by the waitress who befriended him.

Another director might have made one feel the agony of the man in the cave, his increasing sense of hopelessness, and perhaps shown the way in which individuals risked their lives to get close to him with gifts of food and drink, a normal happening in real-life stories of this type. But the crowd in Wilder's eyes is a collective monster, of which Chuck Tatum is only an all too typical representative. Even the dying man's wife, as played by Jan Sterling, is a sluttish figure without charm or beauty. In this extraordinary film, with its dynamic direction and photography (by Charles Lang), Wilder makes his quintessential personal statement about life, which he sees as vicious and vile in a way only Buñuel among the cinema's artists has matched. In all the other major Wilder films some minor concessions have been made to sentiment. Edward G. Robinson's insurance boss in *Double Indemnity,* Jane Wyman's *Time* researcher in *The Lost Weekend,* Nancy Olson's Hollywood studio reader in *Sunset Boulevard*: these people can be said to represent the audience at its most self-flattering, horrified by indecency, trying to help. In *Ace in the Hole* the usual ersatz representative of middle-class values is notably lacking. As a statement against life, as destructive criticism of human beings, *Ace in the Hole* has rarely been matched in the history of commercial cinema.

Since this last artistic statement, Wilder has been content to provide a succession of carefully mounted entertainments practically devoid of personal vision. Occasional attempts to recapture the glitter of the early comedies—*Love in the Afternoon* (1957), *Sabrina* (1954), *The Seven Year Itch* (1955)—have been respectively adipose, styleless, and keyhole-peeping. Only *Some Like It Hot* (1959), a brilliantly funny and brilliantly made farce, suggested the Wilder of the old days. The isolated prestige picture (*The Spirit of St. Louis* [1957]) could have been directed by any competent film-maker, as could *Stalag 17* (1953), the prison camp comedy-melodrama, though *The Private Life of Sherlock Holmes* (1970) was a stylish and civilized diversion.

The great Fritz Lang came to America shortly after Wilder in 1934, when he was already established as the most important director in Germany. After Goebbels offered him the role of chief of UFA and master of the Nazi propaganda machine, he at once left for France, where he made the stagy, mediocre *Liliom* (1934). Arrived in Hollywood, he was hired by Selznick to write (with Oliver H. P. Garrett) and direct the story of the cruise ship *Morro Castle,* which had just burned at sea with the loss of many lives. The project fell through, and instead, Selznick's father-in-law, Louis B. Mayer, borrowed him to make *Fury* (1936) from a script by Norman Krasna and Bartlett Cormack on which Lang himself worked.

The resulting film, seen today, is a great disappointment. M-G-M, in a rare incursion into Warner territory, imposed too many compromises on this pretentious study of lynch law, and the sentimentalized story of the couple caught up in mob violence (Spencer Tracy and Sylvia Sidney) is very tiresome, typical of Krasna's and the studio's superficial approach in many other movies. Even the film's authentic Langian touch, when a woman like some vengeful Valkyrie out of *Metropolis* marches at the head of a mob with torch held high, seems merely calculated and arty in the otherwise humdrum context.

*You Only Live Once* (1937), written by Gene Towne and Graham Baker, is only slightly more interesting. An imprisoned criminal (Henry Fonda) released from jail and his girl friend (Sylvia Sidney) try to establish a decent life away from the world of crime, but their efforts are ill-fated. He loses his job in a garage, and is entangled in a web of doom when he is falsely accused of taking part in a bank robbery and is sentenced to death. Lang believed that man was a victim of fate (a view he no longer holds). His development of the action is accompanied by Leon Shamroy's menacingly Germanic images. At times these are too obvious, almost Mamoulian-like, in such images as the recurrent use of bars of shadows to suggest Fonda's impending doom or the dark bull-frogs like a Greek chorus. Fonda's playing seems nervous and uneasy, out of sympathy with the director. The bank robbery in the rain, with a crippled beggar on a nearby street corner and smudged faces at car windows, represents Lang at his best. But the film is vitiated by a lush romanticism of style.

*You and Me* (1938), made at Paramount, was an artistic and commercial failure. Lang was rescued from it by a 20th Century-Fox contract which resulted in the ordinary *Man Hunt* (1940) and the making of two Westerns which could just as well have been directed by Henry King. Strictly studio products, they were devoid of Lang's vision.

Then, in *The Woman in the Window* (1945) and *Scarlet Street* (1946), Lang was allowed to develop the world of his imagination: night scenes dominating an evocation of an urban environment, the light shining on a rain-swept corner, the raincoated figures drifting by, the sodden reflections in shop windows, the harsh revelations of character in subtle glances and intonations. *The Woman in the Window,* written by Nunnally Johnson, establishes a quintessential Little Man (Edward G. Robinson as a nervous academic) who in a dream envisages the consequences of moral downfall with an available woman (Joan Bennett). Perhaps unwittingly, Lang and the writer provide a fable which the Breen office itself could have composed. The *mise en scène* is cleverly worked out, the performance of Dan Duryea as a repulsive, furtive blackmailer has an almost Gallic quality of realism. One excellent scene shows the professor murdering an intrusive lover of the girl who has enslaved him. A thunderstorm breaks out and as Robinson drives to a

*Joan Bennett, Edward G. Robinson,* THE WOMAN IN THE WINDOW

toll bridge with the body, a sudden beam of light illuminates the features of the corpse, staring out of the rear window in the rain.

*Scarlet Street* reworks the theme of spiritual ruin with the same cast. The obvious moralism here indicates that Lang had decided by now that man's fate is in his own hands, and both films are demands for decency and a sense of responsibility among middle-aged men. It is scarcely surprising that the censors permitted Lang to end *Scarlet Street* with his killer Edward G. Robinson going free, hunted by the voice of conscience. Although the cumulative effect is patly moralistic, Lang gives *Scarlet Street* a good deal of conviction through his direction of the actors and through the excellence of his simulated urban ambience. The scenes between the prostitute Lazy Legs (Bennett)) and her sleazy pimp lover (Duryea) are not particularly well written, but Lang extracts from them a note of bitterness not quite in the script, written by Dudley Nichols. The best sequences are those between Edward G. Robinson and his wife, played brilliantly by Rosalind Ivan. Here the hell of an unhappy marriage is conveyed with a Strindbergian intensity, in scenes superior to the level of the rest of the film.

*Clash by Night* (1952) was less satisfactory, though its cliché-ridden script, adapted by Alfred Hayes from a play by Clifford Odets, has some enjoyable moments, and the evocation of a fishing town is very authentic. *The Big Heat* (1953) is better, partly due to a powerful screenplay by Sidney Boehm. As in several of Lang's German films, we are plunged into a city terrorized by an evil mastermind, here played with icy complacency by Alexander Scourby. With his lavish mansion, mindless family, and conventional upper-set friends, purring an order for murder as casually as he would order a martini, the master criminal reflects Lang's knowledge of people of this kind (he used real felons in the kangaroo court in *M*). Over the fireplace broods the mother who is the only human being he respects (Mrs. Peter Lorre was used as the sitter, another discreet reference to *M*).

Despite the excellence of this film, it is hard not to regret the waste of Lang's talents in Hollywood. Making nothing of interest since 1957, he was generally squandered on dime-fiction subjects, more suited to the lightweight skills of a Siodmak or a Curtiz.

Another refugee from UFA, Edgar G. Ulmer, has been widely admired by Truffaut and Godard without attracting any attention at home. In the 1930s Ulmer made a number of gentle and decent films in Ukrainian

*Glenn Ford, Lee Marvin,* THE BIG HEAT

and Yiddish for national audiences in New York. His *Green Fields* (1931) justly achieved an underground reputation; he went on to make that important film about syphilis, *Damaged Lives* (1933) and a sophisticated horror film, *The Black Cat* (1934).

His Hollywood career is rich and satisfying, though tragically obscure. Perhaps his most effective picture was *Strange Woman* (1946), a story of an unscrupulous schemer, Jenny Hager, who rises to wealth in the Bangor, Maine, of the 1840s. Nicolai Remisoff's art direction creates to perfection the ambience of a fishing port, and even Hedy Lamarr in the central role is convincing. It is, though, the film's visual texture, magnificently achieved by the cameraman Lucien Andriot under Ulmer's supervision, which makes the film a classic. The compositions are reminiscent of late Scandinavian silent films, Sjöström providing an especial inspiration. A composition of a group of women at a window during a local epidemic is a shot not even Welles and Cortez in *The Magnificent Ambersons* could match. The early childhood scenes in which Jenny Hager's true character is disclosed—she sadistically threatens a little boy with drowning—are composed with a sharp intelligence, and throughout the use of pools of darkness, of faces illuminated by the soft glow of candlelight, has a beauty comparable to portraits by Rembrandt.

As a pictorial director, Ulmer was at least the equal of Ingram, but without Ingram's rather static approach to editing. Ulmer's films had a great fluency, a persuasive narrative drive. In *Ruthless* (1948), not quite the equal of *Strange Woman,* he was back on Welles territory in the story of a social climber, played by Zachary Scott, who makes his name by unscrupulous methods on Wall Street. Ulmer used more wide-angle photography here than in any film since *Citizen Kane,* the narrow, low-ceilinged rooms, cluttered interiors, and wonderfully evoked train journey (cut in some versions) conveying a Wellesian visual quality that in some ways refined the master's own techniques. S. K. Lauren, Gordon Kahn, Robert Rossen, and Alvah Bessie all worked on this portrait of the New York tycoon Horace Woodruff Vendig, a fact which explains its remarkable number of sharp-witted lines and situations. The opening sequences, similar to the introductory passages of *Strange Woman,* are extraordinarily effective. The overstuffed interiors, caged birds, and stifling afternoons of an unhappy World War I childhood are conveyed

*Sydney Greenstreet, Lucille Bremer,* RUTHLESS

with exquisite tact, as complex and subtle as passages of Colette's. The near-drowning in a lake is a masterly passage of Griffithian montage and imagery, executed by the great Bert Glennon, who had lost none of the skill he had at the time of *The Last Command*. As the ambitious youth rises through a succession of carefully stylized Frank Sylos sets, he meets well-drawn characters along the way—especially the fat magnate of Sydney Greenstreet, who gives here his best screen performance. At the end, young and old tycoon die together, locked in an embrace of hate in the water under a pier. The film was dismissed by critics, and Ulmer—director also of that first-rate film *The Naked Dawn* (1953)—has languished in obscurity ever since. Hollywood has no place for uncommercial artists like this.

In addition to Wilder, Lang, and Ulmer, the German and Austrian figures in Hollywood in the 1940s were many. Robert Siodmak was a distinguished figure, who in common with Wilder and Lang had worked in Paris before he came to America. His first Hollywood film of consequence was *Phantom Lady* (1944), taken by Bernard C. Schoenfeld from a novel by William Irish (Cornell Woolrich) about a search for a suspected killer's alibi, a woman with a bizarre hat who met him in a downtown Manhattan bar. In Universal's studio Siodmak creates a wholly convincing New York: the *boîte* where a jukebox moans the strains of "I'll Remember April," the train station where the tap of high heels and the rattle of a gate can jar the nerves, the sweat and cigarettes of a jazz dive, and the tropical excitements of a Latin American show. In *The Suspect* (1945), Siodmak moves with equal ease to a London setting, in a story based by the intelligent Bertram Millhauser on the Crippen case about a henpecked tobacconist (Charles Laughton) who murders his wife (Rosalind Ivan) and experiences the agony of blackmail. Once again, the film is entirely Germanic, both in its emphasis on the inevitability of fate and in its swarming, shadow-filled interiors. As the husband imagines murdering his wife, the camera travels along a stairwell, fixing a cold eye on the murder weapon, a stick in a hat stand. Although Laughton was a trifle below his usual strength, Rosalind Ivan and Henry Daniell as the blackmailing neighbor played with an intense brilliance which reflected Siodmak's careful guidance.

Siodmak's next few films were less effective—*Uncle Harry* (1945) was a watered-down version (by Stephen Longstreet and Keith Winter) of the Thomas Job stage play about a poisoning. *The Spiral Staircase*

(1946) was an uneasy excursion into American Gothic with an admittedly good opening sequence in which the pleasures of a hotel Biographic display are matched to the strangling of a girl upstairs. *The Killers* (1946), an extension from Hemingway's story, and *The Dark Mirror* (1946), a study by Nunnally Johnson of psychosis in a twin sister, were handicapped by mediocre writing and poor character motivation. Siodmak's talent reemerged at strength in *Cry of the City* (1948), the most searching of the then popular stories of New York at night. Despite sentimental aspects of the story—reminiscent of *Underworld*—the character drawing by scenarist Richard Murphy and Siodmak's direction of the players are remarkably tough. Against the overworked, conventional figures of the cop Candella (Victor Mature) and his Jewish-Italian rival Martin Rome (Richard Conte), we see the vivid squalor of the abortionist doctor (Konstantin Shayne), the grossly evil masseuse (Hope Emerson), the shyster Niles (Berry Kroeger), and the terrified nurse (Betty Garde) who is half attracted to a criminal patient. Siodmak's best direction can be seen in sequences such as the arrival of the shyster at St. John's Hospital to torment Martin Rome in his bed of pain; the masseuse greeting Rome, the figure seen at first through the glass panel over a door; Niles' murder in a swinging, creaking office chair (a touch Lang himself must have envied); and the escape through the prison tunnel, accompanied by the drumbeats of Alfred Newman's score. *Cry of the City* was proof that the best American films of the Forties utterly escaped the confines of the stage.

Other important Germanic presences were John Brahm, creator of the Gothic masterpieces *Hangover Square* (1944), *The Lodger* (1944), and *The Locket* (1946); Douglas Sirk, who directed such utterly UFA-esque pictures as *Sleep My Love* (1948) and the excellent *Thunder on the Hill* (1951); Frank Wysbar (*Strangler of the Swamp* [1945], *Lighthouse* [1946]); Fred Zinnemann, warm and sympathetic director of *The Search* (1949), *Act of Violence* (1949), and *High Noon* (1952); and Curtis Bernhardt (*Possessed* [1948], *Payment on Demand* [1951]).

Otto Preminger has an altogether less likable and more exploitive directorial approach than the aforementioned figures. For a time the idol of the French and British critics, more recently in eclipse, Preminger remained almost consistently mediocre throughout praise and blame, heavily dependent on his writers and cinematographers. His first important feature, *Laura* (1944), begun by Mamoulian, who was withdrawn by Preminger acting as producer part of the way through shooting, is technically uninteresting, largely achieved in medium shots. It is notable for ingredients other than the direction itself, such as the music of David Raksin; the style of the individual players' personalities—Judith Anderson, Dana Andrews, Gene Tierney, and especially Clifton Webb; and the Fox production gloss. The film's perfect casting cannot be credited to Preminger, since Mamoulian was responsible for it, and the best "touches" in the direction are due to an unusually refined and detailed screenplay of which Jay Dratler was chief author.

*Fallen Angel* (1945), an attempt to recapture the flavor of *Laura,* again had excellent Fox craftsmanship. The art direction of the seedy cafe, the small town room lit by intermittent neon signs from across the street, and the finely wrought "house" photography of Joseph LaShelle to a great extent surmount the only fair writing and the ploddingly obedient direction. *Centennial Summer* (1946) was a misguided attempt at a musical, altogether lacking in the charm it aimed for, and *Forever Amber* (1947) offered little more than the very fine amber-tinted photography of Leon Shamroy. *The Fan* (1949) was a travesty of Wilde; *Angel Face* (1953) was a labored and amateurish

*Courtesy Twentieth Century-Fox.*

*Clifton Webb, Gene Tierney,* LAURA

affair about a psychotic girl played by Jean Simmons. The depressing record of third-rate direction excessively admired in France was interrupted only by *The Thirteenth Letter* (1950), a remake of Clouzot's *Le Corbeau,* a story of poison pen letters set in French Canada. The unusually well-worked-out script by Howard Koch and Louis Chavance inspired Preminger to his best direction to date, and the film achieves a highly effective purposefulness. The characters have an unusual amount of depth for an American film of the period. The admirable Constance Smith and a subdued Charles Boyer act with distinction under Preminger's discreet guidance.

His next few films—*The Moon Is Blue* (1953), which once created a censorship furor and now seems about as daring as a Lux commercial, and *The Man with the Golden Arm* (1955) among them—aimed at "controversial" subjects in the spirit of headline journalism, which more effectively inspired Warners in the 1930s. Slack and flaccid, Preminger's direction failed to match his frequently well-written scripts: Wendell Mayes' clever writing of *Anatomy of a Murder* (1959) was almost ruined by Preminger's loose handling and the lamentably inferior photography of Sam Leavitt. A comparison of this film with LeRoy's not dissimilar *They Won't Forget* shows the difference between a paunchy and a muscular directorial approach. Preminger's only fairly good film of the late 1950s was *Bonjour Tristesse* (1958), in which Arthur Laurents' not disgraceful version of Françoise Sagan's realistic writing touched off a talent dormant since *The Thirteenth Letter. Bonjour Tristesse,* with its casually heartless portrait of life in the South of France, the brown bodies and the indifference of sun-filled days, almost gets close to the irony underlying the hedonism of Sagan.

In the 1960s and 1970s Preminger's work became less and less attractive, including a failed attempt at a serious political drama, *Advise and Consent* (1962), poorly made, straggling in construction, and as dingily shot as *Anatomy of a Murder; Exodus* (1960); *The Cardinal* (1963), which took on the subject of the Catholic Church with pious ignorance and was saved only by the rich photography of Leon Shamroy; and increasingly desperate and futile wooings of the public in treatments of racial problems (*Hurry Sundown* [1967]), youth (*Skidoo* [1968]), or the maimed (*Tell Me That You Love Me, Junie Moon* [1970]). Aside from the excellent first few minutes of *In Harm's Way* (1965), which summarized with skill the atmosphere of Navy shore life in Hawaii before Pearl Harbor, Preminger has gone from folly to

Scene from IN HARM'S WAY

catastrophic folly, apparently still able to raise money on the basis of his previous successes.

Max Ophüls was an Austrian with a less harsh and bitter approach than most of his fellow expatriates. His Hollywood career was brief. He was fortunate that the enlightened producer John Houseman gave him the opportunity to make for Universal one film, *Letter from an Unknown Woman* (1948), which recaptured much of the elegance of his *Liebelei* (1933), also set in Vienna, a film full of snow, sleigh bells, carriages, lights gleaming on ornamental gardens, and trysts at night. Ophüls, in the Houseman production, managed to carry the whole Viennese romantic tradition bodily over to Universal. The art director Alexander Golitzen created a marvelously accurate Vienna aided by Franz Planer's subtly UFA-esque lighting. In the brief sequence in Linz, filled with sunlight, marching soldiers, and church bells, even the slightest hint of an "American" film disappears. Zweig's story of an adolescent girl who bears a pianist's child has been softened by Howard Koch's script. Ophüls' direction overrides any objections, ably assisted by Joan Fontaine's slightly artificial but appealing performance as the young girl, and Louis

*Joan Fontaine*, LETTER FROM AN UNKNOWN WOMAN

Jourdan's subtle suggestion of decadence as the pianist. Ophüls perfectly evokes the feeling of a romantic daydream which reality shatters, the spiral stairway filled with the strains of Liszt, the sunlit room with its clutter of lifetime keepsakes, the theater with its crisp white furs and opera glasses, the anguished farewell in a parked carriage. Though his other American films, such as *Caught* (1948) and *The Reckless Moment* (1949), were subtly elegant, they did not have the charm of this masterpiece.

Three major directors, Julien Duvivier, René Clair, and Jean Renoir, pursued brief wartime careers in the American cinema. Duvivier, who arrived after his great success with *Un Carnet de Bal* (1937), directed *Tales of Manhattan* in 1942. This extraordinarily sophisticated work, dazzlingly shot by Capra's great cameraman Joseph Walker, was somewhat overlooked at the time. Scripted by Ben Hecht among others, it is the omnibus story of the adventures of a tail coat, which begins as a precious object fussed over by a brace of Fifth Avenue tailers, and descends socially to becoming a scarecrow's jacket in a field. Duvivier's direction is masterfully assured throughout. The opening episode is a model of screen construction: a tiny *conte* about a philandering matinee idol (Charles Boyer), his mistress (Rita Hayworth), and her ruthless big game hunter husband(Thomas Mitchell), staged partly in a hunting lodge. Two other episodes surpass it: the carefully modulated sequence in which Charles Laughton plays a struggling composer given his one chance to conduct his work, the tail coat parting at the seams as he stretches out his arms for a cadenza; and the extraordinary scene involving Edward G. Robinson as a Bowery bum who receives an invitation to a high-class college reunion in Manhattan. It emerges that he was a prominent Chicago attorney who had been disbarred; he is pointedly and cruelly humiliated in front of his college mates by his former partner, played, in his finest screen performance, by George Sanders. This masterly episode, directed to perfection and written with an uncompromising realism rare in a Hollywood film, represented Duvivier and the Fox production team at their peak.

In 1943 Duvivier made another collection of short stories, *Flesh and Fantasy,* the best episode in which was an adaptation by Samuel Hoffenstein of Wilde's "Lord Arthur Savile's Crime." Well shot by Stanley Cortez, this was in every way an accomplished version of the story, from

the opening palm-reading scene in which the occultist played by Edward
G. Robinson foresees the future to the final murder on Westminster
Bridge. Another American film, *The Imposter* (1945), though very well
played by Jean Gabin, was not a success.

René Clair was equally typecast. If Duvivier had proven himself commercially with an omnibus film in France he must be given omnibus
subjects in Hollywood; if Clair was a specialist in fantasy, he must be
given fantasies to direct. Fortunately, he was able to preserve the
qualities of delicate imagination which distinguished such French classics

*Edward G. Robinson, Anna Lee,* FLESH AND FANTASY

*Courtesy of Universal Pictures.*

as *Les Deux Timides* and *Sous les Toits de Paris* (1929).

His first American picture, *The Flame of New Orleans* (1941), in which Dietrich gave her most skillful comedy performance, far better than her work for von Sternberg, was a delicious trifle. *I Married a Witch* (1942) was even more attractive. The latter opens in Salem, Massachusetts, at the time of the witchcraft trials. The spirits of Jennifer (Veronica Lake) and her warlock father (Cecil Kellaway) are imprisoned in the roots of an oak tree until a lightning stroke releases them from their earthly cage. Mounted on a broomstick, they set out to revenge themselves on the descendant (Fredric March) of the man who condemned them. The screenplay by Robert Pirosh and Marc Connelly from the novel *The Passionate Witch* (left uncompleted by Thorne Smith at the time of his death) has a gentle charm reminiscent of the best of the Thorne Smith "Topper" comedies, and Clair's execution is expertly lightweight. After making a less skillful comedy about precognition, *It Happened Tomorrow* (1944), and a version of Agatha Christie, *And Then There Were None* (1945), he returned to France to make that delicious Faustian romance *La Beauté du Diable* (1950), with Gérard Philipe.

The great Jean Renoir had a thoroughly unsatisfactory wartime career in Hollywood. He was often handed scripts carefully written to the last detail which he could do little to improve. His first American film, *Swamp Water* (1941), had been turned out by Dudley Nichols a year before Renoir arrived from France. He managed to persuade 20th Century-Fox to permit him to make the film in Georgia. The script, however, was a waste of Renoir's talent, and unlike Stuart Heisler in *The Biscuit Eater* (1940), he did not bring much freshness of observation to the Georgia locale. *This Land is Mine* (1943), also written by Nichols in an obvious and sententious style, was a story of the French Resistance that found Renoir at his most mannered. *The Southerner* (1945), written by Renoir himself and Hugo Butler from the novel *Hold Autumn in Your Hand* by George Sessions Perry, was a more personal but unconvincing account of life in the Deep South, with poor casting (Zachary Scott and Beulah Bondi were miscast as farm people) vitiating any attempt at realism in the direction; and the writing was overladen with moralistic tags. Even *The Diary of a Chambermaid* (1946) was an aggravation: adapted by Burgess Meredith from the stage version of Mirbeau's novel by Andre Heuse, Thielly Nores, and the Grand Guignol writer Andre de Lorde, it had Guignolesque elements and a number of distractions caused by the mixed American, Czech, and Australian cast. The best feature of this artificial film was the brilliant playing of Francis Lederer as the insidious valet, Josef. Like Lang, Renoir was largely wasted in Hollywood.

# 5. Changing Patterns in Drama

The Europeans affected every part of Hollywood film-making except the comedy and the musical, especially the rich range of B pictures (including such special pleasures as the Val Lewton horror films made at RKO Radio, among them *The Cat People* [1942] and *Isle of the Dead* [1945]). Alongside this major development there emerged a new type of American hero, chiefly personified by the cool and detached Alan Ladd and the bitter, amused, and sardonic persona of Humphrey Bogart. Bogart frequently appeared in films with a strong Germanic look at Warners, but he always seemed to work against their grain, not taking their heavy artificial symbolism very seriously. In one director, he found his perfect temperamental match: John Huston. More successfully than Howard Hawks, John Huston managed to rise above the somewhat turgid look and sound of Warners films of the period to create in at least one film, *The Maltese Falcon* (1941), an economical masterpiece of screen construction and execution. In fact, the film looks back to the Thirties and the more spare and uncluttered Warners approach of that time. It has survived the years intact, appealing particularly to our own anti-baroque attitude.

Bogart, like West and Fields before him, conveyed an implicit (and at times explicit) dislike of the Establishment. He therefore became the father of Brando, Dean, Newman, and other later rebels. A direct line can in fact be drawn in the American film from *The Maltese Falcon* to the present day.

This film is drawn as closely from Dashiell Hammett's novel as von Stroheim drew from Frank Norris. The film's resonances are achieved by marvelous casting (Bogart, Mary Astor, Sydney Greenstreet, Peter Lorre) and by the intimacy of the actors' group playing. Huston's direction is admirable, giving an additional edge to his version of Hammett's already bitter writing. In this story of the search for a valuable golden bird given as tribute by the Knights of Malta to the Holy Roman Emperor Charles V, the observation of greed is witty in the extreme. The only touch of emotion is when at the climax Humphrey Bogart as the detective Sam Spade sends the treacherous Brigid O'Shaughnessy (Mary Astor) to jail. Here a cliché image—the bars of an elevator closing on the doomed woman's face, cutting her off from the world—is effectively recharged by Huston's direction.

His *In This Our Life* (1942) was by contrast a mediocre affair about a family in the Deep South. Here the director's detachment seemed to result from boredom with the subject. After a period making several very good war documentaries, Huston returned to Hollywood with *The Treasure of the Sierra Madre* (1948), a B. Traven story with similarities to *Greed,* about a search for gold no less desperate than the quest for the legendary falcon. Max Steiner's score and the turgid photography of Ted McCord combined to make the film see unduly labored, despite the practiced playing of Walter Huston and Tim Holt. *Key Largo* (1948) was even heavier. A Maxwell Anderson melodrama laid in the Florida Keys, its setting is a decaying hotel caught in the grip of a hurricane. The entire cast overacted, Edward G. Robinson supplying his characteristic cigar-chewing turn as an Al Capone-like criminal, Claire Trevor singing a drunken song as his moll, Humphrey Bogart snarling monotonously, and the cameraman (Karl Freund) and composer (Max Steiner) overindulging every Germanic whim. The climax, identical with that in *To Have and Have Not* and *The Breaking Point,* showed Huston inferior to both Hawks and Curtiz as a technician.

*We Were Strangers* (1949) was more effective, a story of a revolt in the Havana of 1933, staged in protest at the Machado regime. A patriotic band of rebels plans to murder a member of the aristocratic Contreras family and destroy the officials attending the funeral by dynamite placed in the grave. The digging of the tunnel through corpses in various stages of decomposition has a tautness and economy not seen in Huston's work since *The Maltese Falcon,* and the final mowing down of the rebels on a flight of steps, for all its indebtedness to *Potemkin,* is a moving sequence.

*John Garfield, Jennifer Jones,* WE WERE STRANGERS

*The Asphalt Jungle* (1950) benefited from Ben Maddow's cleverly written screenplay, which covered the events connected with a robbery of a jewelry store by criminals ranging from a mindless hulk (Sterling Hayden) to a diabolically clever safecracker (Sam Jaffe). Huston's direction has all the shrewdness, expert pacing, and attack that most of his films after *Falcon* so seriously lacked. The scenes involving the opulent but ruined lawyer (brilliantly played by Louis Calhern) are the best written and directed in the film. Characters like this one— smooth and smart on the surface but rotten and frightened within—are of the kind Huston so perfectly understands.

After *The Asphalt Jungle* Huston became increasingly eclectic. *The Red Badge of Courage* (1951) was a carefully wrought version of Stephen Crane which was ruined by studio (M-G-M) interference. *The*

*African Queen* (1952), less expertly put together than his previous films, had the advantage of the celebrated performances of Humphrey Bogart and Katharine Hepburn as a small riverboat captain and a missionary in Africa during World War I. Largely a European director after that, Huston dealt with authors ranging all the way from Pierre la Mure (*Moulin Rouge* [1953]) up through Tennessee Williams (*The Night of the Iguana* [1964]) to Melville (*Moby Dick* [1956]). All of these films were made in a mode of inflated pretentiousness, quite the opposite of Huston's earlier spare laconic wryness. Only occasionally could a return to quality be discerned: in the sumptuous color photography (by Charles G. Clarke) of the Japanese period subject *The Barbarian and the Geisha* (1958), and in the touching treatment of Clark Gable and Marilyn Monroe in the beautifully shot anti-Western *The Misfits* (1961) (which was a companion piece to Martin Ritt's *Hud* [1963]), with Montgomery Clift as a classic figure of the young American rebel. This tightly-knit, bony film, stripped of the self-indulgent extravagance of the European

*Louis Calhern, Sam Jaffe,* THE ASPHALT JUNGLE

movies, was well ahead of its time. In its final scene, which shows Gable and Monroe in a car talking about the passage of time, we see the closing of an era of great stars and the passage of Hollywood itself. The effect is deeply moving, and Huston has not equaled it, even in the harshly realistic *Fat City* (1972).

Like Huston, Samuel Fuller came to the attention of critics as a hard-bitten, highly intelligent director-writer preoccupied with stories of violence. His claustrophobic, gripping, and powerful style made considerably more of such subjects as *I Shot Jesse James* (1949) and *Pickup on South Street* (1953) than his own scripts seemed to offer, and the latter film achieved an almost Middle European intensity and lack of sentimentality in its portrait of squalor. *The Baron of Arizona* (1950) was an undistinguished effort, and *Park Row* (1952) a stuffy, would-be Wellesian account of early newspapers which suffered from poor acting. *House of Bamboo* (1955), a thriller shot in Tokyo, offered some excitingly shot struggles in a city the bizarre intoxications of which brought out the best in the director, and *Run of the Arrow* (1955) and *Forty Guns* (1957) were expertly made Westerns. The latter film in fact rivaled Kurosawa in its use of wide screen, and offered a Freudian gunfight in which the combatants held their pistols like erect penises. Fuller's films of the 1960s continued to offer extremes of violence. *Underworld USA* (1961), the best of these, was a vivid charcoal sketch of the life of criminals, especially well handled in the scenes of the young hero (Cliff Robertson) achieving manhood in a jungle of stone. We see the fat gang leader (Robert Emhardt) brooding beside a swimming pool at night, the Fritz Langian meetings under heavy lamps, the sweating fear of the victims of the mob.

Edmund Goulding was a commercial film-maker with an excellent straightforward style who made such gilt-edged successes as *Grand Hotel* (1932) and the admirably made *The Razor's Edge* (1947), both very superior examples of hokum, but was capable of making realistic, important films as well. His two best works were *We Are Not Alone* (1939) and *Nightmare Alley* (1947).

*We Are Not Alone,* which James Hilton adapted from his own novel, was set in Calderbury, an English village of 1914. The set was re-created with fidelity by the art director Carl Jules Weyl from Hilton's and Goulding's memories (Goulding was born in England and had an early career on the music hall stage). A downtrodden Crippen-like little man (Paul Muni) is married to a nagging wife (Flora Robson), and tries to

*Gene Tierney, Anne Baxter,* THE RAZOR'S EDGE

*Flora Robson, Paul Muni,* WE ARE NOT ALONE

find happiness with a German girl (Jane Bryan) engaged to take care of his child. He is hanged finally (and unjustly) for the wife's murder, but at the end, as his son takes a bath, we discover the child singing a song that indicates the father's life will be continued, that he has achieved immortality through the fruit of his loins. Uncompromised, finely wrought, the film creates to perfection an umbrellas-and-aspidistras environment. We see the sadness of a marriage that doesn't work, the Gissing-like turning of collars to conceal a ring of grime, the promenade with gossips waiting to pounce, the flowered wallpaper, overstuffed chairs, and porcelain jugs of a genteel little hell.

In *Nightmare Alley* Goulding and the writer Jules Furthman explored with equal veracity a similar hell: the hell of the traveling carnival, of cheap versions of spiritualism used to deceive the masses. Stanton Carlisle (Tyrone Power, whose performance reflected Goulding's skill with actors) is a barker who climbs to wealth in Chicago by pretending he can bring back the souls of the departed. His most serious mistake is to enter into collaboration with a more ingenious crook—a psychologist, Dr. Lilith Ritter (Helen Walker), who retains details of her clients' memories on disc, thereby providing Carlisle with information about lost children or lovers. Together, they enter into an affair which results in Carlisle's destruction. He ends his career chewing the heads off live chickens to the delight of the carnival's patrons.

As in *We Are Not Alone,* Goulding turns a calm but jaundiced eye on the details of lives lived at the edge of hope. He re-creates the atmosphere of the carnival with a truthfulness that even a Carné might have envied. The film, which has a Gallic accuracy of detail, is courageous for its period, unsparing and at the same time deeply compassionate. The characters are drawn in Furthman's script with a complexity that stems from William Lindsay Gresham's autobiographical novel. The old-time carnival man reciting Shakespeare, dying from a draft of wood alcohol, and his blowsy wife are played to perfection by Ian Keith and Joan Blondell. The millionaire with his Italian garden and dreams of possessing a long-dead mistress is effortlessly brought to life by Taylor Holmes. The finest performance in the picture is that of Helen Walker as Dr. Lilith Ritter. Her realistic playing presents us with a portrait of evil intelligence seldom equalled in Hollywood films. First seen in a nightclub, when with unblinking eyes she assesses Stanton Carlisle's ambitions, she is shown later obtaining a sexual and commercial dominance over her companion. Their Lake Michigan encounter late at night, Lee Garmes' lighting framing them against dark water, is one of the most explicit expressions of eroticism ever attempted by a major studio.

Although Houston, Fuller, and Goulding worked firmly in the mode of *film noir,* they did not reflect any major tradition in the American film. Other directors of the period did show an acquaintance with the great figures of the silent and early sound cinema, their styles reflecting, however distantly, much earlier influences. Among these was the distinguished craftsman Albert Lewin, who deeply admired Rex Ingram. Beginning at Metro just after Ingram completed his work there, he intermittently continued the Ingram tradition of pictorial beauty at the studio. He was encouraged by Irving Thalberg, and even in one picture not made for Metro, *The Moon and Sixpence* (1943), he made a very Culver City-like production. This picture, made for and in the closest collaboration with the producer David Loew, was his first collaboration with the art director Gordon Wiles, a gifted dilettante whose career went back to Howard's *Transatlantic* (1931). Maugham was delighted with Lewin's screenplay for his novel, which used Maugham himself (played by Herbert Marshall) as the narrator. John F. Seitz' cinematography significantly recalled the work that major cameraman had done with Ingram, opulently decorating a story based on the career of Gauguin. The character of Charles Strickland, the artist stricken with a mortal disease in the South Seas, is rather too lazily played by George Sanders, but the careful, intelligent direction sustains one's interest. And two other roles are wonderfully played: Florence Bates as the old Tahitian matchmaker and Steven Geray, flawless as Dirk Stroeve, the failed painter. At the end, as Strickland's paintings are destroyed in a fire, Seitz' photography changes into vividly exciting color—a cleverly vulgar touch of which Ingram would surely have approved.

More advanced in technique, *The Picture of Dorian Gray* (1944–45), again designed by Wiles, was also a film which Ingram might well have made. Although Lewin's sub-Wildean epigrams made up to fill out the screenplay were not appealing, and although George Sanders as Lord Henry Wotton quite failed to convey the subtle decadence of that character, Lewin's direction had a rich pictorial elegance, a genuine feeling for the peculiar intoxications of the period of the Yellow Book. The film holds together largely through the subdued intelligence of Hurd Hatfield's performance as Dorian, a beautiful death's-head quite different from the golden-haired Apollo that Wilde described (the producer, Pandro S. Berman, wanted Gregory Peck for the role, and Greta

*Hurd Hatfield, Peter Lawford,* THE PICTURE OF DORIAN GRAY

Garbo begged to be given it). The *mise en scène*—the painter Basil
Hallward's studio, Dorian's M-G-M-Regency house, an East End music
hall, the Germanic Bluegate Fields—is realized with fastidious accomplishment. The film's lacquered surface ensures an intense aesthetic
pleasure: the gaslights in glass globes framing Dorian's face against a
background of black and white checkerboard floor; a coachmen's curling
whip circling his face like a premonitory noose; steel-engraving trees
with spidering twigs and fronds accompanying a shooting at Dorian's
country estate near Selby; a nursery with its dusty rocking horse, trailing
"Boy Blue" motto, and in the corner the portrait that keeps the secret
of Dorian's soul. In the smallest minutiae—the striped carriage seats on
the train journey to Selby, the paper snow showered out of a basket as
Sibyl Vane sings, the humpbacked dwarf like some figure out of Leni
showing Dorian to the filthy prostitute's room in Blue Gate Fields—
Lewin and Wiles are unfailingly apt.

None of Lewin's subsequent films was up to the standard of *Dorian
Gray. The Private Affairs of Bel Ami* (1947) was a somewhat luke-

warm approximation of de Maupassant, handicapped by censorship and by George Sanders' inadequacy in the title role. *Pandora and the Flying Dutchman* (1951) was an annoyingly stiff and lifeless creation in which the characters, led by Harold Warrender and James Mason, were continually coming across rare books and intoning phrases found in them. Not even the opulent photography of Jack Cardiff could save what was fundamentally a dumb project, and Lewin's career declined rapidly.

We have noted how Henry King, King Vidor, and John Ford sustained the Griffithian traditions into the 1940s and beyond. The Lubitschian tradition was chiefly sustained by Preston Sturges, although there were Lubitschian touches, as I have remarked, in Wilder and in the work of Mitchell Leisen even after he ceased to collaborate with Wilder and Brackett. Unfortunately, Sturges' comedies, to this writer at least, have not worn very well, except for the scintillating *The Lady Eve* (1941). Uninteresting cinematically, Sturges' films were photographed in Lubitschian medium shot, brightly lit in the Paramount manner, notable for their weary, sophisticated, now dated charm and their metallic, coldly witty lines.

*The Great McGinty* (1940) introduced a gallery of players as vivid as Capra's and made it clear that they would shortly form a stock company. This satire on politics makes fascinating comparisons with *Citizen Kane,* shot in the same year. *Christmas in July* (1940), about a young couple who win a lottery, has a gentle charm, but Sturges eclipsed it the following year with *The Lady Eve,* a comedy of manners in which a beer heir (Henry Fonda) is trapped by card sharp Jean Harrington (Barbara Stanwyck) aboard an ocean liner. The film's energy is typical of its period, and the handling has a cool intelligence. In scenes such as that of Jean surveying prospective male victims through a compact mirror in the saloon, of her father "Handsome Harry" Harrington (Charles Coburn) taking the sucker with a sleeve-full of aces, and of Jean's delicious impersonation of a British heiress, Lubitsch's influence is clear.

*Sullivan's Travels* (1942) was an attractive trifle about a director who abandons his career as a maker of light comedies to discover the truth about poverty. The situation harks back to Lubitsch's "serious" experiment with *Broken Lullaby,* and the scenes of Hollywood life were polished and amusing. *The Palm Beach Story* (1942) was as ritzy and

*Charles Coburn, Barbara Stanwyck, Henry Fonda,* THE LADY EVE

*Joel McCrea, Claudette Colbert, Rudy Vallee, Mary Astor,* THE PALM
BEACH STORY

sleek as *The Lady Eve,* a devastating account of the lives of the very rich, with their quaint pet names, pitiless acquisitiveness, and dizzy round of pleasures, played with great style by Mary Astor, Rudy Vallee, and Claudette Colbert.

Unfortunately, Sturges' fire burned out early, dampened by too much praise, too much vanity and authority (like Welles, he had complete command of his films), and an essentially self-destructive quality of personality. His *The Miracle of Morgan's Creek* (1944) dealt with the birth of a litter of babies, and *Hail the Conquering Hero* (1944) with the public's inane adulation of GIs. Both films were marred by over-emphasis and the unattractive personalities of their stars, Betty Hutton and Eddie Bracken. Sturges' career fizzled out after five years.

George Stevens is a dedicated minor craftsman who tends to be either overrated or underrated by critics. Slow, painstaking, decent, he is a film-maker who likes to bide his time with a project; when he finally settles upon one, he directs it with a measured smoothness that at times be-comes monotonous. He made little of interest in the Thirties and Forties; his musicals—except for a beautiful sequence in *A Damsel in Distress* (1937) in which Astaire sang "A Foggy Day in London Town"—were unremarkable in every way. His Forties comedies *Woman of the Year* (1942), *Talk of the Town* (1942), and *The More the Merrier* (1943) were attractive but rather labored ventures into Cukor territory. More ambitious was a new version of Dreiser's *An American Tragedy, A Place in the Sun* (1951), adapted by Michael Wilson and Harry Brown. It was a handsomely made film, though like the von Sternberg version it quite failed to equal the intensity and power of Dreiser's book. It again substituted an indulgent romanticism for the author's crude but moving realism. The story of a young man (Montgomery Clift) enslaved by the rich and beautiful Sondra (Elizabeth Taylor) but ruined by the factory girl (Shelley Winters) whom he makes pregnant and accidentally kills often looks glossy and false, inferior to Wyler's version of *Sister Carrie.* Stevens was at his best only in a few episodes, such as the soft and subdued love scenes between social climber and pathetic drudge, the killing on Loon Lake, long shots from an immense distance alternating with startling close-ups, the wail of a police siren which interrupts a lover's idyll.

Unfortunately, despite these directorial touches, the film is a travesty of Dreiser's novel. Once again, all of the novel's rich social comment

*Charles Coburn, Jean Arthur,* **THE MORE THE MERRIER**

*Elizabeth Taylor, Montgomery Clift,* A PLACE IN THE SUN

was carefully eliminated. Harry Brown and Michael Wilson updated the novel without adding anything new or perceptive about their own time. An example of the compromise involved—typical in Hollywood films, which is why so few can be taken seriously as social comment—occurs in the final scenes when George is in jail awaiting execution. Sondra visits George in his cell and expresses her love for him. The book makes it explicitly clear that once her lover was in trouble and had become a social undesirable, this rich girl wanted nothing more to do with him. The scene in the film is the antithesis of realism. Dreiser's book was awkwardly written but passionately convincing and filled with deeply felt critiques of the heartlessness of a materialist society. Stevens' film is beautifully made, its style far more polished than Dreiser's prose, but it is empty and cold.

Stevens proved with his next film to be a master of the use of landscape. *Shane* (1953), adapted by A. B. Guthrie, Jr., from a story by Jack Schaefer about a cowboy who rides into a remote valley set-

*Jean Arthur, Van Heflin, Alan Ladd,* SHANE

tlement and assumes for the family there the role of a god, has a strong sense of a lived-in environment. The glacial blue of distant mountains, the dusty, muddy plain, the little house where mother and son defy the elements are expertly conveyed. Unfortunately, Alan Ladd failed to convey the force of personality which would have made the stranger's presence overpowering, and the fine playing of Jean Arthur and Brandon de Wilde did not quite compensate for that deficiency. Loyal Griggs' photography, particularly in a shooting in thick mud, was a major asset.

Stevens' most ambitious and important film was *Giant* (1956), a saga based by Fred Guiol and Ivan Moffat on Edna Ferber's novel about the maturing of a Texas land baron. Although Rock Hudson makes a too solidly reticent central figure and Elizabeth Taylor as his wife ages with a remarkable lack of conviction, the film is of value for its evocation of landscape, the mansion set in a vast plain, oil wells springing up on virgin land, horses galloping against a smoky horizon. Several good sequences interrupt a somewhat halting narrative: a Texas party which perfectly hits off the gross bonhomie of that state; a frantic ride under-taken by the family spinster (Mercedes McCambridge), her agony thrust home by a sudden cut from long distance to a close-up of a spur piercing an unwilling flank; and above all the sequence of James Dean staking out his territory or splashing joyously in a sudden gusher of oil. Dean's performance as the ranch hand turned tycoon comes within hailing distance of greatness, particularly at the moment when, old and bitter, he breaks down drunkenly at a political party in his honor. Stevens' subsequent films, *The Diary of Anne Frank* (1959), *The Great-est Story Ever Told* (1965), and *The Only Game in Town* (1970), were all splendidly made, but devoid of dramatic power.

# PART FOUR
# Toward the Contemporary Film

*George C. Scott*, PATTON

# 1. Wide Screens, Wider Horizons

The most profitable year in the industry's history was 1946, but by 1949, the position had entirely changed. British government taxes had severely affected that particular export market, and there was mass unemployment in this industry; RKO closed down completely: the House Committee on Un-American Activities under J. Parnell Thomas brought about an industry witch hunt, in which ten writers and directors refused to testify whether they were or were not Communists. At the end of that year, acting under the guidance of Nicholas Schenck, Eric Johnston, president of the Motion Picture Association of America, issued what came to be known as the Waldorf Statement, announcing that the industry would not in the future engage known Communists in its service. The collapse of industry morale in the face of the inquiry was widespread, and by 1950 television had begun to be a threat. In 1953, as in 1934, the public started to turn from films. Television figures like "Uncle Miltie" (Milton Berle), the puppet Howdy Doody, and Lucille Ball became more popular than all but a tiny handful of movie stars.

The industry fought back with larger and larger screens and with 3-D, a short-lived device featured in such works as *House of Wax* (1953), an inferior version of Curtiz' *Mystery of the Wax Museum*. As the result of a gamble by Spyros P. Skouras, president of 20th Century-Fox, CinemaScope was introduced as the standard, and *The Robe* (1953) was partially reshot and changed to the new ratio. Among other films that followed were John Sturges' *Bad Day at Black Rock* (1955) and Elia

Kazan's *East of Eden* (1955). Musicals like *It's Always Fair Weather* (1955), directed by Stanley Donen, made good use of the new medium, but its shape was virtually intractable for a domestic subject, and one's chief memory of the period is of people talking across immense spaces, isolated as though they were addressing each other in Grand Central Station.

Cinerama, a still more cumbersome gimmick showed split-screen images of land and seascapes, all jiggling alarmingly on three separate panels, only occasionally jelling for a spectacular effect. Best of all the systems was the short-lived VistaVision, made by Paramount in defiance of the CinemaScope standard. It had excellent definition, as evidenced by John Ford's *The Searchers* (1956) and Anthony Mann's *Strategic Air Command* (1956). But it did not last; the public simply did not appreciate its particular qualities. Todd-AO was less satisfactory, though of the films made in the system, Fred Zinnemann's *Oklahoma* (1955) certainly had its moments.

Another way of combating the public obsession with TV was to provide them with something equivalent to that medium in the cinema theaters themselves. The low- or medium-budget black and white feature, dealing with ordinary people and situations, first emerged in Delbert Mann's *Marty* (1954), a Paddy Chayefsky teleplay about a butcher (Ernest Borgnine) and a simple woman (Betsy Blair) who loves him. The direction mysteriously won immense praise at the time. Mann's next Chayefsky subject, *The Bachelor Party* (1957), was more accomplished, chiefly due to the photography of Joseph LaShelle, conveying the heat, the pressure, of summer existence in New York. The opening sequence, in which a group of bachelors chuckle over a pornographic film, perfectly hit off the prurient, schoolboyish humor of these aging adults, with their sleeves rolled up and beer cans at the ready. Fielder Cook's *Patterns* (1955) was another typical film of the period, harsh, shot in television style with the emphasis on close-ups and foreground effects. Here Rod Serling's overwritten script came constantly to small climaxes for commercials that were not there. The world of big business was unflatteringly shown as an arena for colliding egos, hysterically treated, without the humor of Thirties films. Sidney Lumet's *Twelve Angry Men* (1957) gave an equally clear, and equally mediocre, account of the lives of jurymen, while Delbert Mann's *Middle of the Night*

*James Stewart,* STRATEGIC AIR COMMAND

(1959) was an unsparing, more effective account of the desperations of a middle-aged man. On a similar theme, Laszlo Benedek's *Death of a Salesman* (1951) used theatrical linking devices, in which lights go down on a set, and when they go up, the set has changed.

The Fifties were years in which exposés of particularly depressing aspects of suburban life were popular, a period of humdrum realism and flat, insipid writing in the wake of the blacklist. Daniel Mann's *Come Back Little Sheba* (1952) and its successor *About Mrs. Leslie* (1953) were prototypical: subdued, smoothly directed soap opera studies of an older woman, very well portrayed by Shirley Booth. Young people in these films were shown as insensitive or mindless, while their elders were warm, compassionate, misunderstood.

If the most serious film-making of the Fifties was devoted to an exploration of the lives of people approaching or past middle age, then the Sixties showed the emergence of rebellious youth. Up till 1959 or so, apart from certain rock 'n' roll stars who had fugitive careers in the cinema, the image of youth was largely a "square" one, reflecting the still somewhat square character of young people themselves in America. The crew cut, the Ivy League jacket, the wide-cut trousers of the male college student and the lacquered look of the girls had all the glossy smartness and "correctness" of living advertisements for shampoo. By the mid-1960s the much discussed revolution of taste had begun, with the Beatles and the Rolling Stones. Moreover, youth began, at first peacefully, then with increasing violence, to express mass dissatisfaction with existing institutions, a revolt which had its effect on all aspects of American culture. Unfortunately, this new obsession was not sufficient to save Hollywood from a steady decline. The mass desertion of the silent majority to television meant that feature films were on the way out; by 1972, despite such isolated successes as *The Godfather* and *Love Story*, Hollywood film-makers had started to lose the young audience as well.

# 2. New Directors, New Directions

The new generation of directors which dealt with the rebel as its central theme was headed by Elia Kazan and Nicholas Ray in the 1950s. The sexually explicit blue jeans, the T-shirt, the scowl, the shy half-smile of a Brando or a Dean were enormously potent screen images. Kazan moved from mild-mannered liberal films like *Gentleman's Agreement* (1947) and *Pinky* (1949), which dealt with the Jewish and the black problem in a soft, safe fashion, to the Brando vehicles *A Streetcar Named Desire* (1951), *Viva Zapata!* (1952), and *On the Waterfront* (1954). In *East of Eden* (1955) Kazan offered James Dean as a moody, brooding youth in a small town; in *America, America!* (1963) he depicted the life of a young Greek immigrant to the United States.

Kazan developed the tradition in his best film, *Splendor in the Grass* (1961), based on an almost seminal work by William Inge. Though the action was set back in the 1920s, Inge's was a clearly stated contemporary plea for sexual freedom. Warren Beatty was the natural heir to James Dean, similarly tense, introspective, yet possessed of a great animal magnetism. In this film he played a college athlete who falls in love with a young girl, exquisitely played by Natalie Wood, but is prevented by convention from finding sexual release with her. Intensely physical and sensual, the film creates an atmosphere of eroticism rare at the time in American cinema. When Natalie Wood, near hysterical tears, yet laughing happily, sits up in her bath and expresses a joy in her newfound womanhood, Kazan's direction is at its most sensitive. His gifts lay

*Producer-director Elia Kazan* (no shirt) directs *Natalie Wood* and *Warren Beatty* in a scene from SPLENDOR IN THE GRASS

partly in a piercing understanding of the exposed feelings of the young, the miserable joys of adolescence, partly in a brilliant visual flair which illuminated personal feelings through the kinesthetic use of color.

Nicholas Ray lacked Kazan's energy and dynamic attack, but his films were often in the mainstream. His early *They Live by Night* (1949) was a tender and sensitive account of young people pushed by circumstances into a life of crime. His *The Lusty Men* (1952) dealt with rodeo riders and their marginal existences on the fringe of "regular" society. Like Kazan, he was fascinated by minority groups, outsiders: *Hot Blood* (1956) dealt affectionately with gypsies, *Bitter Victory* (1958) with Arabs, *Wind Across the Everglades* (1958) with the people of the bird-hunting swamp country of Florida, and *The Savage Innocents* (1961) with Eskimo tribes. *Rebel Without a Cause* (1955), like *Splendor in*

*Burl Ives,* WIND ACROSS THE EVERGLADES

*Anthony Quinn, Yoko Tani,* THE SAVAGE INNOCENTS

*the Grass* a seminal film for a generation, contained James Dean's classic performance as an outsider, struggling with parents who utterly fail to understand.

In a direct line with Kazan and Ray, John Frankenheimer dealt effectively in his early films with similar themes. A young man himself in the 1960s, he came out of the field of live television with an enthusiasm for the cause of the young. *The Young Stranger,* his first feature, made in 1957, dealt with the struggles of an adolescent against his dull suburban father. *The Young Savages* (1957) was a plea for the decent treatment of delinquents in a big city. *All Fall Down* (1962), written, like *Splendor in the Grass,* by William Inge, was a beautifully made film about adolescence. Brandon de Wilde is a young boy growing up in a small town, with a dominating mother (Angela Lansbury) and a stupid, well-meaning father (Karl Malden). He worships his elder brother, played by Warren Beatty. Gradually, his illusions about this dominant figure in his life are shattered. He realizes that what seemed to be a be-

*Angela Lansbury, Karl Malden, Eva Marie Saint, Warren Beatty, Brandon de Wilde*, ALL FALL DOWN

loved adult male worthy of respect is in fact no more than an opportunist
jerk and a hustler. At the end, the boy reaches manhood by means of
his anguish, and knows how to face life.

Unfortunately, Frankenheimer's disappointment in the commercial
results of this film—it was ruined by bad promotion—drove him to different subjects. Yet he still remained concerned with the theme of the
outsider.

*The Manchurian Candidate* (1962), written by George Axelrod from
Richard Condon's novel, suggested that Frankenheimer was concerned
to lay bare the realities of the political machine. Once again, Angela
Lansbury emerges as the American monster mother, bent on brain-
washing the son (Laurence Harvey) to whom she is physically attracted,
in order to effect the political assassination of her husband's rival in a
presidential race. The direction is garishly sustained, the portrait of corrupt politics Wellesian in its intensity of observation.

*Seven Days in May* (1964), scripted by Rod Serling from the novel
by Fletcher Knebel and Charles Bailey, more expertly tackles a political
theme. Once again Frankenheimer deals with an attempt to obtain su-
preme power by a fascist clique. In the earlier film, the inspiration for the
revolt lay in Russia; in the later work the seeds of destruction are seen to
lie in the American military system itself. In a distant echo of the generals' plot against Hitler, a junta headed by a martinet (Burt Lancaster)
tries to destroy the career of an aging, ailing President (Fredric March)
and set up a secret base in the Western desert. The film is played with
extraordinary skill, proving that Frankenheimer's intensity communi-
cated itself successfully to his actors. Burt Lancaster as the prospective
Hitler is at his best in the film, dynamically conveying his contempt for
the President in a White House confrontation that is the film's most
expertly written scene.

Frankenheimer's great virtues—his sense of realism, attack, pacing,
and electrifying creative energy—seldom recurred in his later films. *The
Train* (1965), taken over from Arthur Penn, was a botch for which he
cannot be held responsible. *Seconds* (1966), superbly shot by James
Wong Howe, the story of a man given a second chance at life, had a
compelling first third. There is power in such scenes as the introduction
of John Randolph to the meatworks, behind which lies the sinister organization which provides new flesh for old; the meeting with Will Geer,
cleverly playing an evil proprietor; the acquisition of a Rock Hudson
face and figure and the discovery that youth and a home at Malibu are

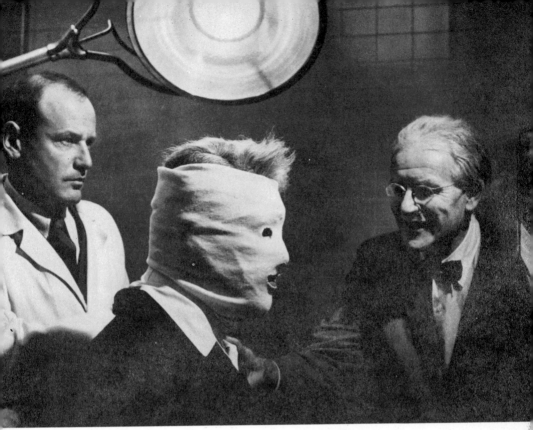

*Richard Anderson, Rock Hudson, Will Geer,* SECONDS

the false allures of the American dream, that the man who seeks Paradise in California has found only the hopelessness of material delights, from martinis to a sad, lost girl at the beach. Frankenheimer moves in this film from condemnation of American sexual dreams and political unscrupulousness to a profoundly angry denunciation of American youth culture. Alas, though, the film fails to achieve the satirical portrait of the Californian rich which would have made it a triumph. The important central passages at Malibu have all the softness of a real dream-come-true. By conspiring with his own target, Frankenheimer shows that corruption has crept up on him, and not even a powerful climax—the hero preferring death in New York to "life" in Malibu, returning to be killed in a horrifying operating room scene—alters the fact that the film has been compromised. Since the commercial failure of this picture, Frank-

*George Macready, Fredric March,* SEVEN DAYS IN MAY

enheimer's films have been mediocre, ranging from *The Fixer* (1968) to *The Horsemen* (1971).

Stanley Kubrick, comparable with Frankenheimer as a major new figure of the 1950s, has chosen to be a European director, making *Lolita* (1962), *Dr. Strangelove* (1966), *2001: A Space Odyssey* (1968), and *A Clockwork Orange* (1971) in England, and therefore falls outside the scope of this survey. Other directors concerned with the theme of the outsider have been Martin Ritt, who in *Hud* (1963) and *The Molly Maguires* (1969), both photographed by James Wong Howe, made distinguished contributions to the genre; and Sam Peckinpah, who has specialized in unsentimental Westerns like *Major Dundee* (1965) and *The Wild Bunch* (1969). Mike Nichols, after a successful commercial career on stage as both performer and director, brought an essentially theatrical technique to bear on the subjects of anguished academics (*Who's Afraid of Virginia Woolf* [1966]); the disaffected young (*The Graduate* [1968]); the bizarre horrors of army life (*Catch-22*

Ben Johnson, Warren Oates, William Holden, Ernest Borgnine, THE WILD BUNCH

[1969]); and the sexual alienations of the prosperous middle class (Jules Feiffer's *Carnal Knowledge* [1971]). Another important director was Donald Siegel, whose tough, confident style was best expressed in *The Line-up* (1958) and *Dirty Harry* (1972).

Perhaps the most important figure of the new American cinema is Arthur Penn, one of the first directors to show the influence of the French and to shift his base of operations to New York. His first feature, *The Left Handed Gun* (1958), was a story about a psychotic gunman told in an elliptical, jagged style which suggested that the director wanted to abandon the formal restrictions of the usual Hollywood film. *The Miracle Worker* (1962), based by William Gibson on the story of Helen Keller, was somewhat conventional and theatrical, a throwback to Penn's early experience in the theater and in television problem drama. Its pretensions were extremely strained, which makes the greatness of *Mickey One* (1965) all the more surprising.

This extraordinary Kafkaesque work written by Alan Surgal is far more effective than Orson Welles' version of *The Trial*, the novel which provides its basic inspiration. Warren Beatty here symbolizes American youth in the 1960s, overwhelmed by the sense of an impersonal bureaucratic state, trapped and on the run. He plays a nightclub comic engaged by a decadent proprietor of a dive to please the jaded customers. With his great cameraman Ghislain Clocquet, Penn creates more vividly than in any other film the pulverizing weight of a mechanical world. He shows Beatty fleeing across immense junkyards where cars are crushed flat and dropped from the teeth of cranes, streets where furtive figures creep into alleyways for shelter, and strange little huts where bizarre figures lurk trying to lure him in. The last scene is extraordinary. It shows the "K"-like protagonist in a *boîte* with a single spotlight pinning him down like a dying butterfly. From behind the spotlight comes an impersonal voice uttering meaningless instructions. The victim goes through his routine in a state of terror, half humorously, half frightenedly, and finally seems to crumble before our eyes. Already, he has become a victim of the system which forces everyone into a required conventional mode.

Unfortunately, Penn did not have a great success with this magnificent surrealist film, and in his future work he pursued his concerns with a keener commercial eye. *The Chase* (1966) was outside of the main body of his work, and is disowned by him as a personal creation. It was an adaptation of a straightforward Lillian Hellman script in which Mar-

*Warren Beatty*, MICKEY ONE

lon Brando appeared as an embattled figure in a town in the Deep South. The film's handsome physical execution did not compensate for a rambling and confused narrative. The film was followed by *Bonnie and Clyde* (1967), which made Penn's name. Overnight, he became an idol of film lovers. Actually, the picture is not strictly speaking a personal invention of Penn's. He came into the project late, after François Truffaut had turned it down. The script was written by David Newman and Robert Benton, two specialists in pop culture who wrote for *Esquire* magazine. Warren Beatty liked the property and his agent William Morris talked Warners into backing it. Penn was a last-minute choice, and simply executed the film with his usual skill.

The credits appear on a black screen, accompanied by Rudy Vallee singing in his reedy tenor "Deep Night." We see rapid cuts of the Barrow gang vaingloriously posing in a series of pastiches of period photographs. Then we observe a blonde girl painting her lips in close-up in a cheap hotel room. Pictures of Roosevelt grin doggily out of shop windows. The film takes us back to 1932, to the black years of the Great Depression, the maverick gangsterdom of the Middle West, and the seedy, doom-struck atmosphere of small-town America on the bread line.

Warners made the picture; the theme harks back to the petty squalor

*Michael J. Pollard, Faye Dunaway, Warren Beatty,* BONNIE AND CLYDE

portrayed by the studio at the time. The Barrow gang—which Dillinger always said gave crime a bad name—could in fact have been the subject of a LeRoy or a Curtiz picture. Instead, Newman and Benton provide a fairy tale for the 1960s, rainbow-colored, funny, sentimental, irresponsible, and violent, complete with hillbilly theme tune, hip stars, and freewheeling post-New Wave camerawork.

*Bonnie and Clyde* is as calculated as a Pavlovian experiment. Because of the under-twenty-five age appeal, all lawkeepers and decent citizens are not only shown as fools and hypocrites but are kept shrewdly on the wrong side of forty. By contrast, the gang is made up of Beautiful People (Bonnie and Clyde themselves), an underprivileged little runt (C. W. Moss), a comically hysterical hausfrau (Blanche Barrow), and a solid sidekick (her husband, Buck). The gang makes its getaways, robs banks —at one stage dragging a stranded and hilariously panic-stricken Blanche onto the running board—and bowls in cute jalopies across the Andrew Wyeth countryside. Then the law puts a stop to the events: Buck is shot and Blanche moans, "Daddy! Daddy!" and Bonnie and Clyde die shamefully but glamorously, tricked into an ambush, in a *Liebestod* punctuated by a motif of machine-gun bullets, photographed in *Saturday Evening Post* rainbow colors.

Neither Faye Dunaway nor Warren Beatty acts in a proper Thirties mode, nor do they seem to understand the feelings of the desperate and the underprivileged. The actress' willowy modern charm is no more appropriate to the lethal, serpentine coldness of the real Bonnie Parker than the actors' sensitive matinée idol's looks have the right style for the shoddy vanity of Clyde Barrow. Their clothes have been updated, and their hair is subtly wrong: to compare the look of the young Paul Muni and Carole Lombard is to see how the Thirties look has been compromised. It is as if the look was too stark for today's audiences.

There are other anachronisms: the murderous couple visit *Gold Diggers of 1933* in 1932 and pass by a theater showing stills of *The Go-Getter,* not released until 1937. Worse still, the small towns that form the background of so much of the action do not resemble hick towns seen in films of the period, and the richly glowing color photography still further reduces the illusion.

Physically, the film is staged with confidence and drive, and several scenes are directed with dazzling skill, such as the capturing of a nervous young undertaker, shocked (this if anything indicates the film's aim at the teen-age market) to discover that his fiancée is thirty-three years old; the police attack on Buck Barrow, his wife's eyes shot away, his head partly blown off, a sequence of horrific and faultlessly realized violence; the escape of the refugees down a blood-soaked river bank to cleanse their wounds in the water; the capture of the sheriff, posed for a photograph with Bonnie by the snap-happy C. W. Moss, the captive spitting into Bonnie's face at the precisely correct climactic moment.

Shot on location by the veteran cameraman Burnett Guffey in the Middle West—fields shimmering with summer heat, dirt roads and remote sand hills blanketed in mist—this is a film with a consistently watchable surface, and two performances—Estelle Parsons as Blanche and Gene Hackman as Buck—are very fine. Penn's command of film rhythm is electrifying. But as a re-creation of reality, of an extraordinarily evil, doomed, and wretched adventure which might have made the subject a great film, *Bonnie and Clyde* can only be described as dishonest, as well as a dangerous incentive to violence in an increasingly psychotic society.

Since *Bonnie and Clyde,* Penn has made two major films, *Alice's Restaurant* (1969) and *Little Big Man* (1971). *Alice's Restaurant,* set in the New England town where Penn lives, is the story of Arlo Guthrie, the son of the famous folk musician Woody Guthrie. The film, which follows the adventures of Arlo and his friends, including the warm and generous Alice who runs the local restaurant, shows sympathetically the development of tribalism among the young. It summarizes to perfection the lives of hippies clashing with police, holding their own versions of Christian gatherings, smoking pot, and enjoying a completely untrammeled sex life. The color has a soft romantic glow, the treatment of character is as warm and sentimental as anything in Griffith, and the handling of landscape frequently reminds one of the American primitive directors. There is a beautiful sequence of a funeral in the snow, exquisitely shot, with sunlight lancing through bare trees and the hippies huddling together in quiet commemoration. Unfortunately, a great deal of the film has a rather forced sense of someone coming from the outside to observe hip culture. Only at moments, as in the visit of Arlo to his father's deathbed, does the film touch a note of genuine feeling. The use of music is attractive and subtle, and Dede Allen's editing unusually fluid, as in *Bonnie and Clyde*.

*Little Big Man* is a personal work, showing Penn's commitment to the cause of minorities, a commitment similar to that of Nicholas Ray. The film in fact reminds one of Ray's *The Savage Innocents* in its sympathetic portrayal of a racial minority group. Based on a novel which had a somewhat picaresque narrative line, it is the story of a young white brought up by Indians who has divided loyalties between the whites and the Indian tribes during the period of General Custer, who appears as a vainglorious fool far removed from the figure portrayed by Errol Flynn and Henry Fonda in earlier treatments of this figure. The sympathy of Penn and of his writer Calder Willingham is clearly on the side of the Indian, and the film is distinguished by a generous portrait of a chief by Dan George. The scenes in the white settlements are scattered and rather strange in their facetious humor, whereas the sequences dealing with tribal life have a fullness of response that reminds one of Ford at his best. The finest sequences are at the outset, when we discover a ruined wagon train and the pathetic relics of a destroyed family, the skeletons of the wagons outlined against the sky, smoke rising up, buzzards wheeling; and the episodes shot in the winter snows of Canada, when the director powerfully evokes a menaced but still courageous Indian world. The entire film is placed in the framework of a taped interview with the ancient protagonist who describes his life as a youth. This device works splendidly, and Dustin Hoffman plays both the old man and the young scout with extraordinary professional finesse.

*Richard Mulligan*, LITTLE BIG MAN

In common with Frankenheimer and Penn, Franklin Schaffner worked in live television in the early 1950s, and like these men he learned at the time a disciplined approach similar to that of early Thirties film-makers and a concern with subjects of social significance. His first directorial assignment was not a personal creation, but did reflect his warm sympathy as a personality. It was *The Stripper* (1963), based on William Inge's play *A Loss of Roses,* by Meade Roberts, dealing with the doomed affair of a filling station attendant (sensitively played by Richard Beymer) and an aging striptease girl (Joanne Woodward). At first the young man seems to offer the sad and tired woman a chance of regeneration, of marriage, but as so often in Inge romantic hopes dwindle into despair. Schaffner used the 20th Century-Fox back lot with the same degree of conviction that Frakenheimer brought to *All Fall Down* in creating the atmosphere of a small town. The film was flawed by the constant recutting of Darryl F. Zanuck and by the miscasting of Joanne Woodward in the title role.

*Joanne Woodward, Richard Beymer,* THE STRIPPER

Schaffner's *The War Lord* (1965) was again based on a very good script (by John Collier). Aside from being a gifted short story writer, Collier was an authority on medieval ritual, and the subject matter, a Frisian invasion of eleventh-century Normandy, was explored with an extraordinary attention to detail in the writing. Once again, the producer interfered with the film, and it came out far from Collier's and Schaffner's intentions. Instead of offering a rich observation of Druid ritual, the film emphasized the sexual elements too heavily, and despite the sumptuous photography of Russell Metty, it came out as a somewhat awkward middle-brow epic.

Schaffner's *The Best Man* (1965) was superior in every way. It was based by Gore Vidal on his own play about a crumbling President of the United States (played with extraordinary skill by Lee Tracy) and the ambitious, Bobby Kennedy-like politician (brilliantly impersonated by Cliff Robertson) who tries to supplant him. The witty and informed portrait of Washington life given by Vidal is enhanced by

Schaffner's levelheaded direction of the players. The best scenes are those involving the women's club leader played by Ann Sothern, who combines a brassy extroversion with a malicious ability to control an army of female voters. The Robertson portrait is also a triumph, the tweedy charm, impeccable face, and all-American build concealing a deadly ambition. Against him is pitched the urbane older figure of Henry Fonda, here giving perhaps his best performance of recent years in a portrayal of damaged integrity inspired in its range of physical detail. In common with most important political films, attempting to come to grips with the corruptions and aspirations of the Senate, the picture was a commercial failure, and Schaffner made no further films of an uncompromised character.

*Planet of the Apes* (1968) offered much of the skillful use of the wide screen which had distinguished *The War Lord,* though inferior matte processing and some watery color photography (Leon Shamroy) muffled its impact. The story—of the world of the future under the dominance of cultivated apes—was rather scratchily developed, and only the expert voices of Kim Hunter, Maurice Evans, and Roddy McDowall, fighting through layers of monkey makeup, served to sustain the interest.

Schaffner's *Patton* (1970) was compromised at every level. The evasive and dishonest screenplay by Francis Ford Coppola and others dealt with the celebrated martinet of World War II who combined bulldozing military tactics with an impatient contempt for his superiors and a ferocious anger at the cowardly or incompetent among his men. Given the opportunity for a full-scale attack on war and its practitioners, the writers and producer chose to present us with a lovable if difficult curmudgeon, played with a splendid crusty charm by George C. Scott. This basic falsity of approach renders the film somewhat less than a serious achievement, even though the execution is tremendously assured. Using newly developed lenses, the cameraman Fred Koenekamp provides splendid vistas of the various areas which Patton conquered. Patton's soliloquies against ruined buildings and in the desert of North Africa are movingly uttered and accompanied by the magnificent noble score of Jerry Goldsmith. The final sequence, after all the stress and storm that has gone before, is highly effective. This strange man who saw himself as a modern reincarnation of Alexander walks away with his white dog against a Spanish landscape. Over his head slowly turn the wings of a giant windmill, reminding the audience of the film's thesis that he is a Don Quixote in a world which puts up obstacles to his weird if somewhat heroic progress. Despite the falsity of the literary parallel, the visual image is superbly striking, and accompanied by Goldsmith's stirring chords, it brings the film to a splendid close.

Schaffner's most recent film is *Nicholas and Alexandra* (1971). Like so many of his movies it is a study in the misuse of power. Unfortunately, there are indications in this account (by James Goldman, based on a book by Robert K. Massie) of the declining Romanov dynasty that Schaffner may also decline, like Frankenheimer before him. The film plods along from episode to episode, deadened by the production hand of Sam Spiegel and the Royal Academy photography of F. A. Young. Only in the last half hour, when the parade of famous figures falls away, can the film be said to achieve a degree of nobility. Schaffner's best direction is seen in the finale at Ekaterinburg, when the royal family is held captive and shot to death in a cellar. The meticulous, thoughtful directorial style works perfectly here, just as W. S. Van Dyke's worked in the last great scenes of the downfall of Louis XVI in *Marie Antoinette*. The long silence before the family sees the cellar door open to admit its executioners is an example of direction at its most controlled. Schaffner is always worthy of respect even when—as here—he is overwhelmed by the subject matter and by a dominant producer.

Of recent directors in the tradition running from Kazan to Frankenheimer, Penn, and Schaffner, the most important is Bob Rafelson. He is in fact the most promising film-maker of the present time, and his writer Carol Eastman (also known as Adrian Joyce) is equally exciting. The film they made together, *Five Easy Pieces* (1969), is an American masterpiece, the most important motion picture out of Hollywood since Schaffner's *The Best Man*. It also served to bring to prominence the most striking of contemporary actors, Jack Nicholson. Unlike his precursors, Nicholson presents the outsider without a touch of glamour. The brooding animal magnetism of a Brando, a Dean, a Newman, or a Beatty is replaced by a sad and somewhat dejected personality enlivened by an acute and all too piercing intelligence. He is, without the dominating sexuality of his legendary forebears, the perfect prototype of the younger man in the 1970s, stripped of illusions and no longer even the representative of sexual fantasy. He is also a happy antithesis of such improbable idealizations of the male as John Wayne, Clint Eastwood, or Cliff Robertson.

In *Five Easy Pieces,* Nicholson gives a performance of sustained brilliance as Bobby Dupea, a drifter who has thrown up the possibilities of a musical career, rebelling against a family of intellectuals in the state of Washington in an attempt to find his true nature as a man in the Californian oil fields. His hoped-for release in physical action is defeated as the romantic daydream of toil dissolves; he realizes he is not compatible with the roughnecks of the fields. His attempt to establish a satisfactory relationship with a beautiful but mindless girl, like Harlow or Monroe a pathetic symbol of American sexual dreams, is also a disaster. They are unable to make contact except through sex, and live in a state of constant anger, victims of an impossible marriage of the intellect and the body. Finally, Bobby makes off to the Pacific Northwest to visit his paralyzed father, but he is unable to communicate either with his high-falutin' relatives or with the parent he loves so much. In a beautifully written, acted, and directed scene he talks with his father against a skyline of dramatic clouds, breaking into tears as he realizes that his contact with the past is as tenuous as his contact with the present.

The last sequence is of the finest quality. Bobby decides to leave both girl friend and family and abandon life entirely. There is nothing left to do except turn up a collar, give a little shiver, and stare ahead at the road as a truck driver gives him a ride to a place where "it is very cold": the country of death. Rafelson and his great cameraman Laszlo Kovacs fix the scene in our minds forever: the filling station and its discreet rest room; the gray surrounding buildings; the dripping autumnal vegetation of the Northwest; the parked truck waiting to go to Alaska; the face of Nicholson, already aging and filled with premonitory shadows, fixed behind the windshield. Religion, love, and family have all failed to work, leaving absolutely nothing at the end but a journey to nowhere.

# Epilogue

The wheel has swung full circle, and we are presently almost back to the situation at the dawn of silent films. Motion pictures are again being shot by young people in the landscapes and city streets of the real America, in wind, rain, snow, and fog. New directors prefer to shoot in real houses, real huts, so that audiences can look through a window to see a real sky. Cameramen like Philip Lathrop and William Butler, and cameramen-turned-directors like Laszlo Kovacs and William Fraker have rejected the studio-bound formalism of their elders and returned to the *plein air* approach of such early figures as Henry Gerrard and Bert Glennon. Once again, New York, instead of Hollywood, has become the focus for film-makers. That city, with all of its abrasions, is still enormously more potent a source of drama and pictorial interest than Los Angeles. Its very tensions and stresses are the essential matter of film-makers who must come to grips with the realities of our time, as Frank D. Gilroy's recent and very accomplished *Desperate Characters* (1971) has proven.

The theme of youth is still the most pressing one in the American film. The direct line of concern has been continued in Peter Bogdanovich's *The Last Picture Show* (1971), which was written by Larry McMurtry, who also wrote the original of the rather better-made *Hud* (1963) of Martin Ritt, on a similar theme of growing up in Texas. Dalton Trumbo's *Johnny Got His Gun,* for all its shortcomings of direction and photographic technique, touches a nerve of reality in its portrait of the handsome young man (played by Timothy Bottoms, a natural heir of Brandon de Wilde who is also in *The Last Picture Show*) destroyed bodily by war. We may expect more location-shot, realistic films about young people in the future, since the theme of the conflict of generations is likely to become even more pressing in the 1970s.

The frequent nostalgia of the otherwise indifferent *Johnny Got His Gun* (1971) in its lyrical and beautiful scenes of hunting and swimming in a flawless landscape before World War I goes all the way back to the Griffithian mode. It is clear that something long lost has been happily regained. A young generation has decisively rejected the loudmouthed angers, the brutal competitiveness symbolized in the city/studio films of the Thirties—just as it has rejected the baroque mode of the subsequent decade. It is cause for rejoicing that at its best screenwriting has never been better than it is today, far removed from the cliché-ridden romanticism which had swamped the screen for so long. It would be hard to think of a previous parallel for the quality of Carol Eastman's screenplay for *Five Easy Pieces* or Frank D. Gilroy's for *Desperate Characters*. At last, as in the Thirties, we are starting to hear again the voice of real Americans, expressing a truly American language. Possibly, with recent advances, brilliant writers like James Purdy and John Updike (whose *Rabbit, Run* was reduced to an unfortunate travesty on the screen) will be attracted to film-making. The fact that Norman Mailer has made films is an encouraging sign, although his work in the field has not matched his fictional or polemical writing. It is encouraging, too —despite indifferent sub-Bergmanesque results—that Susan Sontag has turned her hand to film-making. There seems some evidence that once video cassettes have become standardized like long-playing records and the present confused situation has been sorted out, it will be possible for artists to work in a less trammeled way, making entirely personal films for home consumption. Although there may at the outset be some sacrifice of technical proficiency, the results will no doubt bring the American film closer to the novel or the poem as a means of individual expression.

This is some time away. In the meanwhile, there are major problems in the "new" Hollywood. The industry is, at the time of this writing, all but dead, in the grips of the worst depression since 1934.

Two films, *Love Story* (1970) and *The Godfather* (1972) have broken the pattern of commercial failure. *Love Story* is a reversal to the worst excesses of sentiment of the silent period, and *The Godfather* goes even beyond *Bonnie and Clyde* as the ultimate glorification of the gangster mentality, with the "glamorous" rebel of Marlon Brando finally institutionalized as the hero of the Mafia. But these "swallows" cannot make a Renaissance summer. Because of the depression, the concept of "free" cinema is largely mythical. Producers and packagers are ever more desperate, refusing to permit anything in a script which does not seem to be instantly commercial. The old system could "carry" personal works, just as publishers of best-selling books could "carry" poetry. Nowadays, despite widespread statements to the contrary, it is harder than ever to convey a personal attitude in terms of film. And the interference of producers and distributors is as constant as ever. A director may be permitted to work more closely on scripts than hitherto, and have more license in shooting, but he very seldom acquires the right of final cut of his film. Adjustments, often desperate and ill-advised, are constantly made as the various executives and distributors try to see which market areas are being catered to.

Film-makers, though, are a tough and resilient breed, and despite a crumbling and inefficient system, with the major studios monopolizing distribution, they can still pursue their vision in many instances. Against conflicting interests, they can, if they are possessed of a formidable will, impose their imagination on the public mind. They need to have a degree of energy, whether as writer, cameraman, or director, so that the power of the medium can be fully expressed. Finally, they need to remember that although they are working in a hard-bitten and hard-pressed business they are also artists working in a grand tradition that began long ago with the struggling pioneers of Vitagraph and Biograph. It is to remind them, and their public, of the nature of that tradition that I have written this book.

# INDEX